Drupal 7 Business Solutions

Build powerful website features for your business

Trevor James

Mark Noble

BIRMINGHAM - MUMBAI

Drupal 7 Business Solutions

First published: December 2008

Second edition: January 2012

Production Reference: 1090112

Published by Packt Publishing Ltd.
Livery Place
35 Livery Street
Birmingham B3 2PB, UK.

ISBN 978-1-84951-664-8

www.packtpub.com

Cover Image by Karl Moore (karl.moore@ukonline.co.uk)

Credits

Authors
Trevor James
Mark Noble

Reviewers
Richard Carter
Adam Hill
Jeffrey Smith
Ravishankar Somasundaram

Senior Acquisition Editor
Usha Iyer

Lead Technical Editor
Dayan Hyames

Technical Editors
Apoorva Bolar
Priyanka Shah

Project Coordinator
Vishal Bodwani

Proofreader
Mario Cecere

Indexer
Hemangini Bari

Production Coordinator
Aparna Bhagat

Cover Work
Aparna Bhagat

About the Authors

Trevor James is a Drupal developer based in Middletown, MD, USA. Trevor has been designing websites for 15 years using a combination of PHP, HTML, XHTML, CSS, and ColdFusion, and has been using Drupal intensively for over five years. Trevor's focus is on building web applications and portals for education, non-profit, medical systems, and small business environments.

He is interested in best methods of integrating Web services with Drupal sites, optimizing Drupal site performance, and building custom Drupal content displays using Views, Panels, Display Suite and other contributed modules. Trevor develops front end Drupal-based interfaces that support data intensive websites. He loves teaching people about Drupal and how to use this excellent open source content management framework.

Trevor authored the Packt book, *Drupal Web Services*, published in November 2010. For more on this title visit: `http://www.packtpub.com/drupal-web-services/book`.

Trevor co-authored the Packt title, *Drupal 6 Performance Tips*, published in February 2010. For more on this title visit: `https://www.packtpub.com/drupal-6-performance-tips-to-maximize-and-optimize-your-framework/book`.

Trevor created a 14 hour video tutorial series on Drupal 7 for VTC (Virtual Training Company) in 2011. The video is available via the VTC website here: `http://www.vtc.com/products/Drupal-7-Tutorials.htm`.

Acknowledgment

Thanks to the Packt editorial staff including Usha Iyer, Vishal Bodwani, Gaurav Mehta, and Dayan Hyames for approaching me originally about writing the second edition of this title. It's been great working on the updated version of the book for Drupal 7. As always the Packt editorial staff have impressed me with their professionalism and knowledge of Drupal and open source. They continue to contribute back to the open source community and to the Drupal community with their titles and as always contribute a percentage of the profits from this book back to the Drupal Association.

I thank all the reviewers of the book who worked closely with me to get this finished product out the door.

The authoring process takes a great deal of time and I thank my family for allowing me to devote countless hours to the writing process. Much thanks to my wife Veronica and our lovely twin daughters Francesca and Clare.

This book is for all the new Drupal users out there. I hope you are as inspired by Drupal as I am and this software helps you to build a rich and dynamic site for your small business. Drupal on!

Mark Noble has worked in software development and website design for over 13 years, in a variety of capacities including development, quality assurance, and management. He takes pride in developing software and websites to make businesses run more effectively, and delights in helping users to get their jobs done more easily.

Mark currently works developing websites, using a combination of Java and PHP, to help libraries to manage their collections. He also performs contract work for clients in a variety of industries, developing both traditional desktop applications as well as web-based applications, using Drupal and a variety of other technologies. When he isn't working for a client, Mark enjoys building sites using Drupal. His other hobbies include playing with his family, photography, hiking, travel, and geocaching.

I would like to thank my wife, April, and my kids, Zoe and Theo, for their support during the writing of this book. I know that at times when deadlines got short, I did too. I love you all and I'm looking forward to having some downtime and relaxation with everyone.

About the Reviewers

Richard Carter is the Creative Director at Peacock Carter Ltd (`http://www.peacockcarter.co.uk`), a web design and development agency based in the North East of England, working with clients including Directgov, NHS Choices, and BusinessLink.

Richard is the author of *MediaWiki Skins Design*, *Magento 1.3 Themes Design*, *Joomla! 1.5 Templates Cookbook*, and *Magento 1.4 Themes Design*. He has acted as a technical reviewer *on MediaWiki 1.1 Beginner's Guide*, *Inkscape 0.48 Essentials For Web Designers*, and the *Definitive Guide to Drupal 7*, and is a co-founder of the Drupal North East user group (`http://www.drupalnortheast.org.uk`).

He blogs at `http://www.earlgreyandbattenburg.co.uk` and tweets nonsense at `http://twitter.com/RichardCarter`.

> I would like to thank the author of the book for dedicating time to helping others learn Drupal, which has changed beyond most recognition in the last few years.

Jeffrey Smith has 15+ years experience in the IT industry and about eight months experience as a .NET developer. He loves trying new things which is a blessing and a curse.

He loves technology and trying new things. He is currently ramping up his JavaScript and Ruby on Rails skills. He is a .NET developer by day and experiments with new things at night. He is working on projects that use ASP.NET MVC, C#, Coffeescript, Drupal, JQuery, MongoDB, PHP, Ruby on Rails, Rhomobile, Sproutcore, and the Strobe framework.

Ravishankar Somasundaram has over six years of experience in providing solutions to clients across multiple sectors and domains. Being more passionate about learning and teaching, he also strongly believes that the sole purpose of learning is to make our minds think in different perspectives and facilitates the same in his training sessions through a blended learning approach mainly focused on how to "learn to learn".

In his early schooling apart from winning several prizes in science projects, he was awarded the Title "Junior Scientist" by a committee consisting of people from ISRO in an Inter school Science Fest for a model display on "Evolution of Airplanes through Aerodynamics", this is one of his childhood achievements.

His final year college project aimed at eliminating the scenario of English alone being the medium of programming in all programming languages, which restricts people who don't know English getting into the IT field and implementing their ideas, was selected and funded by **MIT NRCFOSS** and considered a landmark.

Being one of the seven people from India and the only one from Tamil Nadu as an official third party developer of Moodle code, he shares his knowledge by helping people on Moodles official forum and on IRC. He has also presented a paper in the ninth International Tamil Internet conference on "Moodle: For Enhanced Learning" which talks about leveraging Moodle's capability to expand the user base for one of the oldest languages known to mankind—Tamil.

Ravi was a Freelance IT Consultant delivering solutions to firms irrespective of Technical, Non-Technical or Business domains. Currently he works for Thirdware Technologies as a Technical Analyst and Chief Architect heading the R&D Division.

Recently he represented his company at an International conference "Yugma—Unleashing the Innovation potential" with an idea which uses Artificial Intelligence to empower the next generation enterprise mobile solutions.

I am thankful to all the people I have met till date, for they have contributed to the cause of my growth either by being an inspiration or personally guiding and pointing me to the right direction when facing challenging situations or throwing critiques continuously, making me recognize there is always an area for improvement in my career and personal life

Last, but the foremost, I dedicate all my accomplishments to my parents, sister and other relations for all their faith, hope, love, and support.

www.PacktPub.com

Support files, eBooks, discount offers and more

You might want to visit www.PacktPub.com for support files and downloads related to your book.

Did you know that Packt offers eBook versions of every book published, with PDF and ePub files available? You can upgrade to the eBook version at www.PacktPub.com and as a print book customer, you are entitled to a discount on the eBook copy. Get in touch with us at service@packtpub.com for more details.

At www.PacktPub.com, you can also read a collection of free technical articles, sign up for a range of free newsletters and receive exclusive discounts and offers on Packt books and eBooks.

http://PacktLib.PacktPub.com

Do you need instant solutions to your IT questions? PacktLib is Packt's online digital book library. Here, you can access, read and search across Packt's entire library of books.

Why Subscribe?

- Fully searchable across every book published by Packt
- Copy and paste, print and bookmark content
- On demand and accessible via web browser

Free Access for Packt account holders

If you have an account with Packt at www.PacktPub.com, you can use this to access PacktLib today and view nine entirely free books. Simply use your login credentials for immediate access.

Table of Contents

Preface

You can use the Drupal 7 content management framework to build a small business website rapidly. You may add blogs; images and image galleries; maps, e-commerce and shopping carts; social application integration including Twitter and Flickr, and more to your site to connect with your customers and make more money from your business.

Drupal 7 Business Solutions will give you hands-on practical tutorials on how to build a rich and dynamic website for your business quickly using one of the most popular tools in open source.

You'll start by adding blogs and images to your website. Then you'll learn how to add a VIP section to your site so that you can give your logged in users special discounts and other VIP freebies. Next, you will learn to send your customers e-mail newsletters and show them a dynamic events calendar.

The book will then teach you to add e-commerce to your site using the new Drupal Commerce module so you can sell your products online. You'll add YouTube videos, Google maps, and Flickr-based photos to help enhance your business site. You will then learn to incorporate feedback mechanisms for your customers.

The book also explains how to maintain your site, upgrade it, and continue adding dynamic content to it over time so you can market your business successfully with a professional, flexible and optimized website.

What this book covers

Chapter 1, Planning our Site and Setting up Drupal: In this chapter we plan for and map out our website and its content with the Drupal content management system as the backbone. We look at the advantages and benefits of using Drupal to build our site. We install Drupal and set up the website's initial basic configuration.

Chapter 2, Creating the Artisan Bakers Collective Website: In this chapter we continue configuring Drupal and learning how to run a cron task and check the Drupal status report. We enable clean URLs, and add some Basic Page and Article content to our site. We add users to our site and configure basic user permissions. We discuss the various types of home pages we can configure using Drupal. We configure path aliases, set up navigation menus, tweak the order of our menu items, enable core modules; and install contributed Drupal modules.

Chapter 3, Adding Products and Services: In this chapter we build a custom content type using Drupal. We configure the content type and add custom fields to the content type in order to post specific data to our site using the content type's form. We install and configure the Date module to handle adding fields to our content type to collect date and time information. We set up some basic access control to our content type. We also build some taxonomy vocabularies and add tags to our site.

Chapter 4, Interacting with Customers and Visitors: In this chapter we add user roles to the site and extend the user signup form to add fields to collect user profile data. We enable and configure the Comments module and create some specific comments-based actions and triggers.

Chapter 5, Creating a Company Blog: In this chapter we enable and configure the Blog module. We add some blog posts and set up a moderation system for our blogging. We learn how to configure advanced actions in Drupal. We add easy access methods for our site visitors to be able to get to and read our blog posts by enabling blocks that show recent blog posts. We add RSS feeds to our site's blog. We learn how to aggregate content from other websites using the powerful Drupal Aggregation and Feeds modules.

Chapter 6, Newsletters and Calendars: In this chapter we set up e-newsletters on our site using the Simplenews module. We learn how to add a Newsletter and send it via e-mail to our site visitors. We set up a subscription service for the newsletters. We add an Event content type to the site and create a visual calendar of our events using the Calendar module.

Chapter 7, Sharing and Consuming with YouTube, Flickr, Google Maps, and Twitter: In this chapter we learn how to embed YouTube videos on our site. We install and configure the Flickr module to add Flickr photosets and photos to our site via a web service API. We add Google Maps to our site and also learn how to tweet our site content automatically to our Twitter account.

Chapter 8, Freebies and Downloads: In this chapter we learn how to post files including PDFs to our site's content so our site visitors can easily download these files. We configure both public and private file systems on our site. We install and configure the Print module which adds printer-friendly versions of our site's pages, e-mail to friend functionality, and PDF versions of our site's content. We install the dompdf library so we can generate PDFs of our site's content automatically.

Chapter 9, Online Orders and Payments: In this chapter we install and configure the new Drupal 7.x Commerce module to add e-commerce functionality and a shopping cart to our site.

Chapter 10, Image Galleries and Slideshows: In this chapter we use the Views and Views Slideshow modules to set up image galleries and dynamic slideshows of our image collections.

Chapter 11, Maintaining and Optimizing your Drupal Site: In this final chapter we discuss best practices for maintaining and optimizing our Drupal website and its MySQL database. This includes discussions of Drupal performance and some tips for getting the best performance and optimization out of your website.

Who this book is for

This book is for anyone who wants to learn how to set up a website quickly for their business using the super powerful Drupal open source content management software.

Conventions

In this book, you will find a number of styles of text that distinguish between different kinds of information. Here are some examples of these styles, and an explanation of their meaning.

Code words in text are shown as follows: " Let's tweak the label to read `Description of Item`."

A block of code is set as follows:

```
[default]
exten => s,1,Dial(Zap/1|30)
exten => s,2,Voicemail(u100)
exten => s,102,Voicemail(b100)
exten => i,1,Voicemail(s0)
```

When we wish to draw your attention to a particular part of a code block, the relevant lines or items are set in bold:

```
[default]
exten => s,1,Dial(Zap/1|30)
exten => s,2,Voicemail(u100)
exten => s,102,Voicemail(b100)
exten => i,1,Voicemail(s0)
```

New terms and **important words** are shown in bold. Words that you see on the screen, in menus or dialog boxes for example, appear in the text like this: "You'll see a message stating that **Cron ran successfully:**".

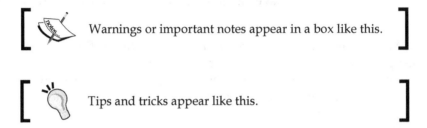

Warnings or important notes appear in a box like this.

Tips and tricks appear like this.

Reader feedback

Feedback from our readers is always welcome. Let us know what you think about this book—what you liked or may have disliked. Reader feedback is important for us to develop titles that you really get the most out of.

To send us general feedback, simply send an e-mail to feedback@packtpub.com, and mention the book title via the subject of your message.

If there is a topic that you have expertise in and you are interested in either writing or contributing to a book, see our author guide on www.packtpub.com/authors.

Customer support

Now that you are the proud owner of a Packt book, we have a number of things to help you to get the most from your purchase.

Downloading the example code

You can download the example code files for all Packt books you have purchased from your account at `http://www.PacktPub.com`. If you purchased this book elsewhere, you can visit `http://www.PacktPub.com/support` and register to have the files e-mailed directly to you.

Errata

Although we have taken every care to ensure the accuracy of our content, mistakes do happen. If you find a mistake in one of our books—maybe a mistake in the text or the code—we would be grateful if you would report this to us. By doing so, you can save other readers from frustration and help us improve subsequent versions of this book. If you find any errata, please report them by visiting `http://www.packtpub.com/support`, selecting your book, clicking on the **errata submission form** link, and entering the details of your errata. Once your errata are verified, your submission will be accepted and the errata will be uploaded on our website, or added to any list of existing errata, under the Errata section of that title. Any existing errata can be viewed by selecting your title from `http://www.packtpub.com/support`.

Piracy

Piracy of copyright material on the Internet is an ongoing problem across all media. At Packt, we take the protection of our copyright and licenses very seriously. If you come across any illegal copies of our works, in any form, on the Internet, please provide us with the location address or website name immediately so that we can pursue a remedy.

Please contact us at `copyright@packtpub.com` with a link to the suspected pirated material.

We appreciate your help in protecting our authors, and our ability to bring you valuable content.

Questions

You can contact us at `questions@packtpub.com` if you are having a problem with any aspect of the book, and we will do our best to address it.

1
Planning our Site and Setting up Drupal

Although several books have been written about Drupal 7, most have been written for developers to help them program sites using Drupal coding standards, enhance sites by using custom modules, and change the appearance of Drupal sites by using themes. In this book, we take a different approach. Throughout the book, we will develop a website for a (fictional) business and meet the needs of this business.

We have included an explanation of all the key features in Drupal that most small-to-medium-sized businesses would want to use on their sites. A thorough step-by-step description of how to integrate each piece of functionality into your website is included, along with an explanation of the business need that is being satisfied by using the functionality.

After reading this book, you will be able to adapt the techniques used in this book to either develop a site for your company on your own, or work with a development firm to create a website that truly meets the needs of your business.

In this chapter, we will introduce our client, the Artisan Bakers Collective and discuss their plans to build a website. We will also introduce Drupal 7 and describe why it is a good fit for our client's website.

In this chapter, we will cover the following topics:

- Plans for the Artisan Bakers Collective website
- The advantages and disadvantages of simple, static web pages
- Advantages and disadvantages of customized PHP and MySQL sites
- Deciding on Drupal for building the website
- Getting started with Drupal

Artisan Bakers Collective

Baker James is the owner of the Artisan Bakers Collective, a popular artisan bakery, café, and store. The past few years have been very good, and he has expanded from one bakery to three. Each bakery is decorated in a retro theme and Baker James is extremely proud of the decor. The Artisan Bakers Collective offers a wide variety of breads and baked goods, but specializes in creating sourdough bread using traditional European-style slow-rise recipes handed down over generations.

Baker James wants to add an e-commerce component to his business, so that he can reach a larger clientele, which he feels will bring in additional revenue. He also gives baking classes and would like to promote this.

Plans for the Artisan Bakers Collective website

Baker James had a website designed for him several years ago, but it has proven to be difficult to maintain and is therefore several years outdated. James would like to build a new website for his businesses that is easy to update and maintain. He would like to provide a destination for his customers where they can visit his bakery online, learn more about the bakery, find out about classes, events, and the featured breads, and receive discounts, if they are loyal customers.

Baker James has several key goals for his site, which are as follows:

- The site must provide an easy method for updating its content so that it's always current
- Baker James should be able to make updates to the website without having to pay a consultant to do so
- He should be able to run a secure and stable website that uses current website development standards
- The overall website should be easy to maintain in terms of keeping Drupal modules updated and keeping the site secure and stable
- It should be possible to add new functionalities to the website without requiring a complete start over

After Baker James came to us expressing his desire to have a new website built, we sat down with him to determine what pages and sections should be added to the website, so that we can plan our development. Based on these discussions, we decided on the following features for the site:

1. **Home Page**: This includes links to other areas in the site, current events, and sample menu items. Baker James may want the home page to have a design and layout different from the rest of the site.

2. **Pages**: This includes pages highlighting bread, other baked goods, and coffee. There will be one method for creating pages—a simple method where each page is developed independently, using a form (in Drupal), that is simple to complete.

3. **Search**: This allows visitors to search the menu for the bakery's goods, based on a variety of criteria.

4. **Ratings**: This allows visitors to rate items on a scale of 1-5.

5. **About Us Page**: This page provides contact information.

6. **Guest Book**: This allows visitors to comment on the bakery and give feedback. Baker James can see when new comments are added, and he can optionally remove comments if they do not meet the site's standards.

7. **Map**: This helps the visitor find all of the Artisan Bakers Collective bakeries, using Google Maps.

8. **Polls and Surveys**: From time to time, the bakery will have polls to see what items patrons want added to the menu, and what they think of the new items on the menu.

9. **Photo Gallery**: This shows the pictures of food on the menu as well as pictures of the restaurants.

10. **Monthly Newsletter**: This is a newsletter that visitors can subscribe to. Baker James will be able to create the newsletter content on the site. Customers can also view the previous editions of the newsletter.

11. **Event Calendar**: This showcases events occurring at the bakeries.

12. **Member Rewards site**: This gives details of the discounts for members who have visited the bakery a specified number of times.

13. **Online ordering**: This will allow visitors to order breads and sign up for classes through an e-commerce ordering system.

14. **Forum**: This is a forum to solicit suggestions and ideas for improvement, to discuss policies, and so on.

15. **Blog**: This will be used by Baker James and his employees for discussing topics important to them, including information on new menu recipes, running a bakery, and more.

16. **Administration Area**: This helps Baker James optimize his website, so that the visitors can make the most of it.

Selecting a foundation for the Artisan Bakers Collective site

In this section, we will explore a range of possible technologies that could be used to build the Artisan Bakers Collective website. The pros and cons of each method will be discussed, and we will choose the final technology that will be used to build the website.

Simple static web pages

Many websites continue to be built by simply creating standalone HTML pages that do not change frequently over time. These pages can be created with a dedicated website design program or with a simple text editor. These pages are then uploaded to the web server, using an FTP client or another transfer client provided by the web host.

Key advantages

There are several advantages of using this method of web development, listed as follows:

- HTML web editor software can make creating web pages as easy as writing a letter, since the interface is similar to Microsoft Word
- Website editors may provide pre-built themes to make the website appealing, without any graphical design experience
- It is a very easy way to get started
- For simple sites, simple techniques are sometimes appropriate
- A website can be created relatively quickly
- Websites can be built for free or for the cost of a website design program
- The hardware requirements are very low, so the website will run on nearly any host

Key disadvantages

Although static web pages can be easy to develop, there are a number of disadvantages that appear after you deploy the website and try to make revisions to it later. The disadvantages are listed as follows:

- Adding a new page to the website may require changes to all of the existing pages on the website
- Changing elements that are common to all pages, such as the header or the footer, may require changes to every page on the website
- When major changes are needed to the website, it may be easier to rebuild the entire site
- It is easy to have errors within the website, leading to pages that cannot be reached, or errors that the visitor may encounter. These errors can include broken links and images, and broken navigation menus
- Advanced functionality cannot be added without custom programming
- Created code can be inefficient or incorrect, leading to websites that do not display properly in all browsers
- Security and optimization techniques created by other developers are not automatically applied to your site

Fully-customized site with PHP and MySQL

You could also build a fully-customized website, built entirely from scratch, using a programming language such as PHP and a database such as MySQL. In this type of system, one or more programmers build custom code specifically for your website. Some common libraries may be used to speed up development, but the majority of the site will be custom-created.

Key advantages

There are several advantages to developing a completely custom-built website for your company, which are listed as follows:

- The final website will be fully customized to meet the exact needs of your company
- New functionality can be added by another programmer, who is skilled in the same programming language, at a later date

- Complex functionality may be easier to develop, when starting with a clean slate
- The website may be much more efficient than a website built on a predefined framework or content management system

Key disadvantages

Unfortunately, developing a completely custom website is a difficult, time-consuming process and has several disadvantages. They are listed as follows:

- Relatively lesser-skilled programmers may create a website that is difficult to maintain and enhance
- Changing the look and feel of the website may require significant re-work, unless the site is designed to allow customization
- The website may require a great deal of work by programmers to create and maintain
- Security flaws may be inadvertently introduced, which could compromise the overall server or private data of your customers
- The site may require more hardware resources than simpler sites and may require significant resources to run at acceptable speeds
- Creating all of the functionality from scratch can prove to be very costly

Drupal content management system

Drupal is an open source content management framework based on PHP and MySQL. To use Drupal, you need to install it onto your web server. After it's installed, you use Drupal to create and edit pages. Drupal handles most of the common functionalities that are needed to build websites of any size, and also handles many complex functionalities with the help of plugin Drupal modules, including:

- User management
- Categorization of content
- Building menus
- Creating a consistent look for all pages
- Adding pictures to pages
- Creating and maintaining blogs
- Creating and maintaining forums
- E-commerce

- Image galleries and other multimedia support
- Contact forms
- Translation and internationalization
- And much more

Although these features alone are sufficient to handle many sites, Drupal also offers a powerful module system that allows developers to create modules that plug in to the core Drupal framework to seamlessly provide new capabilities. Many modules have been created by the Drupal open source community and released for use under open source licenses, free of charge. Modules are available for nearly every conceivable task, but if you don't find what you are looking for, a custom module can always be created to handle your exact needs.

Drupal also provides a powerful theme system that allows you to change the look and feel of your website and have all of the pages changed throughout the entire website, instantly. Hundreds of free themes are available on the Drupal website, and these can be customized to fit your needs. Alternatively, you could develop a custom theme for your own website. Commercial themes can also be purchased.

Benefits of building with Drupal

Drupal offers a number of benefits not found with the other methods of building a website. Many of these are related to the ease of maintenance and the ability to concentrate on business functionality rather than building common, repetitive functionality. The benefits of Drupal are listed as follows:

- You are free to concentrate on building content and functionality to support your business rather than creating basic functionality already provided by Drupal
- The look and feel of the website can be easily changed without rewriting the entire site or changing all of the pages
- All changes to the website take effect immediately, so you can ensure that the changes are correct
- Changes can be previewed prior to the website being updated, to make sure that it works properly
- Revisions to pages can be tracked, and you can require pages to go through an approval process prior to being made viewable
- You do not have to use FTP or other methods to deploy pages to your website. You can also use more stable and secure methods of deploying entire Drupal sites, using tools and software, including git and SVN.

- Development costs are low, as Drupal is available free of charge

- There is an active community that can help to answer any questions that you may have

- Drupal is actively maintained and enhanced, which helps to ensure that potential security issues are rapidly found and fixed

- Drupal can be used effectively by a wide range of people, even if they do not have any programming experience

- Site management can be delegated to a team of people, who can share responsibility for the entire website between them or take individual responsibility for specific areas within the site

- As Drupal is constantly being maintained and updated, you can gain access to new technologies more rapidly

Disadvantages of Drupal

Although Drupal is a very powerful tool, its very power causes a few disadvantages:

- A short learning curve is needed to get started and use the system effectively.

- It is more hardware-intensive than basic static pages. As it's more hardware-intensive and can create performance issues on a server, you may need to make sure that your organization or business can handle the expense of upgrading a server and the overall server infrastructure to support the site. This may include more expensive hosting options

- Additional programming may be needed to customize Drupal modules to do exactly what you want. Alternatively, you may have to compromise on desired functionality, based on what is actually available

- Drupal may be more vulnerable to security issues as there are a large number of sites that use Drupal, and hackers may target Drupal sites as it's a popular open source software used by many site developers

- Along the same lines as security, Drupal sites require frequent module and software updates in order to keep the website secure and stable. This is extremely important in order to keep your Drupal codebase secure

- There may be limitations to the framework, which could make building custom functionality more difficult

Deciding on Drupal

As you may have guessed from the title of the book, we are picking Drupal, and specifically the latest version, Drupal 7, to build the Artisan Bakers Collective websites. Drupal gives us the best combination of functionality, flexibility, security, and ease of use, for our website. In fact, Drupal is an appropriate choice for a range of websites from small sites to large sites and everything in between. Many large-scale enterprise businesses, non-profit organizations, and private companies are using Drupal to power their website. For example, the White House is using Drupal. Chances are, if you are planning to build a website, Drupal will fulfill all of your needs.

At one point it was more complex to search out modules to use on a Drupal site, and this was looked upon as a disadvantage, but in this book, you'll see that it's actually much easier to locate good stable modules to use in Drupal 7.

Getting started with Drupal

In this book, we will jump straight into using Drupal to build a practical website, and not spend a lot of time talking about basic functionalities, the design of Drupal, or theoretical aspects related to Drupal. We will use Drupal 7, the most recent active version of Drupal, throughout this book. Drupal 7 is continuously in development, while Drupal 6 is also still supported and available for use on sites. The roadmap for Drupal already shows that Drupal 8 is in the planning stages.

To start using Drupal, we recommend setting up a development environment on your local desktop (either on your PC or on your Mac). You can develop the website for the client on your local computer using a local server, powered by MAMP (MySQL, Apache, and PHP for Mac) or WAMP (the same for Windows). This allows for quick and robust local development. When you're ready to show the client the site, you can easily transfer the Drupal site files and the database over to the client's web host.

You can also install the Drupal Development Desktop Stack that Acquia provides for download. They call this the Dev Desktop (`http://www.acquia.com/products-services/dev-desktop`), and it packages the entire Drupal core with PHP, MySQL, and an Apache web server.

This section will assume you have chosen either MAMP or WAMP to install on your local computer. We'll be installing Drupal into the web root of your local environment, which is usually `htdocs` or `www`.

You're also going to need to set up a database for your Drupal 7 site to use, since Drupal is database-driven. To do this, navigate to your **localhostphpMyAdmin** application. In MAMP or WAMP, this is easily located through the MAMP or WAMP control panel.

Follow the given instructions for setting up your database:

1. Open **phpMyAdmin** and click on the **Privileges** tab.
2. Click on **Add a new User**:

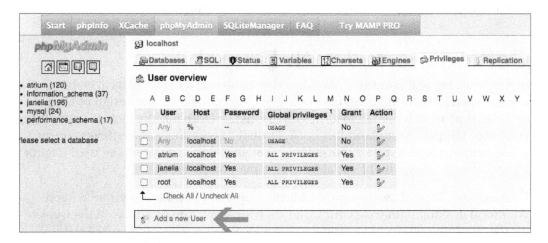

3. Type in a **User name** (here I'll enter the username **drupal7**); set **Host** to **localhost**; and type in a password. Re-type the password.
4. Select the **Create database with same name and grant all privileges** radio button.
5. Then click on the **Check All** link.

6. Click on the **Go** button, to create the database:

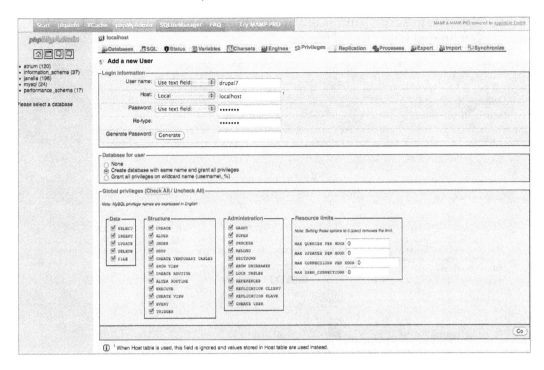

7. Jot down the credentials from above, as you'll need them when you install Drupal.

8. Your blank database is now created and you can now move on to installing Drupal.

You can use the following steps to install Drupal:

1. Navigate to `http://drupal.org`, through your web browser. Click on the **Get Started with Drupal** button.

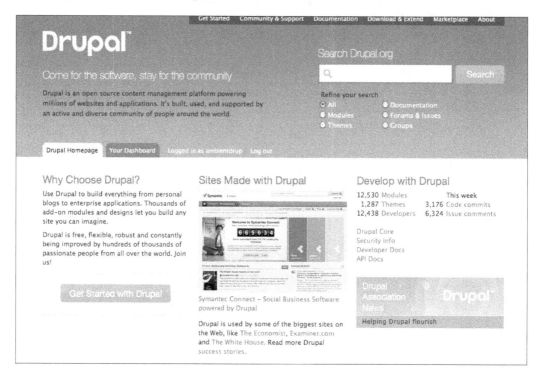

2. On the next page, click on the **Download Drupal 7.8** button. This will launch a **Download & Extend** page. You want to download the 7.x version of Drupal, so click on the `tar.gz` download link to start the download. Save the `tar.gz` file to your web root directory. At the time of this book's release, the Drupal version is 7.8. It may be a different 7.x version when you go to download it.

3. After you download the Drupal installation, you will need to unpack it. The installation is delivered in `tar.gz` format, to unpack which you may need a specialized tool, such as **7-Zip** or **WinZip**. 7-Zip is a freely-available program designed to work with a wide variety of compressed file formats. On the Mac, you should be able to unzip the file by default, without having to download any tools.

4. Unzip/unpack the `tar.gz` file in your `htdocs` or `www` folder. The resulting unzipped folder will be called `drupal-7.8`, by default. This is your Drupal site folder.

5. You can rename the `drupal-7.8` folder to be more specific to the site you're building. Let's rename the folder `artisanbakers`.

6. You can now browse to the location where you have installed Drupal in a web browser, to begin the installation process. If you are installing on your localhost environment the URL of the install will be something similar to `http://localhost/artisanbakers/install.php`. You should see a screen similar to the following screenshot, asking you to **Select an installation profile**.

7. Leave the installation profile **Standard** selected, and then click on the **Save and Continue** button:

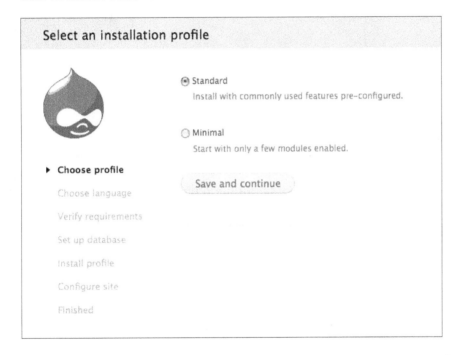

8. Leave **English** set as the default language and click on **Save and continue**:

9. The next screen will ask you to add your MySQL database credentials for the database you originally created for the site. First, make sure to leave the **MySQL, MariaDB, or equivalent** radio button selected. Now, add your credentials, including **Database name, Database username,** and **Database password,** here. Once you add the credentials, click on **Save and continue**.

10. There may be a case where you need to add **Advanced Options** for your database connection. If you are going to be installing and hosting the database on an external server you'll want to expand this **Advanced Options** fieldset and add the path to the externally-hosted server. In our case, we're hosting the database on the same localhost server, so we do not need to expand this fieldset now:

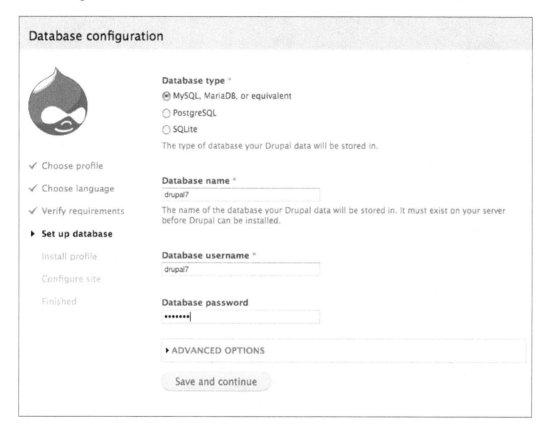

11. Drupal will now proceed with the install.

12. The **Configure site** screen will load next. This screen is split up into various fieldsets. First, you want to give your site a **Site name** and **Site e-mail address**. The site name can be **Artisan Bakers Collective**. For the site e-mail address, type in your e-mail address, for now:

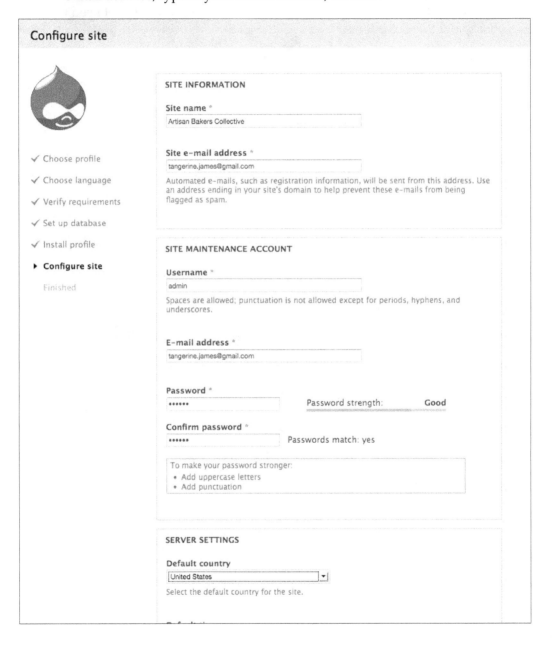

13. Now, you need to set up the **Site Maintenance Account**. This first user account on the site is the super-user administration account. You'll use this account to do all the site development and, later, to maintain the site. For now let's call the super user "admin", so type in admin as the username. You can use the same e-mail address you used previously. Add a password.

14. The password should be strong and include special characters, such as, # or @. You may also want to use capital letters mixed with lowercase ones and also add numbers to the password. Drupal will check the password, using the password strength visual prompt, and this will assist you in constructing a strong password. This is essential for keeping your site secure.

15. For **Server Settings**, choose the **Default country** and **Default time zone** for where you are located. This will automatically use the time zone of your country for all date- and time-related functionalities on your website.

16. Lastly, leave the checkbox next to **Update Notifications** ticked, to check for updates automatically and receive e-mail notifications.

17. Click on **Save and continue**.

18. The installation will complete and you'll see a congratulations screen. Click on the **Visit your new site** link, to launch your Drupal 7 website:

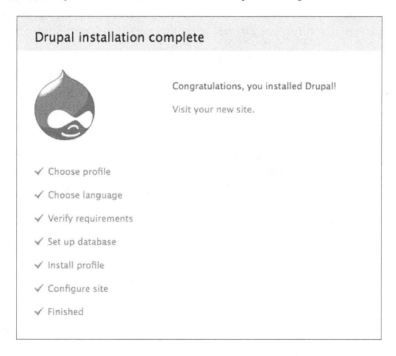

Artisan Bakers Collective on the web

You've successfully installed Drupal 7 and actually already have a fully-functional core Drupal 7 website for your client's business. In *Chapter 2*, *Creating the Artisan Bakers Collective Website*, we'll dive right into the Drupal 7 interface and start adding our client's content and setting up the website, as per our client's requirements.

If you want to see an example of the techniques used in this book as well as a live example of the complete website, you can visit `http://variantcube.com/artisanbakers/`. This site contains all of the examples developed throughout the course of this book. If you have questions about how to use Drupal, please post them on the forum at `http://variantcube.com/artisanbakers/forum`, and I will try to answer your questions, as quickly as possible. You can search on Drupal.org, using the site's default search box. Alternatively, you can visit the Drupal forums at `http://www.drupal.org/forum`, to see if you can find an answer to your question; if not, you can post the question to the Drupal.org community.

Summary

In this chapter, we developed the requirements for Baker James' Artisan Bakers Collective website. We also looked at some of the possible methods of building the website, before deciding that Drupal is perfectly suited for this type of site.

Now that we have our requirements for the website and have decided to build it using Drupal, it's time to get our hands dirty and begin building the website. In this chapter, you successfully installed and configured a development server environment and also installed Drupal. Congratulations! You should be proud of the work you have accomplished so far!

We will start with the basic functionalities that 99 percent of the websites need and then gradually move on to more complex tasks. We will use a step-by-step approach to building the site, so that you can follow along with the examples.

2
Creating the Artisan Bakers Collective Website

In this chapter, we will start building the Artisan Bakers Collective website using Drupal 7. You'll learn how to use the Drupal 7 administrative interface to build your site. We'll look at the differences between the various types of content that Drupal 7 is bundled with and start building our site's pages.

After we get comfortable managing content, we will add web pages to the navigation system, so that customers can easily find all the information that they need. After the navigation has been completed, we will make the site look more visually appealing by adding images. We will learn how to enable core Drupal 7 modules; and how to install new modules.

By the end of this chapter you'll be able to:

- Run cron, check site status report, and enable clean URLs
- Add basic pages
- Add user accounts and tweak user permissions
- Add images to content
- Create a home page
- Add site menus
- Enable core modules and install contributed modules

The Core Drupal 7 look and feel

At the end of *Chapter 1, Planning our Site and Setting up Drupal*, you successfully installed Drupal 7. With Drupal 7 installed you will get a core bare-bones Drupal website that you can begin to customize for your client. Your site's home page should currently look like the following screenshot:

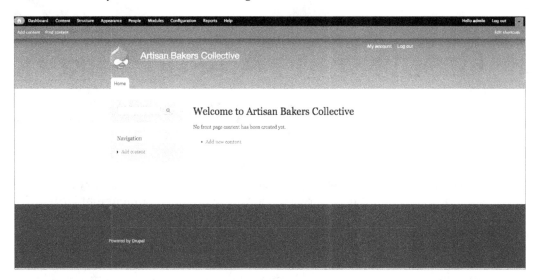

The site displays a blue header area with the Drupal logo icon, a hyperlink to your user account page and to log out of the site. The home tab shows in the primary menu; there's a search box and a **Navigation** block in the left sidebar; and some default home page content. You'll also notice the black horizontal admin menu that is only accessible to you when you are logged into the site as the admin user. This menu provides easy access to the Drupal administrative interface. Finally the footer area in black contains the **Powered by Drupal** text. Every time you install Drupal 7 for the first time you'll see a layout similar to this. The default theme that comes enabled with Drupal 7 is called **Bartik**. We'll talk about Bartik in more detail later in this chapter.

Checking the site's status report

Before we start adding content and pages to our site, let's check the Drupal status report. Drupal provides an easy method of checking on your site's status. This can help you to confirm throughout the project that your site is running smoothly.

In the black admin menu click on the **Reports** link and on the resulting **Reports** screen click on the **Status report** link. You'll also notice here that Drupal 7 provides all of its admin screens as overlay windows. You still see the Drupal website content behind the overlay window and can click on the **X** icon on an overlay screen at any time to close it and return to your site.

The **Status report** screen will load. This screen gives you essential information on your Drupal 7 site including the following information:

- The Drupal version we're using, in this case Drupal 7.8
- Whether your Drupal configuration file is protected. This is good to know in terms of security and you want this to be protected
- A link to run your cron task manually
- The database system you're running on. In this case MySQL and its version number
- Whether the database is up-to-date
- File system info
- Image library info
- PHP version and a link to your PHP.info file
- PHP memory limit
- Whether you have Drupal 7 update notifications enabled
- The type of web server you are running — in this case it will most likely be Apache

- Any errors or warning messages. Notice here, in the following screenshot we have a yellow warning telling us that our modules and themes are out of date. You may also see more critical warning messages with red backgrounds on this screen:

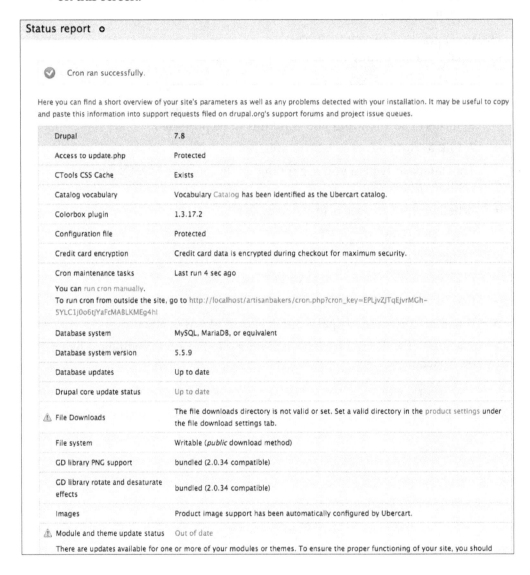

Status report ⚙	
✓ Cron ran successfully.	
Here you can find a short overview of your site's parameters as well as any problems detected with your installation. It may be useful to copy and paste this information into support requests filed on drupal.org's support forums and project issue queues.	
Drupal	7.8
Access to update.php	Protected
CTools CSS Cache	Exists
Catalog vocabulary	Vocabulary Catalog has been identified as the Ubercart catalog.
Colorbox plugin	1.3.17.2
Configuration file	Protected
Credit card encryption	Credit card data is encrypted during checkout for maximum security.
Cron maintenance tasks	Last run 4 sec ago
You can run cron manually. To run cron from outside the site, go to http://localhost/artisanbakers/cron.php?cron_key=EPLjvZJTqEjvrMGh-5YLC1j0o6tjYaFcMABLKMEg4hl	
Database system	MySQL, MariaDB, or equivalent
Database system version	5.5.9
Database updates	Up to date
Drupal core update status	Up to date
⚠ File Downloads	The file downloads directory is not valid or set. Set a valid directory in the product settings under the file download settings tab.
File system	Writable (*public* download method)
GD library PNG support	bundled (2.0.34 compatible)
GD library rotate and desaturate effects	bundled (2.0.34 compatible)
Images	Product image support has been automatically configured by Ubercart.
⚠ Module and theme update status	Out of date
There are updates available for one or more of your modules or themes. To ensure the proper functioning of your site, you should	

Generally, you want all of the table rows in your status report to be green, showing that the site is running in a stable and secure environment.

Cron

One thing you can do on this screen is click on the **run cron manually** link. **Cron** is a script that runs various maintenance tasks and other actions on your Drupal site. It's good to run the cron task regularly and Drupal configures cron to run automatically every three hours. Click on the link to run it. You'll see a message stating that **Cron ran successfully**:

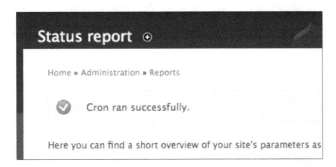

Clean URLs

Another item you'll want to check immediately after you install Drupal 7 is whether your site is using clean URLs. By default, Drupal 7 should auto-detect whether your web server supports clean URLs. Clean URLs are user and **Search Engine Optimization(SEO)** — friendly versions of the default Drupal URL path. By default Drupal will run its URLs or paths with special characters inserted. For example, if you have an **About** page on your site the path to it will be this by default: `http://localhost/?q=about`.

This format can be confusing to visitors because it's more difficult to type and because it contains special characters which make it appear more complex. Some search engines will also not index anything that comes after a question mark in an URL. This effectively makes your site have only one page in the eyes of some search engines. You can convert these to standard URLs by using clean URLs. This will make the same page's path as follows: `http://localhost:8888/about`.

This is a much easier URL for your site visitors to remember and it also makes it much easier for search engines to crawl and index your client's website.

In Drupal 7 clean URLs will be set up automatically for you during the installation process as long as your server supports this technical feature. If this does not happen during installation you can visit the clean URLs configuration page at **Configuration | Search and Metadata | Clean URLs** and Drupal will run an automatic test to determine if your site can support clean URLs. Click the **Save configuration** button. Now your site will be utilizing clean URLs:

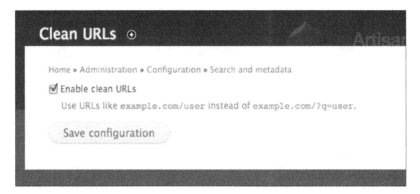

 If your setup does not meet the requirements, there is a wealth of information on the Drupal site at: `http://drupal.org/node/15365` that will help you determine why, and correct any issues. If you continue to have trouble setting up clean URLs, you may need to contact your site host.

We're now ready to add pages and content to the Artisan Bakers Collective site.

Drupal core content—basic pages and articles

This section will describe how to add content, or what you may be used to referring to as web pages. First we need to define some terms that Drupal uses when it deals with web-based content. When we talk about web pages within the Drupal framework, we're going to be generally speaking of nodes. A **node** is the Drupal equivalent of a web page, containing text, images, and other content. So when you add a page to a Drupal site you're adding a node. Additionally, each node in Drupal gets an ID that corresponds to its location in the MySQL database. In Drupal a web page is not a flat file that sits on the web server. It's a node that populates a database as data. Attached files and images get uploaded to the web server and sit in file directories, but the web content in a node gets stored in the database.

When we add nodes to our site we add them using content types. Drupal content types are used to add content to a Drupal site. Generally your client, in this case Baker James, need not know the specific definitions of these Drupal-based terms but it can definitely help you out to know what nodes and node IDs are. You can then explain these terms to your client, if they are interested in learning more about the specific Drupal terms and definitions.

Drupal 7 gives you two content types that you can use out-of-the-box to post nodes to your site:

- **The Article type**: It gives you a form to post news or blog style articles such as press releases, blog posts, or upcoming event announcements. The Article type defaults to a publishing option of **Promoted to front page**, meaning that any time you add an article to your site it will be promoted in teaser format to the home page content area. You can uncheck the **Promoted to front page** publishing option if you do not want a teaser to show automatically on your home page.

- **The Basic Page type**: It gives you a form to post traditional static-like pages such as your site's **About Us** page.

One of the first set of requirements for our client's site is:

- Adding the About the Artisan Bakers Collective page
- Creating a basic menu item
- Adding news and event announcement that we'll feature on the site's home page

Adding a Basic page

At the core of every site are pages that don't change or rarely change. Drupal makes it extremely easy to add these types of pages to a website without having any programming knowledge. We will demonstrate these techniques on the Artisan Bakers Collective site by creating a simple about page. We'll also take a look at how Drupal 7 allows us to set up a dynamic home page.

To add a new **Basic page**, click on the **Add Content** link in your toolbar menu on the top-left side of the site. You will now be presented with a list of content types that Drupal knows how to create. By default, Drupal gives us a **Basic page** type and an **Article** type. Most static-like pages, including our About Artisan Bakers Collective page, will be created using the **Basic page** type.

However, if you want to tag your content or add an image with your text content, the **Article** type may be a better choice, because by default the **Article** type comes with an image field and tagging enabled:

To create our about page, click on the **Basic page** link. Drupal will now present you with a form on which you can enter information about the page. You are required to enter a title that is displayed in the title of the web browser and above the page content when it is displayed on the site. Let's call this page **About Us**.

A typical about page may contain the name of the company, the address of the company, and a brief history of what the company does. We will use this as a guideline when we create our **About Us** page.

You can enter information exactly as you do in the word processor of your choice, using the *Enter* key to separate paragraphs. Drupal will automatically convert the text you enter into correct HTML for display in a web browser. You don't need to worry about learning HTML at this point. However, if you do know HTML, you can use tags to format your pages. The important thing to realize here is that you don't have to enter any HTML, but if you do, Drupal will automatically recognize it and render it correctly when you publish your page.

> Later, we will install a rich text editor module directly into Drupal to allow us to use a **What you see is what you get (WYSIWYG)** approach, to add text and HTML. There are multiple modules available for Drupal that adds a WYSIWYG editor.

The text we'll use for the **About Us** page is shown as follows. Go ahead, type or copy and paste the following code into the **Body** box in your Drupal **Basic page** form:

```
<em>Artisan Bakers Collective</em> is a European styleartisan
bakery serving a large variety of sourdough breads, pastries, cookies,
and coffees.  We sell our goods in-house at our stores and here via
our Website.  You can order breads 24/7 using our convenient online
store.  Artisan Bakers Collectivewas founded in 2010 by Baker Trevor
James to serve as an example website for the <strong>Drupal 7Business
Solutions</strong> book.
<h3>Address:</h3>
1500 Main Street
Anytown, MD
USA

<h3>Phone:</h3>
301-000-0000

<h3>Hours of operation</h3>
<ul>
<li>M-F: 8AM - 10PM</li>
<li>Sat: 7AM - 12PM</li>
<li>Sun: 8AM - 8PM</li>
</ul>
```

Directly under the body text box you'll see a drop-down box for **Text format**. Change this to **Full HTML**. The **Full HTML** text format will allow for HTML tags including the `<h3>`, `<ul>`, and `<li>` tags that you added to the content and will render them correctly.

Scroll down until you see the **Menu settings** tab. We want to add the **About Us** page to our Drupal menu system so that our site visitors can navigate to it easily. Enable the **Provide a menu link** box. Leave the **Menu link title** set to `About Us`. This will become the menu link that your site visitors will click on. Leave the **Parent item** set to **Main menu**:

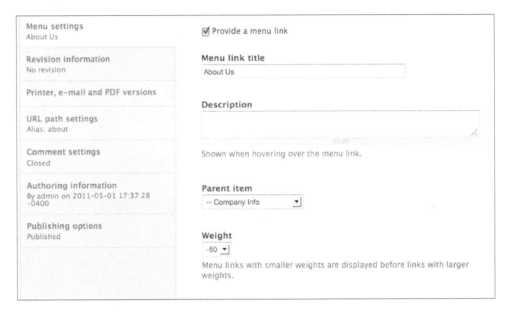

You will also see the **Weight** select box. This refers to the positioning of your page in the navigation menu. If you nest your page under a parent item and there are other items nested in that parent item, you can weight the items so they appear in a specific order.

Now scroll to the bottom of the form and click on the **Save** button. Your **About Us** page will publish on the website and Drupal will show you a green message stating **Basic page About Us has been updated**. You'll see your new **About Us** page and also see that it's been added to the main menu. There is now a new **About Us** tab in the main menu in your header region. You have successfully added your first **Basic page** to the site.

Notice that the **About Us** menu tab is highlighted, as it's the active page on the site. If you click on the **Home** tab, you'll return to the site's home page. Then you can click on the **About Us** tab to launch the **About Us** page again:

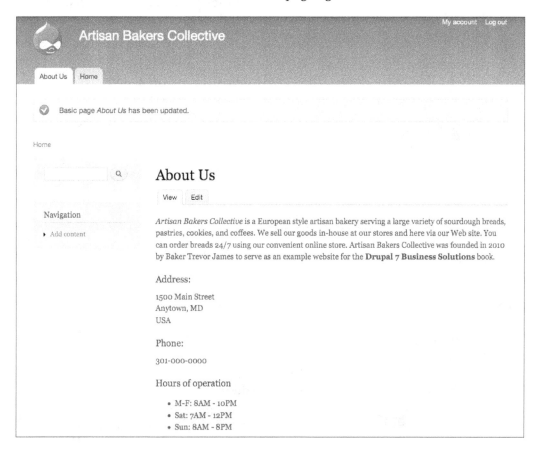

Editing a page

After you have created a **Basic page**, you can change the text on the page at any time by editing the page. To edit a page, first open the page in your browser, and then click on the **Edit** tab.

When editing your nodes, Drupal displays the same form that we used when adding the page to the site.

Security considerations

You can control who is allowed to add pages to your website by using permissions. By default, only the administrator is allowed to create **Basic pages** and **Articles**. If you are working on the site with a team, it is a good idea to create a new user role that gives team members access to only the functionality that they need to do their jobs.

Let's create a content editor role so that other people in our team can add pages to our site. To create a new role, click on **People** through the Drupal admin menu. The **People** overlay screen will load showing you a table of users on the site:

Currently there's one user, the main super-user admin. This **admin** user has the core Drupal administrator role and permissions to do everything on the website. To add a new role click on the **Permissions** tab and then on the **Roles** button. Type `content editor` as the name of the role and click the **Add role** button:

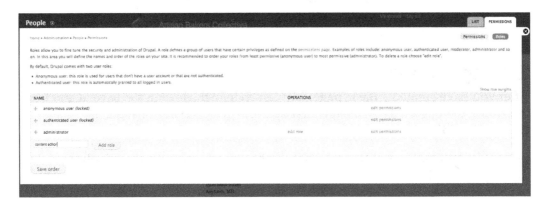

Now that we have a new role, we can assign permissions to it by selecting the **edit permissions** link. The permissions you set will depend on what the user needs to do to perform his or her job and how much you trust the user. In most cases, it is best to give users less permission options in the beginning, and then give them additional privileges as they become more familiar with the site.

For our site, we will give the editor the following permissions, which are located after the **Node** heading:

1. **Basic page: Create new content**: Allows the user to create basic pages for the site.

2. **Basic page: Edit own content**: Allows the user to edit pages that they have created, but not pages created by other users.

3. **Basic page: Delete own content**: Allows the user to delete pages they have created, but not pages created by other users.

A full list of permissions for creating and editing content is shown in the following screenshot:

If you trust the users who will become editors, you could also give them the privilege to edit and delete any **Basic page** content, which would give them the ability to edit and delete pages created by other users.

Once you assign the role's permissions, go ahead and click the **Save permissions** button at the bottom of the **Permissions** page.

If you choose to use other content types such as the **Article** type, you will need to assign permissions to these as well.

We will discuss additional permissions in further sections of this book, so don't worry if you don't know what they all mean now.

Adding users

Now once you save your user permissions you'll be redirected back to your user permissions page. To add users you'll need to go back to your **People** screen by clicking on the **People** link in the breadcrumb navigation menu. If you go back to your **People** screen you can click on the **Add user** link to add a new content editor user to your site. The **Add user** form will load. Here you can give the user a username, e-mail address, password, activate the user account, and assign user the content editor role you just created by selecting the role from the **Roles** set of checkboxes. The **Status** radio buttons refer to whether the user is active or blocked. All users are active by default. If you block a user they will no longer be able to log in to their account but the account will still exist on the site. Also enable the **Notify user of new account** checkbox if you want to send the user their login credentials through e-mail:

Username *

trevor

Spaces are allowed; punctuation is not allowed except for periods, hyphens, apostrophes, and underscores.

E-mail address *

backdrifting07@yahoo.com

A valid e-mail address. All e-mails from the system will be sent to this address. The e-mail address is not made public and will only be used if you wish to receive a new password or wish to receive certain news or notifications by e-mail.

☐ Plaintext-only emails

The *HTML Mail* module can send emails with fonts, styles, and other HTML formatting. If you prefer to receive all your emails in unformatted plain text, select this option.

Password

●●●●●●   Password strength: **Good**

Confirm password

●●●●●●   Passwords match: yes

To make your password stronger:
* Add uppercase letters
* Add punctuation

To change the current user password, enter the new password in both fields.

Status

◯ Blocked

◉ Active

Roles

☑ authenticated user

☐ administrator

☑ content editor

☐ VIP

☐ blogger

☐ moderator

Go ahead and do this, and then click the **Create new account** button. When you create the new account, Drupal will show you a message stating: **A welcome message with further instructions has been e-mailed to the new user username**.

If you revisit your main **People** listing you'll see the new user account listed in the **People** table.

Street presence, setting up the home page

Now that we've added a Basic page called **About Us** to the site, let's go ahead and create our home page. We will cover two possible styles of home pages. The first advantage the home page display that Drupal gives us out-of-the-box. With this core layout and style you can display short snippets of text called **teasers** from other portions of the website on the home page. This type of page is typically used on news sites and blog sites when you want to feature articles with their headline and teaser.

The other type of home page is a more static page similar to our **About Us** page, which contains its own unique content. This type of page is typical of most websites.

Blog style home pages

The first page is the home page that most visitors will see. Drupal makes it very easy to control the appearance and content of the home page.

By default, Drupal uses a blog style format for the home page. Drupal allows you to stick any piece of content you're adding on the site to the home page and feature it using its title and teaser. Drupal calls the part of each page that is displayed a teaser.

The number of posts or teasers you want to show on the home page of the site is governed by the settings on your **Site information** admin screen. Go to **Configuration | System | Site information**. The **Site information** screen contains a section titled **FRONT PAGE**, where you can control the number of posts you want to show on the front page of the site. The default is set to **10**. You can also tell Drupal what node you want to use as your home page here. By default this is set to the front page of the site:

FRONT PAGE

Number of posts on front page

10 ▾

The maximum number of posts displayed on overview pages such as the front page.

Default front page

http://localhost/artisanbakers/

Optionally, specify a relative URL to display as the front page. Leave blank to display the default content feed.

If you browse to your home page now, this will launch the default core Drupal home page. Currently the only content on your home page is the **Welcome to Artisan Bakers Collective** home page title.

Go ahead and click on the **Add new content** link through the shortcut toolbar menu. This just launches the same **Add content** screen that we're already familiar with from posting our **Basic** page. This time let's click on the **Article** link. Now fill out the **Title** field, add a tag or multiple tags to your article post; and type your article text into the **Body** box. Like you did with the **Basic** page you can add HTML code:

Tags

The **Tags** field is a field to enter a collection of tags or terms you want to associate with your article post. Type in a few tags and make sure to separate them by commas.

Adding images to your content

One significant improvement in Drupal 7 is that some of the more complex content type modules and functionalities are now built into the core Drupal, making them a lot easier to use out-of-the-box. This means that amongst other immediate benefits, your article content type comes with an image field as part of its core content type fields.

In *Chapter 3, Adding Products and Services*, we're going to show how easy it is to extend our content types by adding new image fields through the core content type module, but for now we'll use the image field on the **Article** type to populate our nodes with images.

On your **Create Article** form, click the **Browse** button in line to the **Image** field and locate a JPG, PNG, or GIF file on your computer. Then click on the **Upload** button to upload and associate the image with your article. When you upload the image, Drupal will display a small thumbnail version on your article form with a link to the full JPG version and the file size of the JPG noted:

Type some alternate text into the **Alternate text** field so that you are meeting 508 accessibility requirements. Alternate text is read by screen readers and is a recommended requirement to make your site accessible to all users, no matter how they are accessing your website.

We'll take a closer look at how Drupal handles and displays images in *Chapter 3*, when we talk about adding custom fields to our content types.

URL path settings

Now scroll down and click on **URL path settings**. Drupal allows you to rename the path of your article node with a more human-friendly alias. So instead of node/2, you can add an alias for this article. For example, you could type in migoya-sourdough:

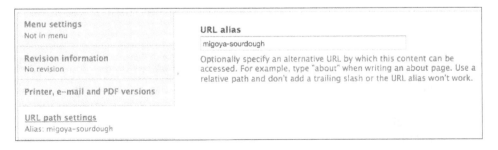

By adding this human-readable URL alias, in this case **migoya-sourdough**, the page will now have this alias instead of the default node/2 when it's displayed in the web browser. This alias will mean more to your site visitor and also make it easier for search engines to crawl your site and index your site correctly for good search results.

Using path aliases

A page alias allows you to access a page using a different URL. There is no limit to the number of aliases you can assign to a page, but in most cases, you will want only one additional path for any given page.

When creating paths, it is a good practice, not to use spaces in the path and to separate words with either hyphens (-) or underscores (_). The hyphen may be better for search engines as some search engines may treat words separated with underscores as a single word. You should not use spaces because technically they are not allowed in URLs. Most browsers will translate any spaces to 20%, but you may run into compatibility issues.

After you have created an alias, you can use the alias to create menus and build other links.

Creating multiple aliases for a page

Sometimes a single path for a page is not enough. For example, if you are migrating to Drupal from an old site, you will probably want to alias the old pages to use the new paths, so that visitors and search engines using the old paths can still find your information. This is possible for any page on your old site which is accessed with simple URLs that do not have extra query information. For example, the URL www.oldsite.com/home_page.html can be aliased, while the URL www.oldsite.com/home_page.html?a=Helllo cannot be.

If you want to create more than one alias, you need to click on **Configuration** and then on **URL aliases**, in the **Search And Metadata** fieldset:

SEARCH AND METADATA

Search settings
Configure relevance settings for search and other indexing options.

URL aliases
Change your site's URL paths by aliasing them.

Clean URLs
Enable or disable clean URLs for your site.

When the URL aliases screen loads you'll see a table showing you all of your node aliases. It should look similar to the following screenshot:

You can create a new alias by selecting the **Add alias** link. Drupal will open a form where you can enter the **real path** and the alias of the path. The real path is the existing system path on the site. For our **About Us** page, this is node/1. The **path alias** is another name that you would like to use to access the page. For the **About Us** page, we can use about. Complete the fields and then click on **Save**:

Now when you visit the **About Us** page your path should be: http://localhost:8888/about. Drupal will show you a message stating: **The alias has been saved**.

Automatically creating page aliases

If your find yourself creating new aliases for pages that follow a defined format, you can use the Pathauto module to automatically build aliases for you. More information on this is available at: `http://drupal.org/project/pathauto`.

Publishing options

Now click on the **Publishing options** tab. By default you'll see that Drupal will automatically promote article content to the front page of the site. You'll recall that this box was unchecked for the **Basic** page type. You can also check the **Sticky at top of lists** box and Drupal will then always keep this article post at the top of your home page above any other content you post. This is a nice way to feature special events or news on your home page:

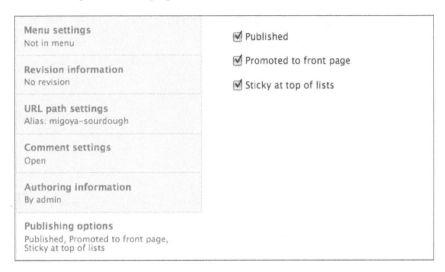

Click on the **Save** button and your article will be published. You'll immediately see your article and the larger scale version of the image you uploaded. Now, if you browse to your site's home page you should also see your article at the top of your home page, promoted and stuck to the top. The home page version will have a medium-sized version of the image you posted. Also notice that your home page gets an orange RSS icon just below the content.

If you click on the RSS icon you'll get an RSS feed showing all of the home page content:

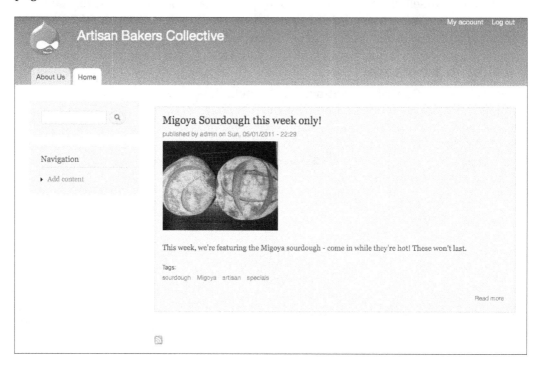

 Since your home page post is sticky you'll see your teaser surrounded by a border and with a light-gray background to denote that it's sticky at the top.

Your site visitors can subscribe to this feed and they'll always get the updated home page content through this RSS subscription:

Additionally, you should see the tags that you added to your article just below the article post on the home page. If you click on a tag you'll launch the tag's specific term page at an URL similar to `/taxonomy/term/tid`, where `tid` is the tag ID in the database. This resulting term page will show all content tagged with that specific term and the header of the page will be the name of the tag:

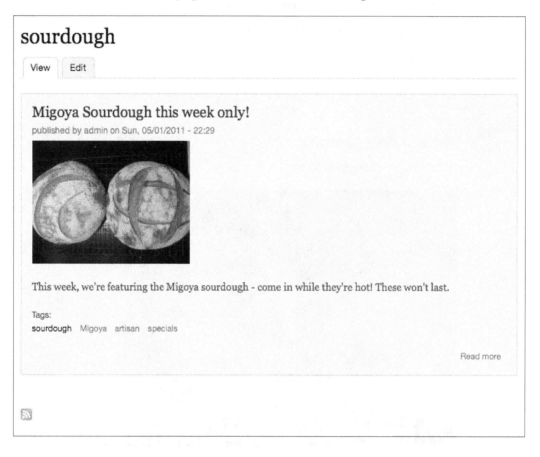

You also get an RSS feed for every term page on your site. This shows you the tremendous flexibility and organization of a Drupal site.

Creating a traditional home page

Another method of creating a home page for Artisan Bakers Collective is to create a specific node in Drupal, and then specify that node as the home page. Let's walk through this process now and then you will have two home page options to present your clients with.

The first step in creating a traditional home page is to create a **Basic** page that will serve as the foundation for our home page. We will create the page in exactly the same way as we created the **About Us** page. Click on your **Add content** link and then click on the **Basic page** link. The **Basic page** form will load.

For this specific example of a home page using the Basic page type let's enter the text as shown in the following screenshot. Of course, you can enter any text you have that meets your client's requirements:

Select the **URL path settings** tab and type in home page as the path alias for this node. Then click on **Save**. The **Basic** page type does not come with an image field by default, so we'll need to add an image to our home page after we publish it initially. We'll look at configuring an image field for the Basic page content type later in this chapter.

After you have created the home page, you need to tell Drupal that you want to use this page, rather than the default page that Drupal assigns out-of-the-box. First, make note of the path in the address bar when you are viewing the new home page. In this example, we've aliased the path to this page as home page. Now, open the **Site information** page by going to **Configuration | Site information**. Scroll down until you see the **FRONT PAGE** section. In the **Default front page** field remove the default node path and add our **home-page** path:

FRONT PAGE

Number of posts on front page

10 ▾

The maximum number of posts displayed on overview pages such as the front page.

Default front page

http://localhost:8888/artisanbakers/ home-page

Optionally, specify a relative URL to display as the front page. Leave blank to display the default content feed.

Click on the **Save configuration** button. If you browse back to your home page you should see your new home page displayed. You'll also notice that Drupal has automatically updated the main menu **Home** link to the correct new home page. This is because the **Home** link in the main menu is set to a path of `<front>`. The `<front>` tag allows Drupal to always point to the correct home page since the `<front>` tag is specifying whatever content is serving as the home page on the site. We'll discuss this in more detail in the next section on navigation.

Deleting a page

If you decide that a page is no longer relevant to your site, you can remove it from your website. There are two ways of doing this. You can either unpublish the page or completely delete the page.

Unpublishing the page will prevent the visitors from viewing the page, but the page will still be stored within Drupal, so it can be republished later if the content becomes relevant again. To unpublish a page, edit the page and then click on the **Publishing options** link. This will expand the **Publishing options** section. Simply deselect the **Published** checkbox and then save the page. Drupal will ensure that the page is removed from all of the menus, so that unauthorized visitors can't view it.

If you want to return to the page later, you will either need to type in the URL for the page or you can find the page through the content manager, which can be accessed at `yoursite.com/admin/content`. This page can also be reached from the **Administer** menu by clicking on the **Content** link. When you visit your main content admin screen, you should see something similar to the following screenshot:

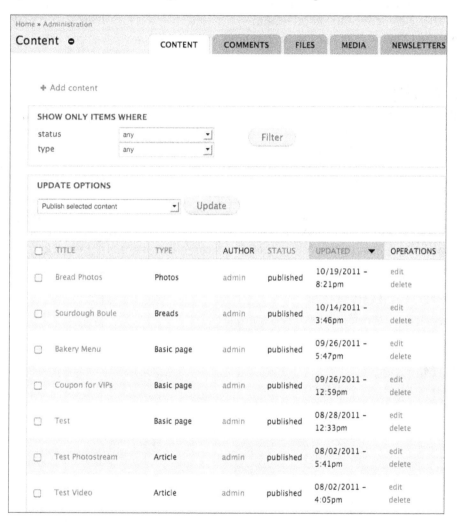

The other method of removing a page from your site is by deleting it. If you delete a page, it will be completely removed from the site and cannot be recovered. To delete a page, edit the page and then click on the **Delete** button at the bottom of the page. You will be asked to confirm that you really want to delete the page. If you click on the **Delete** button again, the page will be completely removed from your site. If you change your mind in between, you can select the **Cancel** link.

Getting around—setting up navigation

As your site gets larger and more complex, you will need to ensure that visitors can easily find what they are looking for. With traditional website development, managing navigation is among the most difficult, time consuming, and error prone tasks. Fortunately, Drupal handles the details of maintaining the navigation system for us, so we can concentrate on making sure that the navigation structure makes sense and is easy for the user to understand.

Building menus

The primary way to organize content in Drupal is by using menus. The Drupal menu system organizes content in a simple outline, where a page can be nested under another page. Drupal handles the expansion and collapsing of menus to hide menus that aren't immediately relevant to the user. This helps to keep the menu short and also ensures that the visitor can easily understand your site layout. You can also create multiple menus for the site. For example, many sites will have a **Main menu** that is displayed on the left-hand side corner of the screen, and a smaller menu that is displayed at the top of the page, and that lets the visitor jump to a specific section of the website. Ultimately with Drupal 7 you can create as many menus as you need.

Types of menus

Drupal offers four different built-in menus:

1. **Main menu**
2. **Management**
3. **Navigation**
4. **User menu**

You can access all of your menus by going to **Structure | Menus**:

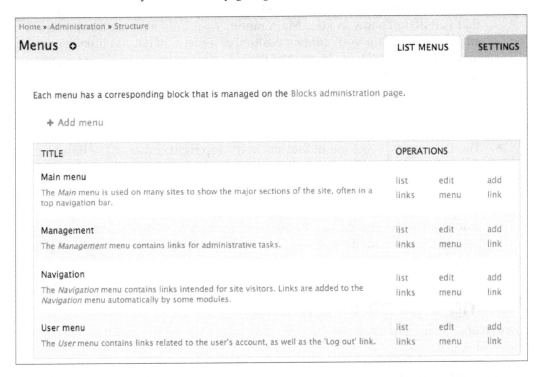

Although you can use these menus for any purpose you want, the standard uses are as follows:

- The **Main menu** lists only the most important pages of the site. This helps your visitors by quickly pointing out the pages that you feel are the most important ones, and allowing the visitors to quickly jump to these sections. The items in the **Main menu** will normally be duplicated in the **Navigation** menu. However, the **Main menu** will only have one level. By default, the **Main menu** is displayed as tabs in the header area of the default Drupal Bartik theme upon installation of Drupal. Currently we have two links in this menu—**Home** and **About Us**.

- The **Management** menu contains all of the administrative links that run along the top black admin menu when you're logged in as an admin user on the site.

- The **Navigation** menu typically lists pages that you want the site visitors to see. This typically serves as a secondary menu to collect and present links that you do not show in your **Main menu**. You could also use this menu as an admin menu for your content editors, or a menu of helpful links for your logged-in site members. In most of the sites, this menu is displayed on the left-hand side of the screen, and allows the user to quickly navigate to any page on the website. The Navigation menu may have multiple levels, which can be expanded or collapsed. This menu provides a lot of flexibility and you can tweak the use of it as per the requirements of your site.

- The **User menu** is the menu that sits in the top right corner of the Bartik theme by default in Drupal 7. This contains a link to the user's account page and a **Logout** link. You can add additional user-specific links to this menu. This menu only shows for logged-in users.

  Additionally you could add a new custom menu to handle additional links. To add a custom menu you would click on the **Add menu** link at the top of your menus administration screen.

Adding a page to a menu

Let's go ahead and add all of our main landing pages for the site and then we'll add the child pages.

Go to **Content** and click on the **Add Content** link. Click on the **Basic page** link to add a new **Basic** page to the site. Call the page **Breads**, add your content to it and then in the **Menu settings** tab, enable the **Provide a menu link** box. The **Menu link title** field should contain your **Breads** title. Type that in. Leave the **Parent item** set to **Main menu** and then click on the **Save** button:

We've created a new node on the site and stuck the node into the main Drupal menu. Now go back to your home page and you should see the new **Breads** link in your main menu. Go ahead and add **Basic** pages for the **Events, Order Online & Classes**, and **Company Info**. Make sure to add each page into the main menu system just like we did previously with the **Breads** page. Refresh your home page and you'll see all parent pages accessible through the main menu. It should look like the following screenshot:

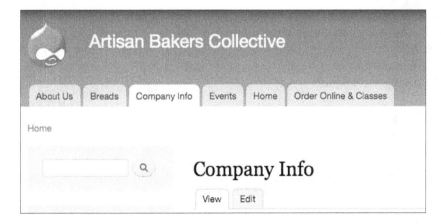

Notice here that we're on the **Company Info** page so that page's menu tab is highlighted in the main navigation. Also notice that the main menu items are not in the specific order that we need. You may want to rearrange your parent menu items at this point to match your outline. Recall that, from our earlier work we've already added two additional parent menu items, **About Us** and **Home**. We're going to move the **About Us** menu under the **Company Info** parent item; and then we'll also rearrange all of our main menu items so that they are in the correct order based on our original menu outline.

Setting the order of menu items

To order and weigh our menu links, go to the Drupal menus admin screen at **Structure | Menus**. Now click on the **List Links** link under the **Operations** column of the menu table and on your **Main menu** row.

You'll load a table that shows all the menu links for the Main menu. Notice that there are 4-pointed arrow icons next to each menu link. These draggable 4-pointed arrow icons sit to the left of each menu link. If you click-and-drag these icons you can move and reorder your menu items.

To do this, click down on the 4-pointed arrow icon to the left of the menu item name and while you're still holding down the mouse button, move the item to the required position in the list. The display of the menu will automatically change as you move the item up or down. By using the graphical editor, you do not need to worry about the relative weights of the menu items and when you move an item, the remaining items are automatically renumbered as necessary. Drupal auto adjusts the weight of the item based on where you drag it. You can also change the nesting of menu links by dragging the item to the left or the right. This allows you to easily and intuitively change the parent of the menu item.

Let's go ahead and order our main menu so it matches our original outline. Also nest your **About Us** page within the **Company Info** parent item. So just click-and-drag that **About Us** link slightly to the right and drop it under **Company Info**. Click on the **Save configuration** link. You should end up with a menu similar to the following screenshot:

MENU LINK	ENABLED	OPERATIONS	

Main menu ⊙   LIST LINKS   EDIT MENU

✦ Add link

Show row weights

MENU LINK	ENABLED	OPERATIONS	
⊹ Home	☑	edit	delete
⊹ Breads	☑	edit	delete
⊹ Order Online & Classes	☑	edit	delete
⊹ Company Info	☑	edit	delete
⊹ About Us	☑	edit	delete
⊹ Employment	☑	edit	delete
⊹ Press	☑	edit	delete
⊹ Customer Survey	☑	edit	delete
⊹ Glossary	☑	edit	
⊹ gallery	☑	edit	

Save configuration

Although the concept of weights is used frequently within Drupal, it may not be familiar to you. When items are displayed in a list, Drupal sorts them according to their specified weight prior to displaying them. This causes the items with a negative weight to be closer to the top of the list, and items with a high weight will to be closer to the bottom of the list. If two items have the same weight, they may be displayed alphabetically, chronologically, or randomly depending on the list being displayed. Each level of a menu contains separate weights, so you don't need to worry about using a limited number of weights for a potentially unlimited number of menu items. If you want to manually weight menu items instead of using the drag-and-drop functionality, you can click on the **Show row weights** link on the top right of the menu table. This will allow you to see the Drupal menu weights applied as you drag the order of the items.

For example, clicking this **Show row weights** now will look like the following screenshot:

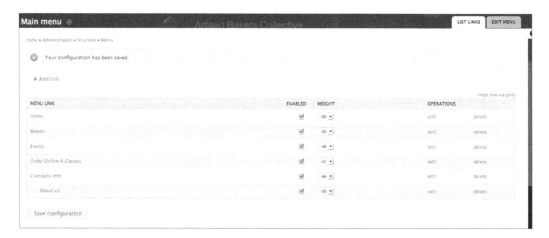

Refresh your home page and you should see your main menu links in the correct order. You won't see your nested child links yet, as we'll need to add a new Drupal module to our site to display these links.

Enabling core modules and installing contributed modules

The functionality that we have used so far is included in the default installation of Drupal and you don't need to do anything special to use it. However, the real power of Drupal is unleashed when you begin enabling the optional modules that are included with Drupal, and when you install contributed and custom modules.

The Drupal installation includes over 20 modules, some of which are not enabled by default. These modules may be disabled by default for several reasons. Some are disabled because they are not needed by every Drupal installation, or they may require extra configuration, or they may have an impact on performance. There are also several optional modules that are enabled by default because they are used by a majority of sites. However, if your site doesn't need the functionality they provide, you can disable them.

You can view a complete list of modules that are available on your site by clicking on the **Modules** link in the administrative menu. The modules admin screen will load showing a list of the core and contributed modules that you have currently installed, and allows you to enable or disable them. The listing for each module includes a short description of the module, along with information about what other modules are required. If you try to enable a module that depends on disabled modules, Drupal will prompt you to see if you want to enable the required modules that are currently disabled.

To enable a module, select the checkbox next to the module, and then click the **Save Configuration** button. If you enable multiple modules at the same time, Drupal will take care of enabling the modules in the correct order and checking any dependencies for you.

After a module has been enabled, the **Administer** menu will be updated with **new configuration options** for the module. There may also be new permissions for the new module. Check documentation for the module to learn more about how to configure the module.

Installing contributed modules

Now, in order for us to view the child menu items that we've added using the instructions presented previously we're going to install a contributed module called Menu block (`http://drupal.org/project/menu_block`). This will allow us to enable our child menu items on the sections of the site where they should be visible.

We have already discussed about enabling core modules to add functionality to your site. In addition to the optional core modules, many developers from across the globe have contributed modules with custom functionality to Drupal. Custom modules add support for a wide range of functionality, including the following:

- Integration with third-party websites such as YouTube, Amazon, and Flickr
- Administration assistance, including backing up your site, maintaining your database, and tracking site usage
- Creation and display of custom content
- E-commerce and advertising
- Extensions to the core Drupal menu system
- Layout tools for building complex layouts
- Tools for building complex lists of content

If you want to add a specific piece of functionality to your site, chances are that there is already a module available that does just what you need. A complete list of modules can be found at: `http://drupal.org/project/modules`.

The modules that are available depend on the version of Drupal you are using. The Drupal site tells you which versions of Drupal each module is compatible with, and also allows you to filter the available modules based on your version of Drupal.

Installing the Menu Block module

We're going to install the contributed module Menu Block on our site so we can extend the display options of our current core menu system. The Menu Block module is an actively maintained contributed module, which is located here: `http://drupal.org/project/menu_block`.

Installing modules in Drupal 7 is much easier than previous versions of Drupal. Now you can simply add the path to the module's FTP location directly into a field on your Drupal site and then Drupal will install the module automatically through that path. Here are the steps to install a contributed module:

1. Locate the contributed module page. Our Menu block module page is here: `http://drupal.org/project/menu_block`.

2. At the time of this book's release, the version of Menu block that we'll be installing is 7.x-2.2. This is the latest Drupal 7 version.

3. Roll your mouse over the **tar.gz** link in the module release table for the 7.x version and you'll see it's a link to the FTP location of the module on the Drupal server. In this case you should see: `http://ftp.drupal.org/files/projects/menu_block-7.x-2.2.tar.gz`.

4. Now in a separate browser tab go to the **Modules** admin screen in your Drupal site by clicking on **Modules** in the admin menu.

5. Click on the **Install new module** link.

6. This will launch the `Install` form. You'll see a field for **Install from a URL**. You want to click-and-drag the FTP link from the Drupal.org site and then release the link into that field:

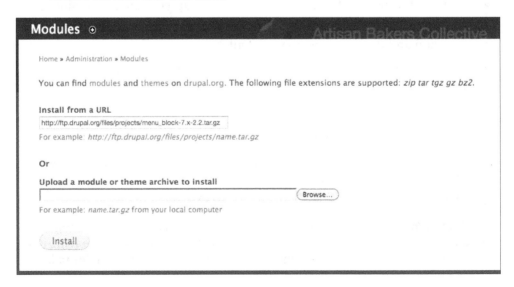

7. Now to install the module click on the **Install** button.

8. Once the module installs Drupal will show you an **Update manager** screen telling you that the **Installation was completed successfully**:

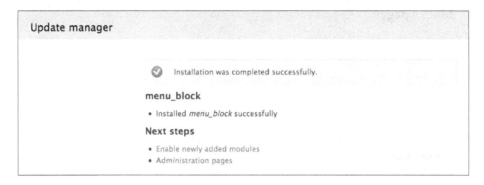

9. The next step is to enable the module. Drupal 7 also makes it a lot easier by allowing you to click on a link to **Enable newly added modules** through the **Update manager** screen.

10. Once you click on this link the **Modules** screen will load. Now scroll down in your modules list until you see the Menu block module in the `Other` table. Enable the checkbox and then save your module configuration:

ENABLED	NAME	VERSION	DESCRIPTION
☑	Menu Block	7.x-2.2	Provides configurable blocks of menu items. Requires: Menu (enabled) Required by: Menu Block Export (disabled)
☐	Menu Block Export	7.x-2.2	Provides export interface for Menu block module. Requires: Menu Block (disabled), Menu (enabled)

Notice that on the Install module form you can also **Upload a module or theme archive to install**. This allows you to upload the `tar.gz` file of the module you want to install if you've downloaded the ZIP file from Drupal. org. So there are two methods for installing. You can also use the traditional Drupal install method of course which is to upload the module to your `/sites/all/modules` directory and extract it there.

11. Depending on the module that you install, there may be settings specific to the module. Once we install the Menu Block module Drupal shows us a message on the **Modules** screen telling us how to configure our module. In this case to add a Menu Block to our site we need to visit the **administer blocks page**:

- To use menu blocks, find the "Add menu block" link on the administer blocks page.
- The configuration options have been saved.

12. After the module has been enabled, you should check the permissions for the module to determine if any changes are necessary. This is done on the **Permissions** page, which can be accessed by clicking on **User management** and then **Permissions**, from the **Administer** menu. In our case the Menu Block module does not provide any new permissions. Now that the custom module has been installed, you can use the module to enhance your site.

Using the Menu Block module

Now let's return to our menu items and set up our block menus of child elements for each section of our site. Let's create the block menu for our **Company Info** section first. This section will contain all of our about related child links, as per our original menu outline including: **About Us**, **Employment**, and **Press**. I've added the **Employment** and **Press** nodes on the site and I've added URL aliases for each that correspond to being in the **Company Info | About Us** section. This means that each page in the **About Us** section will have an URL alias that follows the following pattern: about/*. So for example, our employment node will have the following URL alias: about/employment. I've also changed the **Company Info** link in the main menu to point to the /about node. It's still our parent item for the section but it will load the **About Us** page. If you view your main menu links at this point they should look like the following screenshot:

Now to add a Menu Block go to your blocks administration screen at **Structure |
Blocks**. Click on the **Add Menu Block** link at the top of the screen. Leave the **Block
title** field blank. In the **Administrative title** field type in `Company Info Menu Block`.
Leave the **Menu** select box set to **Main menu**. Leave the **Starting level** set to **1st level
(primary)**. Leave **Maximum depth** set to **unlimited**:

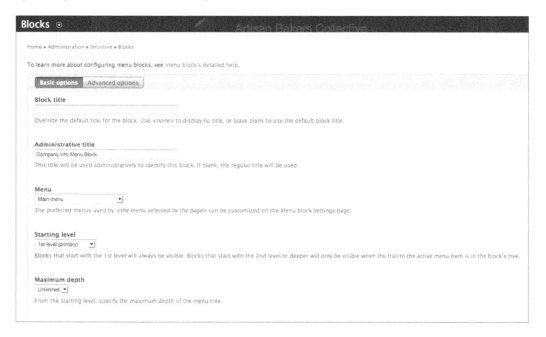

Now click on the **Advanced options** tab. In the **Fixed parent item** select box choose the **Company Info** as the fixed parent item for this Menu Block:

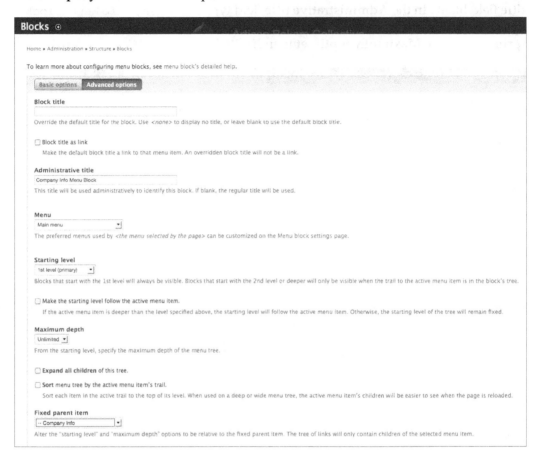

Now scroll down and in the **Pages** tab make sure the **Show block on specific pages** is selected to **Only the listed pages**. Then in the text box type in about and on the next line about/*. This will show the block only on the **Company Info** pages as they are using the about/* wildcard URL alias. Click the **Save block** button.

Now on your **Blocks** admin screen scroll down until you see the disabled **Company Info Menu Block**. Enable the block in your **Sidebar first** region. Then click on **Save blocks**:

Now go to your main **Company Info** node. You should see the correct **Company Info Menu Block** showing in your **Sidebar first** region. Click on the links in the Menu Block and each of the nodes should be showing the same Menu Block in their Sidebar first. You now have a menu showing dynamically on just your Company Info related pages:

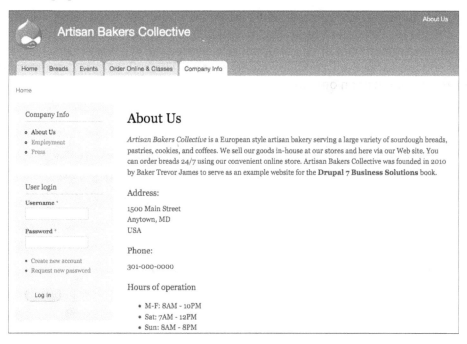

Summary

Congratulations! We have covered a lot of ground in this chapter, but we now know how to leverage the power of Drupal to create the core pages and menus of your website. You also learned how to enable and install contributed modules. The techniques that you have learned in this chapter can be applied to a wide range of websites and will probably be used in every website that you create with Drupal.

In the forthcoming chapters, we will continue to enhance the Artisan Bakers Collective website with new functionality. Although we will be using more advanced techniques in the future chapters, we will continue to refer back to many of the techniques you have learned in this chapter, especially:

- Installing and configuring contributed and custom modules
- Creating new pages
- Creating menus
- Creating dynamic lists of content
- Organizing blocks of content on our site
- Creating dynamic layouts of content

As you have seen in this chapter, Drupal makes creating and maintaining a site fun, and frees you from complex programming or detailed coding.

In the next chapter, we're going to add a custom content type to our site and add custom fields to our content type. This will help us to extend our core content and also allow our site to hold and contain more custom data. We'll also learn how to tag our content using the Drupal taxonomy system. This will help to organize and categorize the content on our site.

3
Adding Products and Services

In the previous chapter, *Creating the Artisan Bakers Collective Website*, we laid the groundwork for our site and added a few pages that are common to nearly all sites on the web. In this chapter, we will use Drupal to build a custom content type to store individual bakery items that appear on the Artisan Bakers Collective Breads menu. We will also explore different ways of displaying the content, to make the menu look its best.

At the end of this chapter, you will understand:

- How to use Drupal's core content types structure to build new content types
- How to display and theme content types and their custom fields to customize the overall display of content on your site.

Building a custom content type

In this section we will set up a custom content type for the Artisan Bakers Collective website. Our custom content type will be used to display our bakery's goods including its breads and pastries. The content type will contain the following:

- The name of the bread or pastry
- A description of the bread or pastry
- The price of the item
- A picture of the item

You could, of course simply add this content using the default core content type that Drupal 7 ships with; either a **Basic page** or **Article**. However, creating a custom content type in Drupal to hold specific fields related to your specific content is the best practice and also will help to keep your site organized, extensible, flexible, and searchable. This will also give you practice in creating content types using Drupal 7 and adding custom fields to those types.

Introduction to content types

In this section we'll learn about Drupal's core content type and fields system.

Goal

Learn how to build content types and add custom fields in Drupal 7.

Drupal 7 offers you a core content type system that can be used to develop new types of content throughout a website. This is a fantastic method of building content that fits nicely into a template, and of ensuring that all of the content has the same format and all the required fields are filled out correctly. Some examples of good content that you can add to your site using a custom content type, along with examples of possible custom content type fields, are as follows:

- **Movie:** Title, Director, Production Company, Year Released, Rating, and so on
- **Meeting:** Subject, start time, end time, organizer, topic, location, and so on
- **Book:** Title, Author, Year Published, Age Group, and so on
- **Home Listing**: Address, price, number of bedrooms, number of bathrooms, garage type, lot size, and so on

Drupal's content type structure supports a large number of field types that can be used to build custom content types. Some of these fields include:

- **Boolean**
- **Decimal**
- **Float**
- **Image**
- **Integer**
- **List**
- **Long text**
- **Term reference**
- **Text**

You can see a full list of all the core fields that Drupal's core content types support by clicking on the **MANAGE FIELDS** link of one of your core content types like the Article or Basic page. Then select the **Select a field type** fields' drop-down box. You'll see all the core fields listed as shown in the following screenshot:

Using specific field types when you build your new types helps to ensure that the information that is entered is valid. It will also help you to view and filter the display as content is added to your site. Drupal 7 now ships with these custom fields as part of its core so you can easily add them to all your content types without having to install additional contributed modules. Additionally Drupal 7 has made the taxonomy a field in its core, so you can now add term reference fields to your content types in order to show specific vocabularies and tags on specific content.

Designing the menu item

In this section we begin the process of setting up a custom content type in Drupal.

Goal

Design a content type to represent breads and pastries that are available at the bakery.

Steps

When you start designing your site it is a good idea to think about what content types you will need, and design the types before building them. It is relatively easy to add new fields to a type, but if you do so you may need to modify all of the existing content, which can be extremely time consuming.

Even seemingly simple types, such as an address, require some thought—depending on what addresses will be used. For example, if the addresses entered are only from the United States, typical fields are Street 1, Street 2, City, State, and Zip Code. If the address has to include international addresses, typical fields are Street 1, Street 2, City, State/Province, Zip/Postal Code, and Country. If the address is only for a single country, state, or city, you can eliminate or automatically fill out some of the fields, to make entering information more convenient for your editors and users. The types of validation that you do will also depend on what expected values can be entered. For example, for truly international sites, it is impractical to include every state or province in a drop-down list for users to select from. On the other hand, if you know that addresses are only within a specific country, giving a list of states or provinces is very easy.

Step 1: Determining how the content type will be used

The first step in creating a new content type is deciding how the type will be used. You need to think about whether there will be a large or small number of entries, whether the information will be entered by experienced users, inexperienced users, or the general public. You also need to consider where the information will be displayed on the site, and in what format.

By collecting this information at the beginning, you can use it to guide future steps.

Step 2: Determining what fields need to be included

Think about what fields need to be included in the content type. You can do this in a number of ways:

- Use the fields from an existing paper form
- Use the fields from an existing backend system that the website will interface with
- Create fields based on the business process that you are adding to the website
- Brainstorm the possible values with a group of co-workers
- Look at example data to find commonalities, and then create a new field for each piece of common data

If you have tried several methods and still can't determine what the fields should be, you may want to try breaking the type into several separate but related types, or hiring a consultant to help you. Alternatively, you may have simply found a type that is not a good candidate to be created using a custom content type.

Each content type in Drupal automatically contains a field for a title, which is a single line of text; and a field for the description, which is a block of text. These fields can be renamed or hidden from view depending on your requirements. You will find that most content types that you create will use these two fields.

For our Breads and Pastries menu item, we will include the following fields:

- The name of the baked good item (using the default **title** field)
- A description of the item (using the default **body** field)
- The price of the item
- A rating for the item
- Information displaying dietary concerns or allergies (gluten free, vegan, vegetarian, and so on)
- What times of day the item is available
- The type of the item (bread, pastry, sourdough, European, flatbread, cake, and so on). Here, we'll use a Drupal tag to determine this
- Whether the menu item is available seasonally
- When the menu item is available, if it is only available seasonally

Step 3: Determining what type each field should use, and what validation should be done

After you have a list of the fields that you want to include in your new content type, you need to think about what information the field will contain, so that you can select an appropriate type for the field. You will want to consider whether the field contains basic textual information, numeric information, references to other content, dates, vocabularies and tags, or some other type of information.

As you decide what types should be used, you should also consider how long each field should be, and whether it should be restricted to specific values, or if editors can enter anything they want in the field.

For our content type, the fields will use the following types:

Field	Type	Validation
Item Name	Text (single line)	Must be provided, no length requirements
Item Description	Text (multiple lines)	Must be provided, text should be at least 10 words long
Item Price	Decimal	Must be a number greater than 0.00
Ingredients	List (Text)	This will be a free form list of key ingredients that visitors can search or select on.
Dietary Concerns	List (Text)	This will be a free-form list of possibilities that editors can add to as new allergens are added; it can be left blank if there are no allergens for the food
Meals	List (Text)	Must be filled out; possible values are Breakfast, Lunch, Dinner, and Dessert. Multiple items can be included if it is available at more than one meal
Type of Item	Term reference	Must be filled out; new tag values can be added by the editor. Default tag values are: bread, sourdough, pastry, cake, muffin, cupcake, cookie, European rustic, pain ordinaire, and baguette.
Seasonal	Integer (true/false)	Must be filled out; default value is false
Seasonal Start	Date	Can be left blank if Seasonal is false; can include month, date, and year
Seasonal End	Date	Can be left blank if Seasonal is false; can include month, date, and year

Step 4: Determine who will be viewing and editing the content type

In this final step, you need to consider who will enter the content and who will view it. This will help you to determine which permissions are to be added for each content type.

Our Breads and Pastry item type does not need specific permissions for each field.

Creating the content type

In this section we build our custom content type.

Goal

Build the `Breads` and `Pastry` item content type.

Now, that our item content type has been fully designed, we can begin implementing the content type for the Artisan Bakers Collective website.

Steps

To create a new content type, we load the Content Types management screen by going to **Structure | Content types**. Now, click on the **Add Content type** link as shown in the following screenshot:

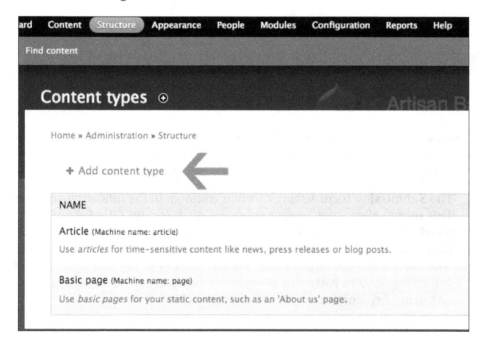

Drupal will load a form that asks for the **Name** and **Description** of the new type. We will use the following values:

- **Name:** Breads & Pastries

- **Description:** This content type is used to add bread and pastry items & goods to our bakery site so we can easily organize our baked goods for display on our site.

 Notice that as you type in the content type name, Drupal will auto complete the machine name for the content type. This is the name of your content type for the database.

The **Add Content** screen also contains additional options for **Submission form settings, Publishing options, Display settings, Comment settings**, and **Menu settings:**

1. The **Submission form settings** section is shown in the following screenshot. This section allows you to customize the labels for the **Title field label**, which we will rename to **Item Name**. You can also disable, make optional, or necessitate a preview before submitting. If required all your content editors who use the form to add content will be required to preview the node before submitting it. Let's leave this set to **Optional**. You can also add some help text in the **Explanation or submission guidelines** box:

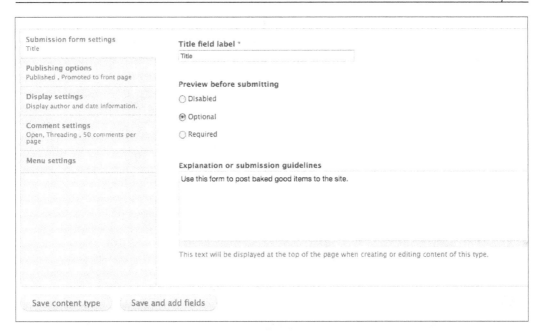

2. The **Publishing options** allows you to tell Drupal to auto publish your content type's nodes by selecting the **Published** checkbox. It also allows you to choose whether to promote your nodes to the front page of the site via Promoted to front page, whether the nodes should be sticky at top of lists by default, and whether you want to create a new revision for each node published. Let's leave the **Published** box checked but the other boxes unchecked.

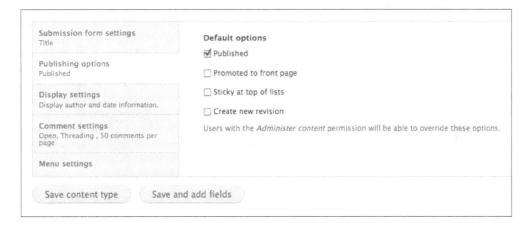

3. The **Display settings** allow you to choose to display author and date information on the nodes. For these baked good item nodes we'll uncheck the box to display the author information. This display setting makes more sense for news or blog posts.

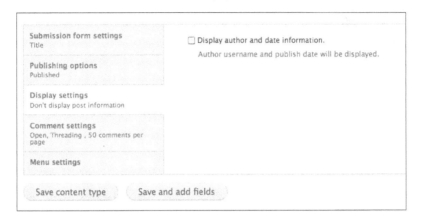

4. The **Comment settings** section allows you to control whether or not visitors to your site can comment on this type of content. We would like to get feedback on our baked good items so we will enable comments by leaving the default comment setting set to Open. Most of the default settings are perfect for our needs.

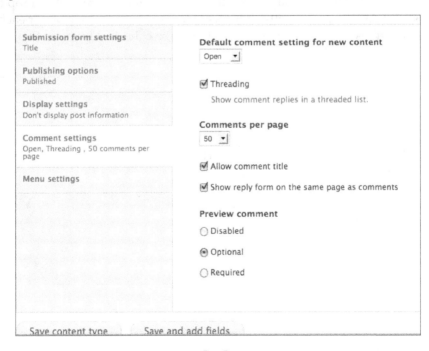

5. Finally the **Menu settings** allow us to tell Drupal which menus to associate with the content type. Since the **Baked Goods** items that we post will most likely live under the **Breads** parent menu item in the **Main menu** let's leave the **Main menu** checked for now:

6. Click the **Save and add fields** button. This will save your content type and move you to the next step in the process where we'll add our custom content type fields.

7. On the next screen Drupal will tell you that **The content type Breads & Pastries has been added**. You'll see the **MANAGE FIELDS** screen and the **FIELD** table will show you the **Title** and **Body** field along with widgets to add new custom fields.

8. If you want to change the label name of your **Body** field you can click on the **edit** link in your **Body** field row. This will launch the **Body** form. Let's tweak the label to read Description of Item:

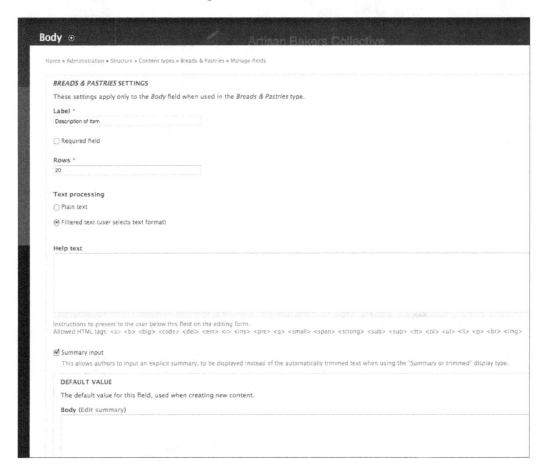

9. You can also make the field required, by checking **Required field**, tweak the rows length of the text box, change the text processing, add help text, add a default value, and change the number of values. Leave everything set to the default here besides the **Label** tweak.

10. Click the **Save settings** button. Let's go ahead and add custom fields now.

Adding a price to the menu item

In this section we add a custom field to our content type.

Goal

To add a field which will store the price of the baked good item.

Steps

Now that we have created the content type, we can set up the custom fields for our type based on the design we did earlier. This is done as follows:

1. To create a new field, add your custom field via the **MANAGE FIELDS** screen's **Add new field** widget.

2. For the `Price` field, set the field **Label** to `Price`, the **Field name** to `price` and the **Field** to **Decimal**. Then click **Save**.

3. After you click the **Save** button, Drupal will display a **FIELD SETTINGS** form that contains specific settings for this field type. Leave **Precision** set to **10**, **Scale** set to **2**, and the **Decimal marker** set to **Decimal point**. Click the **Save field settings** button.

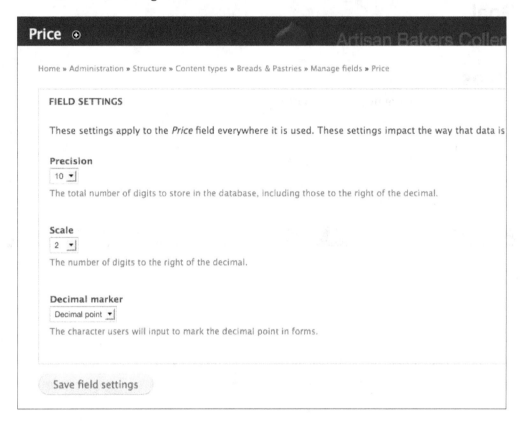

4. On the next screen let's make the **Price** field a required field, by checking **Required** field, set the minimum value to 0.00 and a maximum value if you want to include this. You should also add the $ symbol to the **Prefix** field so that all of our prices are prefixed with **$**. Add 0.00 as the default value price.

BREADS & PASTRIES SETTINGS

These settings apply only to the *Price* field when used in the *Breads & Pastries* type.

Label *

Price

☑ Required field

Minimum

0.00

The minimum value that should be allowed in this field. Leave blank for no minimum.

Help text

Add item prices here.

Instructions to present to the user below this field on the editing form.
Allowed HTML tags: <a> <b> <big> <code> <del> <em> <i> <ins> <pre> <q> <small> <span> <strong> <sub> <sup> <tt> <ol> <ul> <li> <p>
 <img>

Maximum

The maximum value that should be allowed in this field. Leave blank for no maximum.

Prefix

$

Define a string that should be prefixed to the value, like 'S ' or '€ '. Leave blank for none. Separate singular and plural values with a pipe ('pound|pounds').

Suffix

Define a string that should be suffixed to the value, like ' m', ' kb/s'. Leave blank for none. Separate singular and plural values with a pipe ('pound|pounds').

DEFAULT VALUE

The default value for this field, used when creating new content.

Price

0.00

5.   Click **Save settings**. You have successfully added your custom price field and you should see it in your content type **MANAGE FIELDS** screen.

Adding ingredients, dietary concerns and meals fields

In this section we add additional custom fields to our content type.

Goal

Add fields to determine ingredients, dietary concerns, and specific meals an item is available for. We'll use the same field type of **List (text)** for each.

The Ingredients, Dietary concerns, and Meals fields are going to be select lists. We will allow the editor to select multiple options from each list.

Steps

1. Add a new field with the label and name set to **Ingredients**, and with the type set to **List (text)** and the widget set to **Select list**. Click the **Save** button.

2. On the next screen set the **Allowed values** list to:

   Wheat flour

   White flour

   Yeast

   Salt

   Malt extract

   Beer

3. Click the **Save field settings** button. The next screen will be similar to the settings screen you completed on the **Price** field. Complete it and click the **Save settings** button.

4. Add **List (text)** select fields for your **Dietary info** and **Meals** fields using the same process outlined above. For **Dietary info** choose the checkboxes/radio buttons as the form element widget. When you add your allowed values you should separate them into key/label pairs. The key is the machine name

that will be stored in the database. The label will be presented to the content editor entering the item. So use the following as a guide:

- `vegan|Vegan`
- `vegetarian|Vegetarian`
- `glutenfree|Gluten Free`
- `wheatallergy|Wheat Allergy`
- Also note that if you do not enter values in key/label pairs, Drupal will do this for you automatically based on the values you enter.

5. Click the **Save field settings** button. On the following screen you can choose a default value radio button of **N/A**.

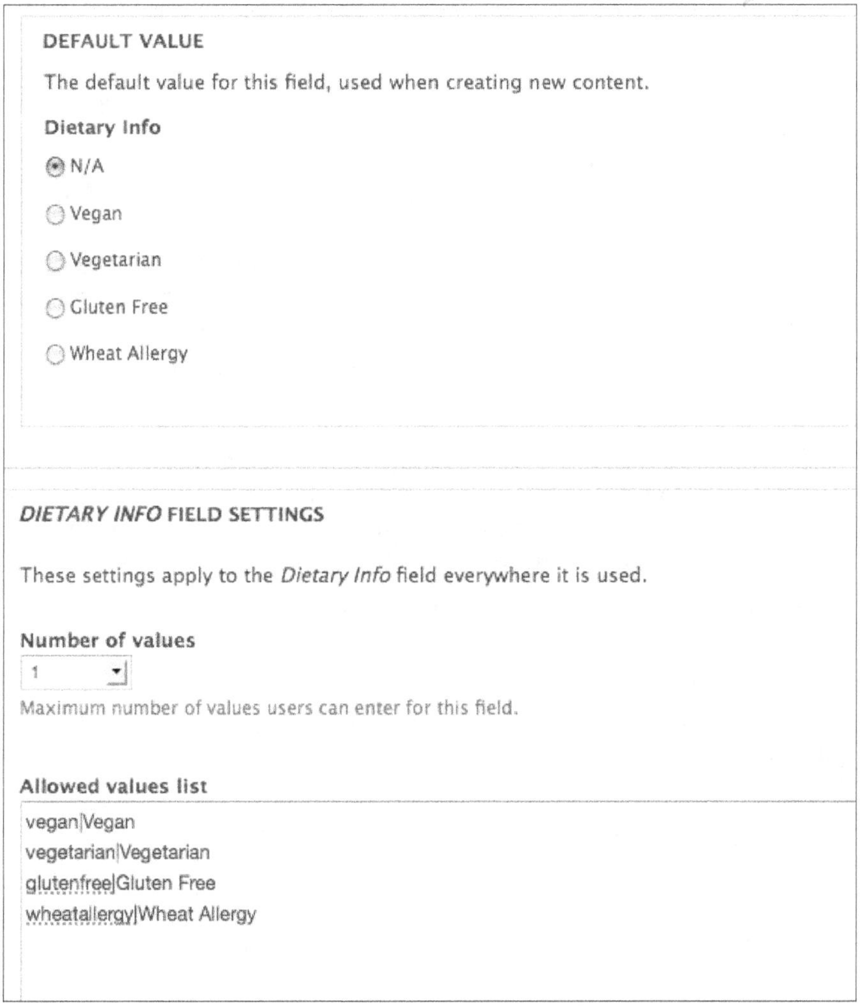

DEFAULT VALUE

The default value for this field, used when creating new content.

Dietary Info

◉ N/A

◯ Vegan

◯ Vegetarian

◯ Gluten Free

◯ Wheat Allergy

DIETARY INFO FIELD SETTINGS

These settings apply to the *Dietary Info* field everywhere it is used.

Number of values

`1`

Maximum number of values users can enter for this field.

Allowed values list

vegan|Vegan
vegetarian|Vegetarian
glutenfree|Gluten Free
wheatallergy|Wheat Allergy

Adding seasonal information to the menu item

In this section we use the Date module to add date and time specific custom fields to our content type.

Goal

Create fields that store information on whether or not a menu item is seasonal, and if it is seasonal what dates the menu item will be available on.

Additional modules needed

Date (`http://drupal.org/project/date`) — This will allow us to add specific **Date** fields to our type. You'll need to install and enable this module first before adding the **Date** custom fields. For installing modules see sections in *Chapter 2, Creating the Artisan Bakers Collective Website*. Make sure you enable all of the date modules including **Date**, **Date API**, **Date Popup**, **Date Repeat API**, **Date Tools**, and **Date Views**.

Baker James likes to rotate his menu seasonally to ensure that he always includes the freshest ingredients for his baked goods. To support this, we will allow him to specify whether each item is seasonal or not, and if it is seasonal what dates the menu should be available on. The display of the menu will take these dates into account, to display only those menu items that are currently available.

Steps

1. We will begin by adding the **Seasonal** field, which is a text field, using the **List (text)** type and **Select list** widget. We will ensure that the valid values are only **Yes** and **No** by adding these values to our **Allowed values** list. Click the **Save field settings** button.

2. To add the start and end dates, you will need to add a second field, using a **Date** field.

3. The start and end dates are implemented as single **Date** fields using the jQuery pop up calendar, where the ending date is required if a starting date is entered.

4. Begin as we did for adding the **Price** field and **Seasonal** fields, by setting the **Label** and **field name** to `Seasonal Dates` and `field_seasonal_dates` respectively. Set the field type to **Date** and the widget type to **Text Field with Date Pop-up calendar**. Click **Save** to add the field and enter the advanced information as shown in the following screenshot:

5. We can now enter the **FIELD SETTINGS** for our date field. The basic options that you need to select are as follows:

6. Click **Save field settings**.

7. We can now enter advanced information for the seasonal dates. Because the hour and minutes are not important in this case, we will remove them from the display. We will also make sure that the fields are not required, because not all dishes will be seasonal. The advanced options are set as follows:

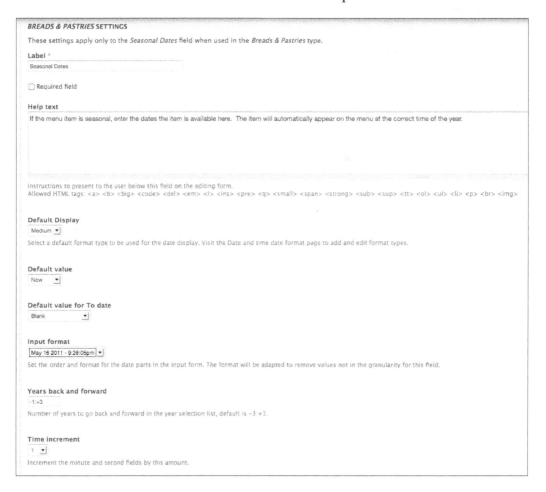

For the **Input format** of the date field you can select a specific format that matches your client's requirements for how they want to display dates on their site. In our case we'll change the date format to **May 16, 2011 – 9:28:05pm** so it's more human-friendly and readable in terms of the formatting.

Adding an image

In this section we add a file upload field to allow for adding image files to our content type.

Goal

Allow Baker James to optionally add an image of the item for display on the item's page.

Steps

1. Create a new field called **Item Image** and set the field name to `field_item_image`. Set the type to **Image** and the widget will default to **Image**.

2. After you click **Save** to create the field, you can enter the settings for the field. The first settings will show the default **Upload** destination, set to **Public files**. If you want to ensure that each item has a picture, you may want to add a **Default image** to be used. A default image will typically be a generic image with a graphic showing that an image was not found or is not available.

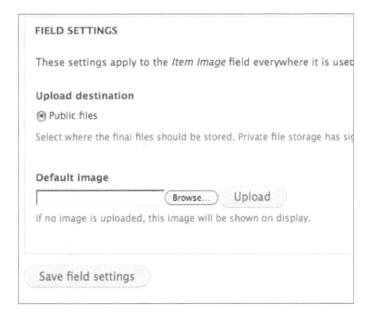

3. Click **Save field settings**.

4. On the next screen you can add specific **Allowed file extensions**, specify a **File directory** for images to be uploaded to(item_images), set a maximum and minimum image resolution, **Maximum upload size**; enable the Alt field and Title fields and what the preview image style will be set to. You can also tell Drupal to accept multiple values in case you want your content editors to upload multiple images per node. You should have a form that looks like the following:

Allowed file extensions *

png, gif, jpg, jpeg

Separate extensions with a space or comma and do not include the leading dot.

File directory

item_images

Optional subdirectory within the upload destination where files will be stored. Do not include preceding or trailing slashes.

Maximum image resolution

300 x 250   pixels

The maximum allowed image size expressed as WIDTHxHEIGHT (e.g. 640x480). Leave blank for no restriction. If a larger image is uploade

Minimum image resolution

150 x 100   pixels

The minimum allowed image size expressed as WIDTHxHEIGHT (e.g. 640x480). Leave blank for no restriction. If a smaller image is upload

Maximum upload size

30 MB

Enter a value like "512" (bytes), "80 KB" (kilobytes) or "50 MB" (megabytes) in order to restrict the allowed file size. If left empty the file size

☑ Enable *Alt* field

The alt attribute may be used by search engines, screen readers, and when the image cannot be loaded.

☑ Enable *Title* field

The title attribute is used as a tooltip when the mouse hovers over the image.

Preview image style

thumbnail ▾

The preview image will be shown while editing the content.

ITEM IMAGE FIELD SETTINGS

These settings apply to the *Item Image* field everywhere it is used.

Number of values

1 ▾

Maximum number of values users can enter for this field.

Upload destination

◉ Public files

5. Click **Save settings**.

Alternative solutions

Another possible solution for attaching images to content types is to install the WYSIWYG, IMCE, and IMCE Bridge modules. This allows for adding a feature-rich text editor to your Body and Text fields; and to upload images directly inside these fields via the text editor buttons that IMCE provides. The IMCE module gives you some additional options for controlling the width, height, alignment, CSS attributes, and horizontal and vertical spacing. The editor can also browse their entire **Files** directory for images they've already uploaded to the Drupal site. More information about each of these modules is on the respective project pages:

- IMCE: `http://drupal.org/project/imce`
- IMCE WYSIWYG Bridge: `http://drupal.org/project/imce_wysiwyg`
- WYSIWYG: `http://drupal.org/project/wysiwyg`

We will install and use all three modules in *Chapter 5, Creating a Company*

Controlling access to the content type

In this section we modify user permissions to set up specific access permissions for our content.

Goal

Modify the permissions of our Content editor role so that editors can create new Breads and Pastry Items.

Steps

1. We can easily control who can create our new content type's nodes by editing the permissions for each role. Begin by going to **People** and then click on the **PERMISSION** tab.

2. The **PERMISSION** screen contains detailed permissions for each content type that you have created. These specific permissions are listed in the **Node** section. We will allow the content editor role to perform any type of action with the new content type, as shown in the following screenshot:

PERMISSION	ANONYMOUS USER	AUTHENTICATED USER	ADMINISTRATOR	CONTENT EDITOR
Breads & Pastries: Create new content	☐	☐	☑	☑
Breads & Pastries: Edit own content	☐	☐	☑	☑
Breads & Pastries: Edit any content	☐	☐	☑	☐
Breads & Pastries: Delete own content	☐	☐	☑	☑
Breads & Pastries: Delete any content	☐	☐	☑	☐

Once you select the permissions click the **Save** permissions button.

There is one additional field we need to add to our new content type before we can start using it. We want to add a field for Type of Item. This field will allow our content editors to select from a pre-determined list of terms that will help to categorize our item types. To do this we first need to learn more about the Drupal concept of taxonomy and how to add new taxonomy vocabularies and tags to our site.

Using taxonomy to categorize content

Taxonomy is a powerful way of classifying the content on your site. After the content has been classified, you can group or filter the content based on the categories that have been set for the content type. When we use the Views module later in the book we'll be able to filter our lists of content on the site by specific tags and vocabularies. This provides a huge amount of possibilities for presenting content on our site.

If you only have a few pages of content, or if you are grouping based on only one category, the taxonomy module is probably overkill for your needs. But the power of taxonomy is readily apparent if you have hundreds of pages of content and complex categorization needs, or when you are classifying content based on multiple categories.

When you define taxonomy, you can decide whether the terms in the category are predefined, or if the editors can add new tags as they add new content. It is best to use predefined tags or terms if the terms are well-defined and are not likely to change. For example, the Bakers Collective site will use predefined values for the Type of Item category. Allowing terms to be dynamically added would be very useful if the terms change frequently, if new categories can be created, or if the initial list of terms is too large for pre-entry to be practical.

You can also create a hierarchy of terms by relating taxonomy categories to each other. For example, if you are categorizing animals by their scientific name, you could create categories for Kingdom, Phylum, Class, Order, Family, Genus, and Species. Each would relate to the category above it. This allows you to easily categorize animals without needing to repeatedly enter the links between the higher level categories.

Drupal uses the following terms to describe its classification system:

- Taxonomy: This is the highest level of the classification and tagging system. Taxonomy means that you can create vocabulary categories that are made up of tags or terms in your Drupal site. Drupal ships with a core Taxonomy module to support this.

- Vocabulary: A group or category of terms that are used to describe one aspect of a piece of content. Some example categories are: color, size, and genre. You can add a vocabulary for breads and then add specific tags to that vocabulary. The tags would be the bread names, for example.

- Terms or tags: A specific identifier within a vocabulary. Red, blue, green, small, medium, large, action, comedy, and romance are all possible terms. A term is also equivalent to a tag. On our site tags could include specific types of bread including Baguette, Sourdough, Ciabatta, Pain Ordinaire and so on.

- Another large benefit in Drupal 7 is that all vocabularies become field level items so you can add specific Term reference fields to your content types.

Create a vocabulary for Type of Baked Good

In this section we add a vocabulary to our site using Drupal's core taxonomy module. This will allow us to add tags to our content.

Goal

Build taxonomy to store information about what type of baked good an item is.

Additional modules needed

Taxonomy (Core).

Steps

To create a new taxonomy vocabulary, you need to load the **Taxonomy** screen at **Structure | Taxonomy**:

Click on the **Add vocabulary** link and Drupal will display a form allowing you to enter the **Name** and **Description** of your new vocabulary:

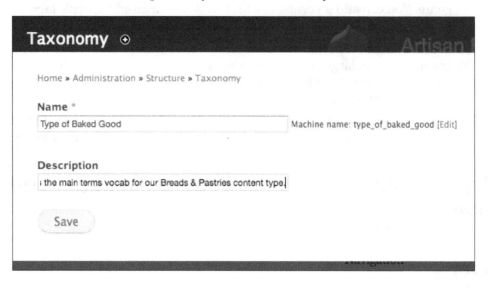

After you save your new vocabulary, you will be returned to the **Taxonomy** screen, which will now include your new category, as follows:

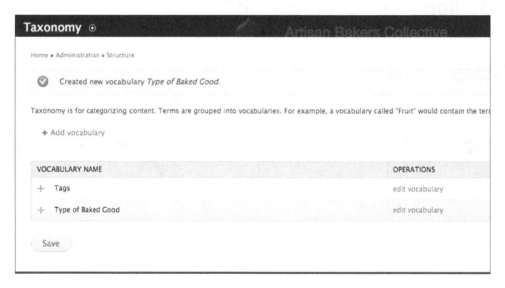

Adding terms to the vocabulary

In this section we begin the discussion of how to add tags to our content in Drupal.

Goal

Create the terms that will be used in the `Type of Baked Good` vocabulary.

Additional modules needed

Taxonomy (Core).

Steps

1. Now that our vocabulary has been created, we can define the terms that can be used within this vocabulary by clicking on the **add terms** link. A single term includes the name of the term and the description of the term. You can also use the **RELATIONS** options to define a hierarchy of terms. You can also include a specific URL alias for your term.

    The information for the term `Sourdough` is shown as follows:

    Name *

    Sourdough

    Description

    This is the tag for any baked good item that is made with sourdough leaven.

    Text format Filtered HTML ▾

    - Web page addresses and e-mail addresses turn into links automatically.
    - Allowed HTML tags: <a> <em> <strong> <cite> <blockquote> <code> <ul> <ol> <li> <dl> <dt> <dd>
    - Lines and paragraphs break automatically.

    URL alias

    sourdough

    Optionally specify an alternative URL by which this term can be accessed. Use a relative path and don't add a trailing slash or the URL alias won't work.

    ▾ RELATIONS

    Parent terms

    <root>

    Weight *

    0

    Terms are displayed in ascending order by weight.

    Save

2. Click **Save** and then add the remaining terms using the same method. Our final list of terms for our **Course Type** is shown in the following screenshot:

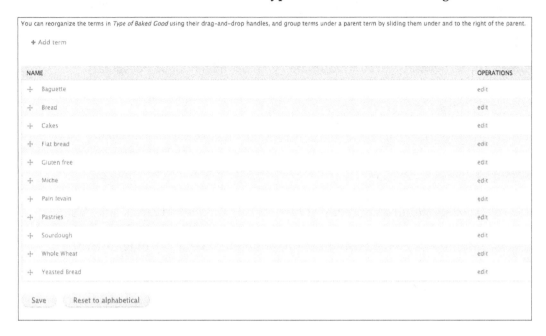

These terms can be sorted and nested by clicking and dragging the arrow cross hair icons. For example, you can sort and organize all your terms in alphabetical order to make it easier for your content editors to choose a term when they post content using your new content type. By default Drupal will organize the terms alphabetically.

Adding the Term reference field

In this section we add a term reference field to our content type so we can add tags to our content.

Goal

Add a **Term reference** field to our Breads and Pastries content type to allow for tagging of our content type's nodes using our new **Types of Baked Good** vocabulary.

Steps

1. In the **Add new field** row of your content type, add a label called **Type of Baked Good**, and a **field** name of `field_bakedgood_term`.

2. Select **Term reference** as the **Type of data to store** and **Select list** as the widget as shown in the following screenshot:

3. Click **Save** to save the basic information and Drupal will prompt you on the next screen for the **Vocabulary** to reference. Choose the **Type of Baked Good** vocabulary you just built on your site. Click **Save field settings**.

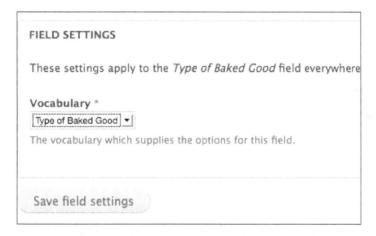

4. On the next screen you can add any additional specific settings for your **Term reference** field. The only item that we will change on this screen is the **Number of values**. Let's set that to `Unlimited`. Click **Save settings**.

5. Let's now drag our **Type of Baked Good** term reference field and drop it just below our **Description of Item** but before the **Price** field. Let's also drag the **Item Image** just above the **Price** field. Your final **Breads & Pastries** content type fields screen should look like the following screenshot:

6. We're now ready to add nodes using our new content type

Adding content with the content type

Now that we have built our content type, we can begin to use this type to add the specific **Bread & Pastry** item nodes to the site.

Creating a new Breads and Pastries item

In this section we add new content to our site using our custom content type.

Goal

Build **Bread & Pastry** items using our new content type, for display on the website.

Steps

1. We will start by clicking on the **Add content** link in the toolbar menu. Drupal will now open the same list of possible content types that we saw when we built our static pages in *Chapter 2, Creating the Artisan Bakers Collective Website*. However, now our new **Breads & Pastries** type is also available.

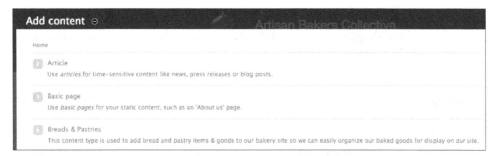

2. Click on the **Breads & Pastries** link and Drupal will present you with a form based on the custom fields that we have created.

3. Complete all of the fields for the new content type, and then click the **Save** button.

4. Once the node has been created, the default display will look like the following screenshot:

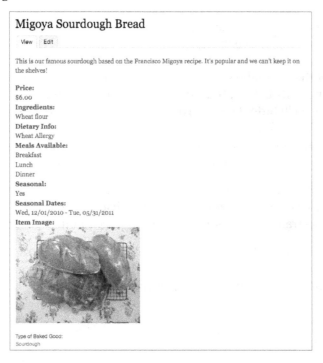

Customizing the display of the content type nodes

Although the default view works for some content types, most of the time you will want to customize the look of your content type so that it is clear and appealing to visitors.

We can improve the display of this content type's node display. We will discuss various ways of doing this in this section.

Modifying the order of fields and the display of the field labels

In this section we modify the display options for our fields in our content type.

Goal

Customize how the fields of our content type are displayed, to maximize usability for our visitors.

Steps

Now that we have created a node with our new content type, you'll notice that the field labels are showing above the field data. You can control the display of your content type's fields in terms of hiding or displaying labels and field data. Our client wants to display the field labels inline to the actual field data. So instead of the **Price** label showing above its field output, the display should be inline so **Price: $6.00** is all on one line. Also, we'll hide the **Item Image:** label text, so only the image displays. Finally, we'll arrange some of our fields so that the image displays first and the **Type of Baked Good** tag shows up directly below the image. Drupal allows us lots of flexibility in how we organize and display our field elements.

To do this go to **Structure | Content types** and click on the **Manage display** link next to **Breads & Pastries**. This will open up the display screen. First, let's click and drag our fields to arrange them how we want to present our content.

Then hide the **Item image** label by changing the label widget to **<Hidden>**. Then, change the label widgets for the other items to be **Inline**. The format widget allows you to hide or change the format display of each item's content.

You should get a screen that looks like the following:

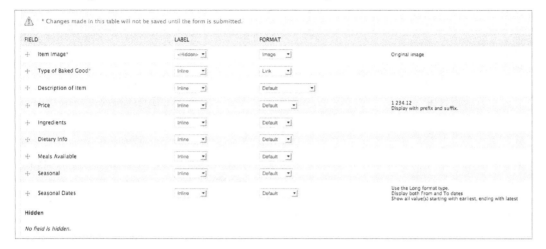

Click **Save**.

Now go back to your node and refresh. Your node should now display the fields based on the display settings tweaks you made. The presentation of the baked good item should be much more streamlined and professional now.

If you need additional customization for your content type, you can theme the content.

Summary

Now, that you have finished this chapter, you should understand how to build a new content type and use that content type on your website. By using custom types for your content, you can make adding content easy for editors, and make the look of your content consistent for users.

In the next chapter, we will make the website more interactive by allowing guests to interact with the site through comments, ratings, polls, and user surveys. This type of functionality is very popular with web users because it allows them to become a part of the site. It is also a fantastic way to learn more about your customers so that you can continue to provide better services for them.

4
Interacting with Customers and Visitors

Baker James thinks that his bakery is the best in the region and to make sure that his food stays on the top, he is always seeking feedback from his customers both when they are in the bakery, and when they are visiting the Artisan Bakers Collective website.

In this chapter, we will:

- Create a variety of functionalities that will allow the site's users to interact with the website and help them feel that they are a part of the community, in addition to giving valuable feedback to Baker James.
- Allow users to:
    - Register on the website.
    - Comment on content.
    - Respond to polls.
    - Answer surveys.

Working with users

In this series of tasks, we will explore Drupal's user functionality, which allows you to add users to your site and specify the functionality that they can use. We will also discuss the concept of roles, which allow you to create a group of permissions that can easily be assigned to users. Finally, we will discuss how to assign roles to the users.

Allowing user registration

In this section, we'll set up the user account process on the website.

Goal

Allow users to register on the website so that they can access additional content that is not available to unregistered visitors.

Drupal contains a sophisticated system of user management and permissions that allows you to easily control who can access your website and what they can do on the website.

Steps

In this section we're going to configure default **Account settings** for our site, as follows:

1. Settings related to user registration are controlled from the **Account settings** configuration screen, which is available by selecting **Configuration** from your toolbar menu and then clicking on **Account settings** in the **PEOPLE** section.

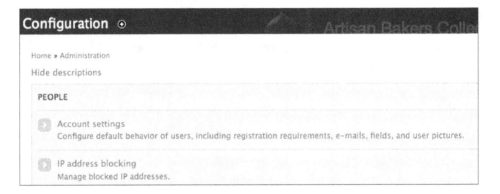

2. The **Account settings** screen shows us that the name given to any anonymous visitor to our site is, Anonymous. The screen also allows you to set your **Administrator role**, by default it's set to the core Drupal administrator role. We'll leave these two settings as is.

3. The default **REGISTRATION AND CANCELLATIONS** settings will allow visitors to register for an account but administrator approval is required to make the account active. Baker James wants to control access to the site and wants to approve user registration requests before they are activated. This will help him recognize special customers to include in his VIP club and

make sure that only the customers living near his restaurant are registered. Let's also leave the **Required e-mail verification when a visitor creates an account** checkbox selected. This will force the new user to confirm their e-mail before their account is activated.

4. **When cancelling a user account** can be set to a number of options. Let's leave this set to **Disable the account and unpublish its content**.

5. The next section allows for you to enable user signatures and pictures. This will allow your users to type in signatures and add user pictures to their posts and content. Let's enable both.

6. Leave the picture directory set to its default. We won't upload a default picture; and leave picture display, upload dimensions and upload file size set to their defaults.

ANONYMOUS USERS

Name *

Anonymous

The name used to indicate anonymous users.

ADMINISTRATOR ROLE

Administrator role

administrator ▾

This role will be automatically assigned new permissions whenever a module is enabled. Changing this setting will not affect exi

REGISTRATION AND CANCELLATION

Who can register accounts?

○ Administrators only

○ Visitors

⊙ Visitors, but administrator approval is required

☑ Require e-mail verification when a visitor creates an account.

New users will be required to validate their e-mail address prior to logging into the site, and will be assigned a system-gener registration.

When cancelling a user account

○ Disable the account and keep its content.

⊙ Disable the account and unpublish its content.

○ Delete the account and make its content belong to the *Anonymous* user.

○ Delete the account and its content.

Users with the *Select method for cancelling account* or *Administer users* permissions can override this default method.

PERSONALIZATION

☑ Enable signatures.

☑ Enable user pictures.

Picture directory

pictures

---

7. The final section at the bottom of the form is settings for specific e-mails that you would send to your new users. These include the welcome e-mails, account activation, blocked accounts and cancellation, and password recovery e-mails. We'll leave these all set to their default for now but just be aware that you can customize them based on the client's own custom e-mail content.

8. Click **Save configuration**.

Extending the user signup form

You can add custom fields to the user account creation form. This is helpful if the client wants to collect additional data besides the user's e-mail address and username. For example, we could add a field asking the user what their favorite baked good is? This is a flexible method of building a dynamic user profile system.

To do this click on the **Manage fields** tab of the **Account settings** screen. Type in the label for your new field; the field name, and select a field widget. This process is the same as adding custom fields to our content types in *Chapter 3, Adding Products and Services*.

Click **Save**, then click the **Save field settings** button on the next screen. Leave the max length set to 255 characters.

On the next screen, we can tell Drupal to make the field required and also to display the field on the user registration form. In our example let's leave the **Required field** box unchecked but check the **Display on user registration form**.

Click the **Save settings** button.

Now, we can test out the account registration process. Log out of the site and in the site's user login block, click on the **Create new account** link.

The user account node will load at user/register. You'll see fields for **username**, **e-mail address**, and the custom field you added.

Go ahead and create a new account. As soon as you click the **Create new account** button Drupal will show you the following message telling you that your account is pending approval:

 Thank you for applying for an account. Your account is currently pending approval by the site administrator. In the meantime, a welcome message with further instructions has been sent to your e-mail address.

Additionally, the administrator of the site, or the client in this case will receive an e-mail notifying them that a new user has signed up for an account and needs to be approved. This e-mail will be sent to whatever account you have specified as the main website-based administrator e-mail in the website information settings at `Configuration | Site information`. Additionally, the new user will receive two e-mails. The first will notify them that the account is pending approval and the second will notify them when the account is activated.

Now, log back into the site as the admin user and browse to your main **PEOPLE** screen. You'll see the new account in the **PEOPLE** table. Notice that the account status is set to **blocked**:

	USERNAME	STATUS
☐	sourdoughfan	blocked

This is because you need to approve the account before it's activated. To approve the account click the **Edit** link and select the Active radio button under the status header. Scroll down and click the **Save** button. Now, the new user account is active and the user can log in.

Drupal assigns a default authenticated user role to the new user since you have not specified another custom role to add. We'll set up custom roles in the next section.

Create a VIP role

In this section we create a VIP role on the site.

Goal

Create a VIP role that will be used to give special customers enhanced privileges that normal customers do not have. Customers must be granted VIP access; they cannot sign up for it.

Steps

In the previous section we created a user account on the site. The account was assigned the generic authenticated user role that Drupal gives all users. Our client wants to give people who have accounts on the site privileges including coupons and other items that normal anonymous customers do not get. To do this we should create a specific role on the site that our client can assign to new users:

1. Drupal allows you to manage roles for the website on the **People | Permissions** screen. Go to **People | Permissions**.

2. Now, click on the **Roles** tab. Drupal will display a list of the roles currently available on your site, and also provide you with the ability to add a new role, as shown in the following screenshot:

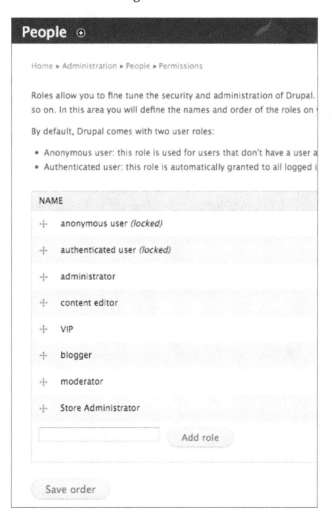

3. Enter **VIP** for the name and then press **Add role**. Drupal will now add the role to the **Roles screen** as shown in the following screenshot:

4. From the manager, you can edit the role, which will allow you to modify the name for the role, or delete the role.

5. Once the role has been created, you need to update the permissions for the role so that the user can perform the tasks that they need to. To modify the permissions, click on the **edit permissions** link for the role.

6. Drupal will then display a list of all of the available permissions, arranged by category. By default, all permissions are disabled. This prevents new user roles from gaining unwanted access. When a user is assigned to more than one role, their actual permissions will be a combination of the permissions of each role. This means that you should give each role as few permissions as possible, and assign multiple roles to a user in order to fully define each user.

7. For our VIP role, we will add the **View comments**, **Post comments**, **Skip comment approval**, and **Edit own comments**. Also give the role **View published content**, and **Use search permissions** and then click the **Save permissions** button to finish the changes.

Assign users to the VIP role

In this section we assign the VIP role to our user accounts.

Goal

Change a registered customer to a VIP customer and let them know that they have been given additional privileges.

Steps

1. Now that we have built the new VIP role, we can assign users to the role. Baker James wants to assign his VIPs manually, but you can also allow visitors to request a different role, or assign roles at sign-up.

2. We have already created a user account so we can edit that account and assign the VIP role to the sourdoughfan user. Click on the **edit** link next to the user account, and then check the box for the role that you want to add to the account in this case VIP.

3. Click **Save**.

Working with comments

In this group of tasks, we will explore Drupal's built-in functionality to allow users to comment on content. We will cover setting permissions to determine who can comment and also describe the approval process for comments, to help prevent unwanted messages from being posted on your site.

Enable comments for a content type and node

In this section we enable comments on our content type.

Goal

Allow registered users to leave comments on nodes published with the Breads & Pastries content type. All comments must be approved before they are published, unless the customer is a VIP customer, in which case their comments will be automatically approved.

We're going to enable commenting on the Breads & Pastries content type so that users of our site can post comments on any Bread & Pastries node.

Go to the content type screen and edit the Breads & Pastries content type. Click on the **Comment settings** tab. This will launch the comments settings for the content type. Let's make sure that the **default comment setting** is set to **Open**, that we're using threading; 50 comments per page, allowing a comment title, showing replies, and that **Preview comment** is optional:

Save your content type. You can always override the comment settings per node if you only want to allow commenting on specific nodes. For example open up the node we published earlier at /node/9 and edit it. Scroll down and click on the **Comment settings** tab. You'll see you can open or close commenting on a specific node and this will override your overall content type comments settings.

We're now ready to add comments to the Breads & Pastries nodes.

Adding new comments

In this section we add new comments to our nodes.

Goal

Demonstrate how visitors will add comments to nodes on the site.

Steps

When a page has been created with comments enabled, you will find a link at the bottom of the page, which a visitor can click to create a comment. By default this link will show up differently for your different user roles. Currently we are only allowing our VIP role users the ability to post comments, so they need to log in first. Anonymous commenting is disabled on the site. Site visitors will see a link under the node content stating: **Log in or register to post comments**:

If you log in as the VIP role you'll see the following **comment** fields on the node:

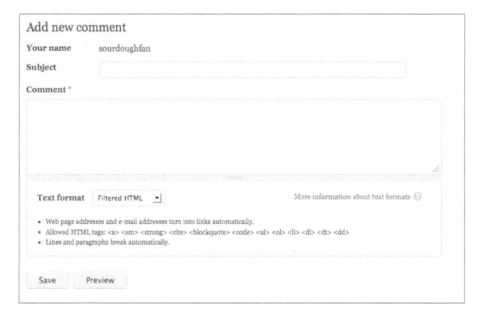

The comment form is built into the actual node itself and asks the user for the **Subject** and actual comment text. The comment will be tied to their user account.

After the visitor has entered a comment, he or she can click **Preview** to review the comment and can also make the changes that he or she wants. Otherwise, he or she simply clicks on the **Save** button to save the changes.

If the user has permissions to post comments without approval, the comment will be automatically published. If the user does not have permission to post comments without approval, the comment will be placed in the moderation queue. Since this user is a VIP role they can post comments without approval. The comment should show up immediately as shown in the following screenshot:

Manage comments

In this section we set up management of our comments.

Goal

Demonstrate how to manage comments, view unpublished comments, and either publish the comment or delete it.

First, let's give our anonymous users approval to post comments. This will allow them to post comments but an administrator will need to approve and publish the comments. Go ahead and post an anonymous comment. When you do this you'll receive a message that states: **Your comment has been queued for review by site administrators and will be published after approval.**

Now, let's log in as an administrator and manage and approve our comments.

Steps

In this section let's take a look at all of the comments posted on our site and learn how to manage them.

1. Comments can be viewed by going to your **CONTENT** screen and clicking on the **COMMENTS** tab.

   The comment manager contains two tabbed screens — one for published comments and another for unapproved comments.

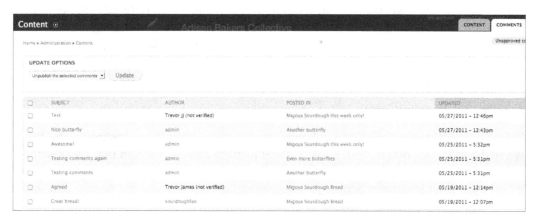

2. Click on the **Unapproved comments** tab to view your comment approval queue. To approve a comment, simply select the checkbox to the left of the comment that you want to approve, make sure that the **UPDATE OPTIONS** drop-down list is set to **Publish the selected comments**, and then click **Update**.

3. If you want to delete a comment, select the comment that you want to delete, change the **Update options** to **Delete the selected comments** and then click **Update**.

Notification of new user comments on site

In this section we'll set up automatic notifications to send to our site administrator when new comments are posted on the site.

Goal

Set up a notification system so that website administrators are notified whenever a new comment has been posted on the site. This will help them to manage comments in a timely manner especially those that need to be approved before publishing.

Additional modules needed

Actions and Trigger (Core).

In order to notify administrators when new comments have been posted on the site, we will need to do two things. First, we will need to build an action that creates and sends the e-mail. The second thing we need to do is create a trigger that tells Drupal when the e-mail should be sent.

Steps for creating the e-mail action

1. Let's begin by creating the action:

2. Actions are created by using the **Actions** screen, which is accessed by selecting **Configuration** and then **Actions**, from the **SYSTEM** section:

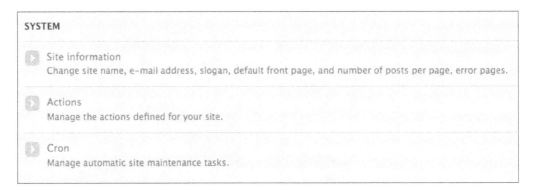

3. As you can see in the following screenshot, there are several basic actions that can be used. Alternatively, you can create your own advanced actions.

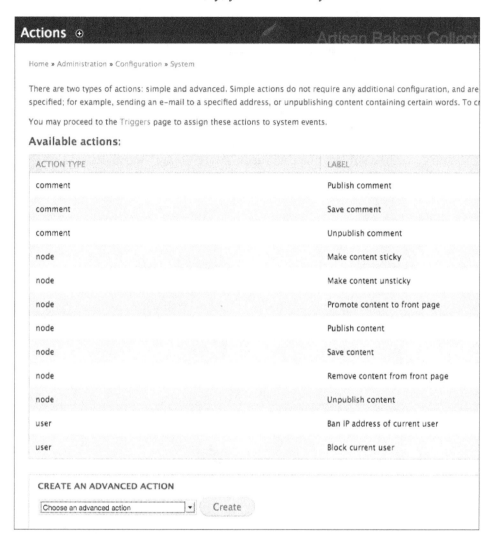

4. As there is no basic action for sending an e-mail or message to a user, we will need to create a new advanced action.

5. Begin by selecting **Send e-mail...** from the **Create an advanced action** drop-down list and then click **Create**.

6. Drupal will then display a form where you can enter information about the e-mail that is to be sent. The label can be tweaked to read `Send e-mail` when `comment is submitted`; the recipient should be the client administrator. You can add a subject line that reads `There's a new comment ready for review and approval`; and any custom message you want to add:

7. Click on **Save** and the action will be added to the **Available actions**. You can modify the e-mail at any point by clicking on the **Configure** link, or you can delete the action by clicking **Delete**.

Steps for creating the new comments trigger

We now need to create the **Trigger** that will determine when our new e-mail is to be sent:

1. First, let's make sure our core Drupal Triggers module is enabled. Go to your Modules administration page and confirm that you have checked the **Trigger** module to enable it. Save your modules page.

| ☑ | Trigger | 7.8 | Enables actions to be fired on certain system events, such as when new content is created. |
| | | | Required by: Mime Mail Action (disabled), Simplenews action (disabled) |

2. Now, go to your **Site configuration | Actions** page and click on the **Triggers** link via your **Actions** screen. This will launch the Triggers screen.

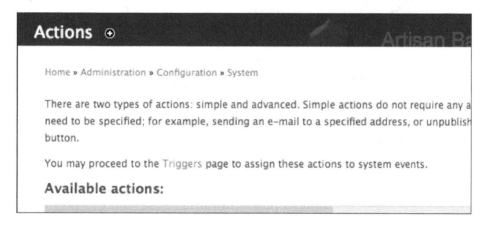

3. To access the manager for comment-related **Triggers**, click on the **comments** tab in the **Triggers** screen. Drupal will display a list of all possible **Triggers**, that you can assign actions to, as shown in the following screenshot:

4. Change the action for **TRIGGER: WHEN EITHER SAVING A NEW COMMENT OR UPDATING AN EXISTING COMMENT** to **Send e-mail action you just set up** and then click **Assign**. Drupal will add the action and save the form. The administrator will then be automatically e-mailed each time a comment is saved or updated.

5. If you want to disable this action in the future, simply click the **unassign** link in the Trigger manager.

Set up user ratings for content

Baker James wants feedback about the baked goods he creates because he wants to know what should be kept on the menu and what could be rotated off. He would like to allow visitors to add some more information about the baked good when they rate it, so we will enable ratings when the visitor adds comments.

To set up a rating system, we're going to install and configure the **Fivestar** rating module. Fivestar is currently in development status for Drupal 7 but we can use and test the module in our localhost environment before deploying it to a production website.

Add Fivestar content ratings to a node

This task will explain how to implement user ratings. For the client site, this will demonstrate how to allow users to rate menu items.

Goal

Allow customers to rate their favorite menu items so that Baker James can get feedback on his food, keep popular meals, and remove unpopular food.

Additional modules needed

Fivestar (`http://drupal.org/project/fivestar`) and the Voting API module (dependency): `http://drupal.org/project/votingapi`. Currently, there is a stable release of Fivestar module for Drupal 7: **7.x-2.0-alpha1**.

Steps

1. Install and enable the **7.x-2.0-alpha1** version of the Fivestar module per earlier module installation instructions. The Fivestar module will show up in the Voting section of your module's administration screen. Also make sure to install the **Voting API** dependency module. Save your module configuration.

▾ VOTING			
ENABLED	NAME	VERSION	DESCRIPTION
✓	Fivestar	7.x-2.0-alpha1	Enables fivestar ratings on content, users, etc. Requires: Voting API (enabled) Required by: Drupal (Field type(s) in use – see Field list)
✓	Voting API	7.x-2.4	Provides a shared voting API for other modules. Required by: Fivestar (enabled)

2. Now, select the content type that you want to add ratings to. In our case we'll edit the **Breads & Pastries** type.

3. Click on the **Fivestar** voting tab and the Fivestar configuration screen will load.

4. Check the **Enable Fivestar rating for the "vote" tag** option, and customize the display of the rating widget if you'd like, or just leave it set to its defaults. We have also enabled **feedback** when the user comments on our menu item and saves their Fivestar vote.

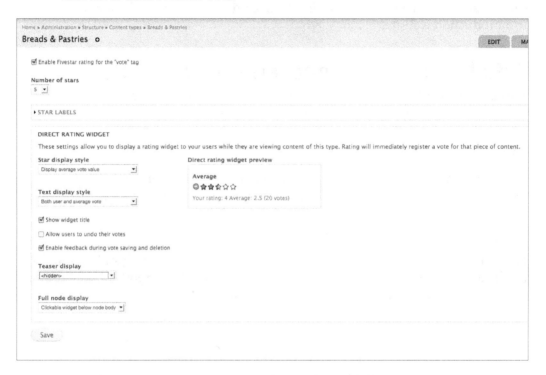

Save the **Content Type** and your changes will be automatically applied.

5. The final change you need to make to your site is to allow users to rate content on the website. This is done by modifying the permissions for the user roles. Go to your permissions screen at **People | Permissions** and scroll down in the permissions table until you see the Fivestar rows. We want to make sure that the VIP role has permission to rate content. You could also give this permission to other roles including anonymous users if you wanted to, but this will be a benefit perk for our VIP role.

PERMISSION	ANONYMOUS USER	AUTHENTICATED USER	ADMINISTRATOR
Fivestar			
rate content	☐	☐	☑

6. Now log in to the site as a VIP and go to the Migoya Sourdough node at node/9. You should see the Fiverstar rating widget just below the **Seasonal date** fields and content. It will say **No votes yet**:

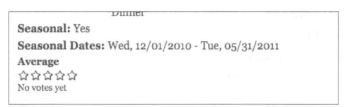

Click on any of the stars in the rating widget to rate the content. Your vote will be saved and the widget will turn a color based on the vote you gave it. It will also show **Your rating** and the average rating tallied based on all votes.

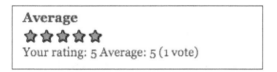

So the rating shows your vote of 5 on the scale of 1 to 5 and the average vote in this case is **1 vote** in total.

Adding a rate this node block

In this section we'll add a rating mechanism to our content by enabling a Fivestar module provided block.

Goal

Show a block in the sidebar of the site to allow logged in VIP users to rate content easily.

Steps

The Fivestar module ships with a block that allows your site visitors to easily rate content via the block as it shows in the sidebar or specific region of the node where the block is placed. This allows for an easier call to action to vote on the node.

1. Go to your **Structure | Blocks** screen.
2. Scroll down to your disabled blocks section and look for the **Fivestar: Rate this** node block.
3. Enable it in one of your sidebar regions.
4. Save your blocks
5. Go to a node on your site and you should see the new Fivestar block showing up in the region where you placed it.

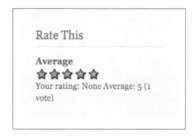

6. Go back to your **Blocks** administration screen and click to configure the Fivestar block.
7. If you click on the **Roles** tab you can choose to show the **Rate This** block for only your VIP role. Check the VIP role and Administrator role boxes and then save your block.
8. Now, when you log in as either of those roles you'll see the **Rate This** block but it will be hidden for all other roles.

Change the display of the ratings

In this section we'll customize the display of our Fivestar ratings.

Goal

Customize the rating display to make the ratings more dramatic.

Steps

The Fivestar module provides you with a wide assortment of images that can be used when displaying or selecting a rating. These are accessed by selecting **Configuration** and then **Fivestar**, from the configuration **administration screen**.

The top section contains a variety of different icons that are used for display. For our site, we will use the **Flames** setting, because that works well with our bakery theme. This is shown in the following screenshot:

If you select one of the widgets in the **Color Scheme** section, you can customize the colors used in the display to suit the theme of your site. Click **Save configuration** and then check out your Fivestar rating block again. You should now see the Flames icons as the rating scale.

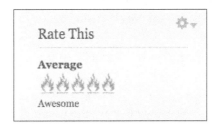

Working with polls

Polls are a great way to quickly gather information from your users. Visitors like to answer short polls, especially if the results are immediately available and the questions are interesting. In Drupal, polls can contain only a single question, along with a set of predefined responses that the user can choose from.

Create a poll

In this section we'll use the **Poll** module to create a poll on our site.

Goal

Create a poll to allow Baker James to get feedback from customers. The first poll will ask customers what their favorite bread is from the Bakers Collective menu.

Additional modules needed

Poll (core).

Steps

In this section we'll enable and configure the Poll module.

1. We begin the process of building a poll by ensuring that the **Poll module** is enabled. The Poll module is included as a part of the Core Drupal installation.

2. Once you have confirmed that this module is available, select **Add content** and then **Poll** from the main **Navigation** menu. Drupal will open a new form, where you can enter information about the poll.

3. First, enter the question you want to ask, in this case: What is your favorite Bakers Collective bread?

4. By default, you are given the space to specify two choices, but you can include additional choices by clicking the **More Choices** button. For our site, we are allowing visitors to select between the following choices: Sourdough, Baguette, Whole Wheat, Gluten Free, Ciabatta, and Flatbread.

5. The **Poll status** controls whether or not visitors can enter new votes into the system. If you want to manually manage the duration of the poll, you can simply close the poll by editing the poll and setting the **Poll status** to **Closed** when the poll is over.

6.   The **Poll duration** can be used to automatically close a poll after a specified interval. The poll can be kept open for various intervals from one day to one year. We'll keep our poll running for **1 week**:

7. When you click **Save**, Drupal will add the poll to the website, and allow you to vote in it, as shown in the following screenshot:

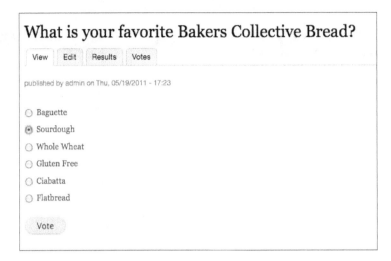

8. The final step to setting up the poll is making sure that the users can submit answers to the poll. This is controlled via user permissions. Go to your Permissions screen.

9. There are several permissions available to control access to the polls, as shown in following screenshot:

10. The only permission we want to grant is the ability to vote for all users. We'll also allow VIP users to cancel and change their votes. Select these options, and then click **Save permissions**.

Adding the poll to the home page

In this section we'll add a poll to our home page.

Goal

Add our new poll to the home page on the right-hand side, so that customers will see the poll and have easy access to vote.

Steps

In this section we'll add a poll to our site's home page.

1. We can add the poll to the home page by enabling the **Most recent poll** block. Go to your blocks' administrator screen.

2. The **Most recent poll** block is disabled by default. Let's enable it in our sidebar second region.

3. Click to save your blocks' configuration.

4. Go to our home page and you'll see the block in your right sidebar. You can add the block to any region of your theme via the blocks' administration page.

5. We can now configure the display by clicking on the gear icon and then on the Configure block link. We will restrict the poll to only be displayed on the home page, as shown in the following screenshot. You can enter `<front>` in the **Show block on specific pages** text field making sure that **Only the listed pages** is selected.

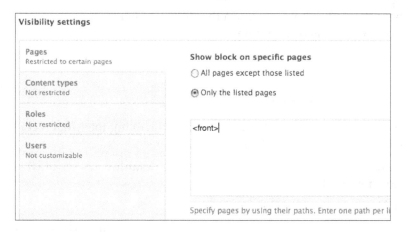

6. Go ahead and cast a vote via your home page block.

7. Your voting block will show the results immediately once you vote, as shown in the following screenshot:

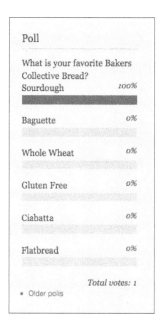

Submitting a poll

In this section we'll submit a poll.

Goal

Demonstrate how a customer will submit his or her answers to our poll.

Steps

Visitors can easily submit an answer to the poll by selecting their preferred option and then clicking on **Vote**.

After voting, the display will be updated to show the results of the poll.

Viewing poll results

In this section we'll view our poll results.

Goal

Demonstrate how Baker James can view the poll results, and show the results of the poll to customers who have already answered the poll.

Steps

Users with the permission to view voting results can view a list of all of the votes that have been cast for a poll. This is done by viewing the poll and clicking on the **Votes** tab, to list all the votes, as shown in the following screenshot:

What is your favorite Bakers Collective Bread?

| View | Edit | Votes |

This table lists all the recorded votes for this poll. If anonymous users are allowed to vote, they will be identified by the IP address of the computer they used when they voted.

Visitor	Vote	Timestamp ▼
admin	Sourdough	Thu, 05/19/2011 - 17:40

This view is useful for ensuring that all votes are legitimate, and for comparing votes submitted by registered users and anonymous users. For registered users their user name will be displayed; for unregistered users, the IP address of the machine from which they submitted their vote will be displayed.

Adding user surveys

User surveys allow more complex methods of querying visitors for information. Surveys support multiple questions that are asked at one time and questions that require more complex answers than a simple selection between a finite number of predefined choices. Baker James will use the user survey to get more comprehensive feedback and information about his customers' experience and what they expect from the bakery in the future.

Creating a user survey

In this section we'll create a survey form on our site.

Goal

Add a survey to the website that asks visitors for their opinion on various aspects of the bakery including specifics about what new food items they are interested in, what their favorite visiting times are, how frequently they visit, and so on.

Additional modules needed

Webform module (`http://drupal.org/project/webform`).

Steps

In this section we'll install and configure the Webform module:

1. Install the **WEBFORM** module on your site, and activate it by using the Modules admin screen. Save your modules' configuration.

▾ WEBFORM			
ENABLED	NAME	VERSION	DESCRIPTION
☑	Webform	7.x-3.11	Enables the creation of forms and questionnaires.

2. There are several core settings provided for controlling the basic aspects of the **WEBFORM** module. These can be accessed by clicking on **Configuration** and then **Webform settings**. For our site, all of the default values are acceptable. Bear in mind here that you can actually enable your other content types as Webform-enabled meaning that you can then add Webform field components to multiple content types. For now let's just leave our Webform type enabled.

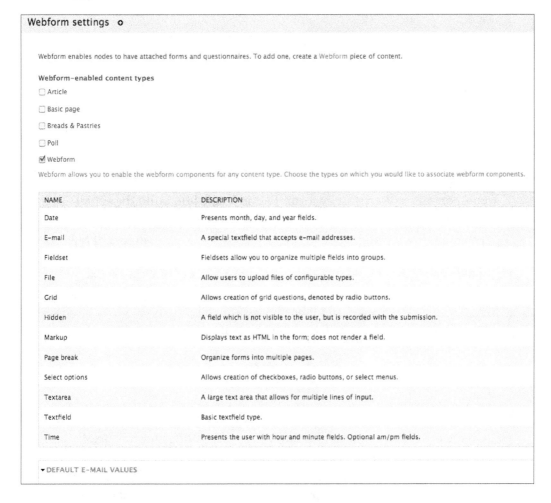

3. To build a new Webform, select **AddContent** and then **Webform**. Drupal will display a form that allows you to build your survey.

4. The first section of the form allows you to enter a title and description. We will fill this form out as shown in the following screenshot:

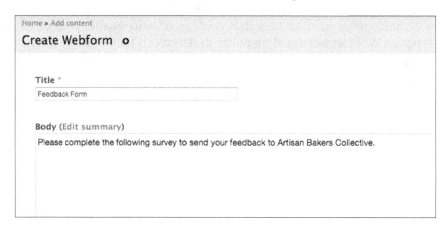

5. Click the **Save** button.

6. The next section of the form controls allows you to add fields or **Form components** to your survey form. This is where you build the actual form fields.

7. To add a new question, enter the question in the New component **NAME** field, and select the type of field from the drop-down list **TYPE**. You can make it a required field by selecting the **MANDATORY** checkbox.

8. Let's first add a text field to collect the site visitor's e-mail address. Type in Your E-mail Address and then choose e-mail as the type, make it required and click the **Add** button to add the component field.

9. On the next screen you can customize specific settings for this text field. Let's leave the defaults and click the **Save** component button.

10. Now, add a select field asking the site visitor how frequently they visit the bakery. Choose **Select options** as the type and make it mandatory. Click **Add**.

11. On the edit component screen you can choose whether to allow for multiple values. For this specific question we'll only accept one unique value per user so leave the Multiple box unchecked.

12. On the edit component screen type in your options in *key | value pairs*. You should have an **Options** box that contains the following *key | value pairs*:

13. You can also select whether you want the list to be in **Listbox** format. This will present the list as a select box instead of a series of checkboxes or radio buttons.

14. Click **Save component**.

15. Add another Select type question asking the site visitor what their favorite baked good is. This time allow for multiple answers as shown in the following screenshot:

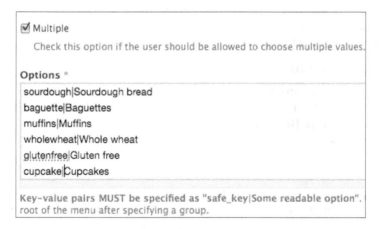

16. Other questions can be entered in a similar manner. For example you may want to add a general comments field using the Textarea type but not make this field required.

17. When you have finished entering all of your questions, click the **Save** button.

18. If you click on the **E-mails** tab above your Form components screen you can control whether or not survey results are mailed to a user, and if they are mailed, who they should be sent to. We won't automatically e-mail survey results, so this section can be left as it is:

19. Clicking on the Form settings tab you can add a Confirmation message that the user will see once they submit the feedback form. You can also set up a custom redirect; and specify the submission limit. This is helpful if you want to secure your form and only allow a specific number of submissions from any one user. For our purposes we'll leave this set to unlimited for now but if you start noticing a lot of spam submissions you may want to tweak this to only allow a specific number of submissions.

20. You can also specify the roles that can submit the form here. We'll leave the permissions enabled for both anonymous and authenticated users.

21. Save your form configuration.

22. Finally, we will add a menu item for this form, called **Customer Survey** which will appear in our main menu. To do this edit the form and check the **Provide a menu link** box. Then specify the Menu link title and set the Parent item for the menu link.

23. Save the form by clicking the **Save** button.

Our form is almost ready to use. We're going to add one more layer of security to the form to help prevent any unwanted spam submissions before we start using it.

Protecting the survey with Captchas

We'll install the CAPTCHA module to add spam prevention to our Webforms and surveys.

Goal

Add a Captcha to the survey to help prevent automated entry into the survey, to prevent spam.

Additional modules needed

Captcha module (`http://drupal.org/project/captcha`).

Steps

In this section we'll add CAPTCHA fields to our form.

1. Begin by installing and activating the Captcha module on your site. Once installed browse to your modules page and enable both the **CAPTCHA** and **Image CAPTCHA** modules:

2. We will then need to configure the CAPTCHA module settings. These are accessed by going to `/admin/config/people/captcha` or by visiting the **Configuration** screen and clicking on the CAPTCHA link.

3. Change the **Default challenge type** to **Image (from module image_captcha)**.

4. Check the box next to **Add CAPTCHA administration links to forms** option, as shown in the following screenshot:

This will allow us to add the Captcha field to our Webform survey.

5. You can also configure Captchas for several predefined forms, specify whether or not users have to answer Captchas for each form they submit, specify whether or not incorrect answers are logged, and what the various options for each type of Captcha are.

6. Save your CAPTCHA configuration.

7. You can view examples of each type of Captcha by clicking on the **Examples** link at the top of the screen.

8. Now that the Captcha has been configured, you can edit or simply view the Webform survey node we created earlier. There, you will find a new section titled **CAPTCHA: no challenge enabled**, which you can expand.

9. Click the **Place a CAPTCHA here for untrusted users** link to expand this section. You can now select the **Challenge type** that visitors will be presented with, as shown in the following screenshot:

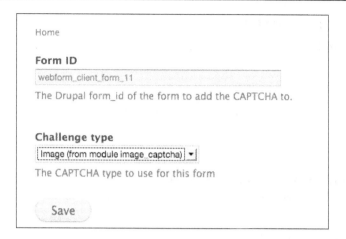

10. Click the **Save** button to save your settings. An untrusted user will see a Captcha when he or she attempts to submit an answer. If you view your form now as an anonymous user you should see the following **CAPTCHA** field displayed on your form:

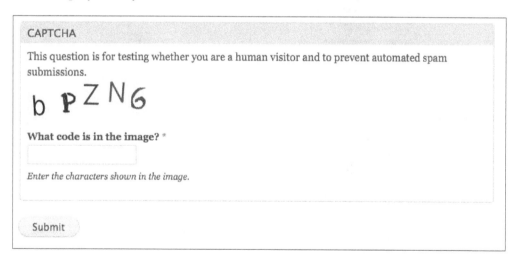

To summarize, we want to add a CAPTCHA field to our Webforms so we can prevent spambots from submitting our Webforms. The CAPTCHA field adds an additional layer of protection and prevention for our site's Webforms. This forces a site user to type in the CAPTCHA image and prove that they are indeed a human and not a machine which is trying to resubmit a form maliciously over and over.

Answering a survey

In this section we'll complete our survey.

Goal

Demonstrate how a visitor will fill out the survey to submit new answers.

Steps

When the users click on the **Customer Survey** link from the menu, they will be presented with the survey form that is to be filled out.

After they have entered all of their responses, they will need to answer the Captcha question, if they are not registered users.

The users then click **Submit** to send their responses to the site.

If any required information is missing, or if the Captcha is entered incorrectly, the user will be asked to correct this information, and then they can try to submit their responses again.

Once the information has been successfully submitted, the user will be taken to your completion page, which was set up when you created the survey.

Viewing survey results

In this section we'll view our survey results.

Goal

Demonstrate how Baker James will view the results of surveys.

The Webform module offers different ways for site administrators to review the survey submissions. These are all accessed by opening the survey and then clicking on the **Results** link.

Submissions view

The **Submissions** screen shows a list of all of the responses to the survey, as shown in the following screenshot. This view can be sorted, so you can easily identify duplicate submissions. You can view individual responses, and delete them if necessary. You can also view and edit each submission via the following screenshot:

Analysis view

The **Analysis** page groups responses so that you can view statistics of the survey and easily see how the answers for each question are broken down. A partial view is shown in the following screenshot:

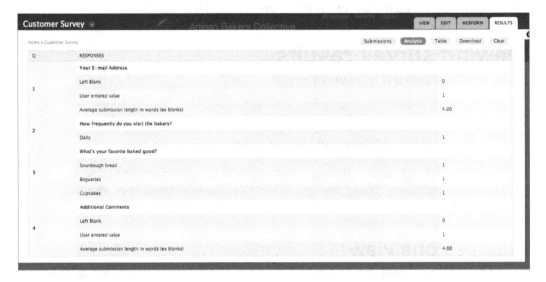

Table view

The **Table** view displays all of the results of the survey in a single, easy to read format, as shown in the following screenshot:

Download view

The **Download** view allows you to download all of the survey responses into a comma-delimited file, which can then be opened in a program such as Microsoft Excel, for further analysis.

Clear

Clicking on the **Clear** link will remove all of the survey responses from the site. This can be useful if you are testing the survey and want to restart, or if you want to restart the survey at the beginning of each month.

Summary

In this chapter, we explored various methods of soliciting feedback from visitors to your site, including comments, ratings, polls, and surveys. Using these techniques will help you to improve the products and services you provide to your customers.

In the next chapter, we will create a company blog to allow Baker James how to promote his restaurant to interested readers. We will also load feeds from other websites into the Artisan Bakers Collective site, to leverage content from other sources.

5
Creating a Company Blog

A **blog** is a series of typically short postings that are displayed in reverse chronological order. Blogs normally allow users to comment on each posting. With a regularly updated blog or blogs, you can ensure that your site always has fresh content, which ensures that both visitors and the search engines keep coming back.

In this chapter, we will:

- Create a blog where Baker James can discuss the Artisan Bakers Collective bakery, baking, the bakery business, and more. He plans to use the blog to make the site more interactive and to draw search engine traffic.

- Each employee will also be given the opportunity to have his or her own blog, where they can create blog entries if they so choose. Employee blogs will be monitored, and posts will be added to an approval queue before they are released to the public at large.

- Finally, we will demonstrate how users can view the blogs using RSS feeds and add related blog posts to their own blogs.

Creating blogs

In this section, we will discuss how to set up the core Drupal blog module so that a user can create blogs. We will demonstrate how Baker James creates blog posts, look at ways to moderate blogs, and use alternate editors to build the blog.

Setting up the blog system

In this section, we will enable the core Blog module and post a blog entry.

Goal

Set up the blog system, so that Baker James can begin posting to the blog.

Additional modules needed

Blog (core)

Steps

In this section, we'll enable and configure the Blog module:

1. Enable the core **Blog** module through the **Modules** administration screen. Save your module configuration:

   | | Blog | 7.2 | Enables multi-user blogs. |

2. Drupal will allow any user with the Blog entry: Create new content permission to create a blog. To make it easier to control who can create blogs, we will create a new role called blogger. To build a new role, click on **People** and then the **PERMISSIONS** tab. Then click on the **Roles** link.

3. Enter **blogger** as the role name and then click **Add role**, as shown in the following screenshot:

   blogger   Add role

4. Once the role has been created, click on the **edit permissions** link, so that we can define what this role can do. We will select the following settings:

PERMISSION

Node

Bypass content access control
View, edit and delete all content regardless of pe

Administer content types
Warning: Give to trusted roles only; this permissi

Administer content
Warning: Give to trusted roles only; this permissi

Access the content overview page

View published content

View own unpublished content

View content revisions

Revert content revisions

Delete content revisions

Blog entry. Create new content

Blog entry. Edit own content

Blog entry. Edit any content

Blog entry. Delete own content

Blog entry. Delete any content

5. These settings will allow users to maintain their own blog, but not modify anyone else's blog. Also make sure to give the role other specific permissions on the site, so that they can access content, view comments, and more. Save your blogger role's permissions.

6. Now add a user to the site and assign the new blogger role to that user account.

Adding a new blog post

In this section we'll add a blog post to our site using the Blog content type.

Goal

Demonstrate how Baker James will add new posts to his blog.

Steps

Creating a blog post is similar to building content pages. A blog is a content type in Drupal so you add blog content using a blog content type form just like using the Article and Basic Page forms for those content types. We'll first add a blog post after logging into the site as Baker James' main administrative account. This is the admin user.

1. We will start by clicking on the **Add content** link and then on the **Blog entry** link in the **Add content** screen:

2. Drupal will display a form where you can enter the **Body** of the post as well as a **Title** for the post, as shown in the following screenshot:

    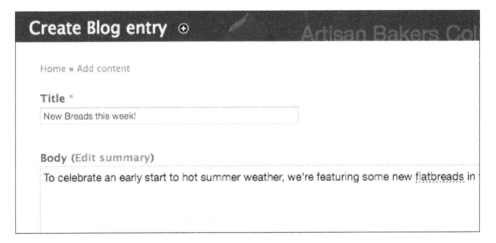

3. Once you are satisfied with the text of your post, simply click on the **Save** button and your new post will be saved. Like all content types on the site you can add an URL path alias; and set specific comment, authoring and publishing settings. We'll leave these set to their defaults for now.

4. If you would prefer that visitors didn't comment on a specific post, you can disable comments by expanding the **Comment settings** section of the form and selecting the **Closed** option.

5. After you have saved the post, the final blog entry will appear as shown in the following screenshot:

New Breads this week!

| View | Edit |

Submitted by admin on Tue, 06/07/2011 - 11:36

To celebrate an early start to hot summer weather, we're featuring some new flatbreads in the bakery this week! We'll have crepes on sale in the morning hours and papadums and focaccias on sale throughout the day.

admin's blog

Add new comment

Your name   admin

Subject

Comment *

6. Notice that under the blog entry there is a link to **admin's blog**. The blog module automatically associates the blog post with the user account that posted it. So as the admin user posted this blog entry, it will now show up on the admin user's blog list. If you click on **admin's blog** you'll see all of the blog posts that have been published by the admin user. The blog posts will show up under a heading that is titled **admin's blog**. Additionally, the blog listing will contain a link to an RSS feed for that specific blog:

admin's blog

✚ Post new blog entry.

New Breads this week!

Submitted by admin on Tue, 06/07/2011 - 11:36

To celebrate an early start to hot summer weather, we're featuring some new flatbreads in the bakery this week! We'll have crepes on sale in the morning hours and papadums and focaccias on sale throughout the day.

Read more

- ° If you click on the RSS icon, you'll launch the RSS feed for this specific blog.
- ° If you click on the **Blogs** link in the page's breadcrumb, you'll launch the overall **Blogs** page and listing that Drupal 7 provides. This page will list all blog posts from all user blogs. After each blog entry there's a link to the specific user's blog.

Blogs

✦ Create new blog entry

New Breads this week!

Submitted by admin on Tue, 06/07/2011 - 11:36

To celebrate an early start to hot summer weather, we're featuring some new flatbreads in the bakery this week! We'll have crepes on sale in the morning hours and papadums and focaccias on sale throughout the day.

Read more   admin's blog

---

7. Additionally, this main **Blogs** page also contains a link to an RSS feed that will contain all the most recent blog postings. So by using the Blog module, Drupal core provides multiple entry paths to blog content. You can view all blog posts, a specific user's posts, or a specific post.

Adding moderation for blog posts

In this section, we'll set up moderation and workflow options for our blog posts.

Goal

Configure the blogging systems so that posts must be moderated prior to publication, to ensure that the posts are appropriate. We will also add a moderator role that can edit posts or delete them, as necessary.

Additional modules needed

- Blog (core)

Creating the moderator role

Before we can set up moderation for the blog posts, we will need to create a moderator role. We can create it by using the following steps:

1. Begin going to your **People** administration screen, click on the **PERMISSIONS** tab, and then **Roles**.

2. Now, enter moderator as the name of the new role and click on the **Add role** button, to build the role.

3. Next, click on the **edit permissions** link to set up the permissions for our moderator role. The only specific permission that is needed to publish the blog posts is **Administer content**, as shown in the following screenshot:

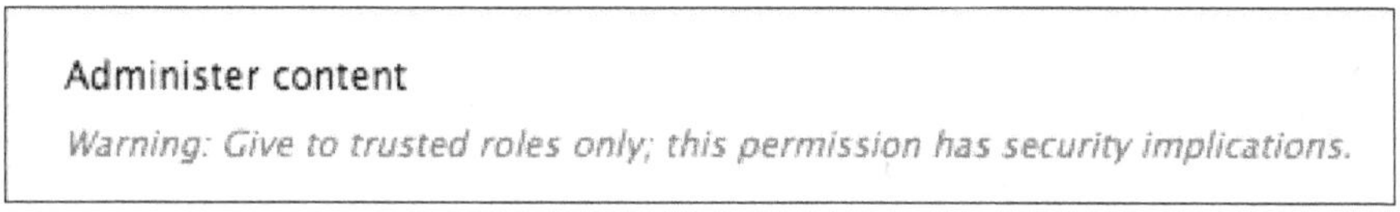

Administer content

Warning: Give to trusted roles only; this permission has security implications.

4. The **administer content** permission will also allow users assigned to this role to create, edit, or delete content, so you need to make sure that you assign this permission carefully. After you have selected the desired permissions, click the **Save permissions** button.

Setting up moderation for the blog posts

If you allow many users to post blog entries, it may be useful, when moderating the blog postings, to ensure that all posts conform to the standards you set. To do this, we will use Drupal's publishing functionality.

1. We will begin by editing the Blog content type by selecting **Structure** and then **Content types**, from the Administer menu.

2. Then click on the **edit** link next to the **Blog entry** content type.

3. Expand the **Publishing options** section, and deselect the **Published** checkbox, as shown in the following screenshot:

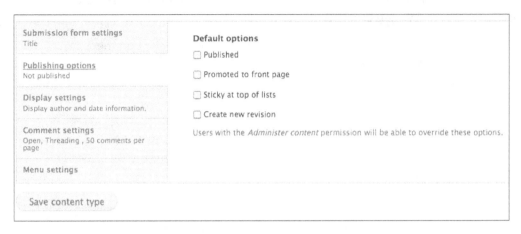

4. Also deselect the **Promoted to front page** checkbox. We'll let the moderator determine whether a post should be promoted to the home page of the site when they publish it.

5. Click on the **Save content type** button to update the blog entry type.

6. With this setting turned off, all posts will need to be manually approved. You can view all of the posts that need to be approved in the **Content** screen which is accessed by selecting **Content** from the toolbar menu.

7. To view only those posts that require moderation, change the **status** field to **not published**, and click on the **Filter** button.

8. Drupal will show only those items that should be moderated, as shown in the following screenshot:

9. To approve a post, you can select the checkbox next to its title, set the **Update Options** to **Publish selected content**, and then click on the **Update** button. Alternatively, you can edit the post and select the **Published** checkbox in the **Publishing options** settings for the post.

Automatically moderating content based on keywords

In this section, we'll set up automatic moderation based on specific keywords that are flagged by our Drupal configuration.

Goal

Add the automatic moderation of posts, based on the content entered within a post.

Additional modules needed

- *System* Actions (core)
- Trigger (core)

Steps

An alternative to forcing all posts into moderation is to allow posts to be automatically published, but to force specific posts to be moderated if they do not meet your guidelines. This can help you cut down on your moderation time and allow most posts to be available immediately after they are written.

If you haven't done so already make sure to switch your default Blog type publishing options back to published. We'll use the **Published** option as our default.

1. We will begin by creating a new action that will unpublish a post. Select **Configuration** and then **Actions**, from the toolbar menu to open the **Actions** manager.

2. Select a new action of **Unpublish content containing keyword(s)** and click on the **Create** button:

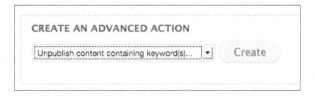

3. Drupal will now display a form on which you can enter the keywords that a post should contain if it is to be held for moderation. Enter the words separated by commas. If a term that you want to filter on includes a comma, you must enclose the entire term in quotes:

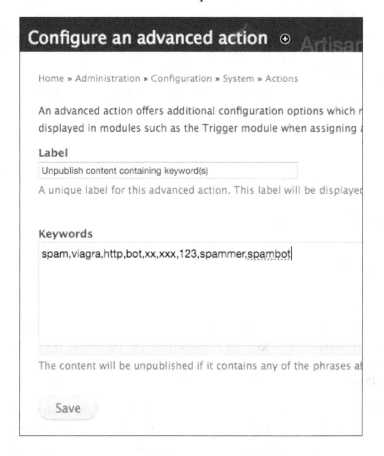

- For a publicly-accessible blog, you will want to enter common terms used in spam such as viagra, and so on. For an internal company blog, you may want to moderate based on competitor names, or terms that may indicate derogatory posts. When you are satisfied with your list of terms, click on the **Save** button. It's important to add potential malicious keywords so that we can prevent spammers from populating our site with comments full of malicious keywords and spam.

4. We now need to trigger the new action when a new blog post is created. Select **Structure** and then **Triggers**, from the Administer menu.

5. In order to ensure that both new posts and edited posts are clean, we will set the trigger so that when a user either saves new content or updates existing content, our new Unpublish content containing keyword(s) action is carried out.

TRIGGER: WHEN EITHER SAVING NEW CONTENT OR UPDATING EXISTING CONTENT

Unpublish content containing keyword(s) ▾   Assign

6. Click on the **Assign** button to save your changes. All posts that meet our criteria (that is, they contain any of the specified keywords) will now automatically be unpublished and put in the moderation queue. Go ahead and test posting a blog entry with the restricted keywords. The post should be unpublished automatically.

There are additional contributed Drupal modules including Mollom (http://drupal.org/project/mollom) that can be installed and configured to prevent spammers from attacking your website. Mollom is a web service-based application that you can integrate with your Drupal site. This means you need to sign up for an account with Mollom first and then integrate your Mollom account information into your Drupal site using the Mollom module.

Enabling customers to read your blogs

In order to make the most of our blogs, we need to make sure that our customers can easily find and read them.

In this section, we will explore various ways of displaying the blogs to our customers.

Displaying a list of available blogs

In this section, we'll display a listing of all the available blogs on our site.

Goal

Modify the website to display a list of available blogs, so that visitors can quickly find their favorite blog.

Additional modules needed

- Blog (core)

Creating a blog menu

Now that we can create new blog posts, we need to let our visitors know about them. We will add both a menu that links to our blog and a block showing the most recent posts in the blog:

To enable the menu link for our blog, go to **Structure | Menus** in the toolbar menu. Then click on the **list links** link in the **Navigation** menu row. At the bottom of the list of menu items, you will find the **Blogs** menu item, as shown in the following screenshot:

1. To activate the **Blogs** menu, simply select the **Enabled** checkbox and then click the **Save configuration** button at the bottom of the screen. The new **Blogs** item will now show up in the **Navigation** menu. If you want to change the name of the menu item, you can click on the **edit** link in the Operations column.

2. Now, log out of the website and you'll see the **Blogs** link in the main **Navigation** menu block.

3. When a user clicks on the **Blogs** link, they will be taken to a page that contains the most recent posts for all blogs, as shown in the following screenshot:

4. From this page, users can read recent posts, create a new blog entry (if they have permissions to post), comment on posts, or see all the posts that a given user has made by clicking on the link to the user's blog.

Creating a blog block

In this section, we're going to add a block to our site showing the most recent blog posts:

1. The blog block is enabled by selecting **Structure** and then **Blocks**, from the toolbar menu. This will open the **Blocks** manager screen.

2. The **Recent blog posts** block will be in the **Disabled** section. Change the **Region** to the **Sidebar first** and then click on the **Save blocks** button.

3. After saving the blocks, the **Recent blog posts** block will be displayed on the leftmost side of the screen. It will look similar to the following screenshot:

Recent blog posts

- Flatbreads on sale today!
- New Breads this week!

More

Creating an RSS feed for newsreaders

In this section, we'll add an RSS feed to our blogs.

Goal

Publish blogs using RSS feeds, so customers can follow blogs in their favorite newsreader.

Additional modules needed

- Blog (core)

Steps

Each blog automatically has an RSS feed created for it. **Really Simple Syndication (RSS)** is a technology that allows readers to automatically retrieve posts from one or more sites, into a feedreader. The feedreader checks for new content at specified intervals and then automatically downloads new posts if they are available. This is a fantastic way for a user to get updates from his or her company on a regular basis.

1. To add an RSS feed from your site to their feedreader, a user clicks on the RSS link icon, which appears at the bottom of all the blogs, and looks like the following screenshot:

   The actual sign-up process will vary somewhat, depending on the web browser that the site visitor is using. In Firefox, the process is as follows (other browsers will also use a similar process). In Chrome for example the RSS feed will be displayed in a raw XML format. First click on the RSS icon. This will launch the RSS feed on your Drupal site. The blog feed should be at this URL: `/blog/feed`

2. In Firefox you can subscribe to the feed using your Live Bookmarks, or specify another method by clicking on the select box.

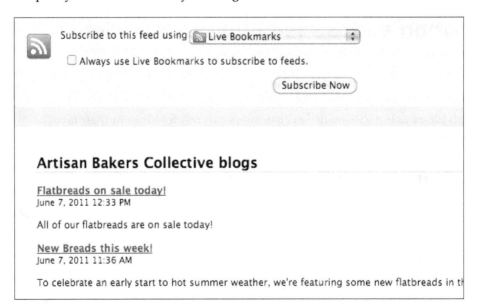

3. After clicking on the **Subscribe now** button the user will be subscribed to the feed.

4. The users can select from several common browsers' feedreaders including Google, Yahoo, and Safari, or they can select an application of their choice. To complete the subscription, they simply click the **Subscribe Now** button.

Adding subscription buttons

In this section, we will configure the AddThis module to allow for sharing of our content on social networking sites.

Goal

Allow the user to easily add blog posts to their favorite apps by providing AddThis and share icons.

Additional modules needed

Add This (`http://drupal.org/project/addthis`).

Steps

You can make subscription to your blog easier and more obvious to visitors by adding a set of share icons that will automatically share your blog posts to their favorite social networking app:

1. Begin by installing and enabling the AddThis module on your site.

2. The settings for the AddThis module are accessed by selecting **Configuration** and then **AddThis** settings from the **System** section.

3. Here you can determine what pages to show to the **AddThis** button; on node pages and in node teasers. Let's check the node pages box.

4. Let's leave the rest of the settings set to their default for now. Click on **Save configuration**.

5. We now need to activate the **AddThis** block. Open the block manager by selecting **Structure** and then **Blocks**, from the toolbar menu. Change the location of the **AddThis** button block to the **Sidebar Second** region, and then click on the **Save blocks** button. Now load your blog page and you'll see the **AddThis** block.

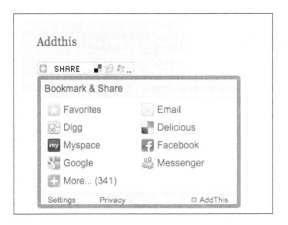

° Also make sure to grant your user roles permission to view the **AddThis** widget in the **AddThis** permissions table.

° You can also limit the display of this block to only show on the main blog page. To do this, click on the **configure** link for the block and then set the visibility settings as shown in the following screenshot:

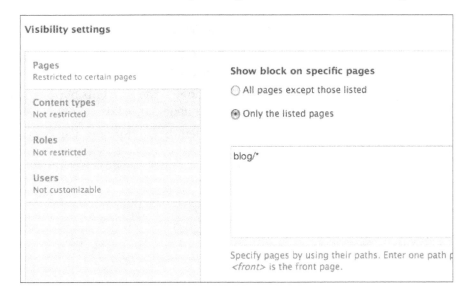

Including information from other blogs

In this section, we will add content from blogs on other sites that is relevant to the customers of our site. This can help customers recognize you as an authority in your area and make the site more useful to them.

Allowing your site to read content

In this section, we'll configure the core Drupal Aggregator module.

Goal

Set up the core Aggregator module to collect posts from other blogs and display them on the Artisan Bakers Collective site.

Additional modules needed

Aggregator (core)

Steps

In this section, we'll enable and configure the Aggregator module. This module will allow us to feed in content to our site from other external websites.

1. Activate the Aggregator module through the modules administration screen.

2. The Aggregator module configuration can now be accessed by clicking on **Configuration** and then **Feed aggregator**, from the **WEB SERVICES** table.

WEB SERVICES

RSS publishing
Configure the site description, the number of items per feed and whether feeds should be titles/teasers/full-text.

Feed aggregator
Configure which content your site aggregates from other sites, how often it polls them, and how they're categorized.

---

3. There are several settings available to the **Feed aggregator**. These can be found by clicking on the **SETTINGS** tab. These settings are shown in the following screenshot:

For our site, the default values are all acceptable. If you plan to import many feeds from different sources, it is a good idea to categorize them so that your visitors can easily find the information they want. The Artisan Bakers Collective site will have two categories: Baker Blogs and Recipes.

4. To add a new category, click on the **LIST** tab. Then click on the **Add category** link on the **Feed aggregator** screen. Drupal will display a form that allows you to enter a **Title** and **Description** for your category, as shown in the following screenshot:

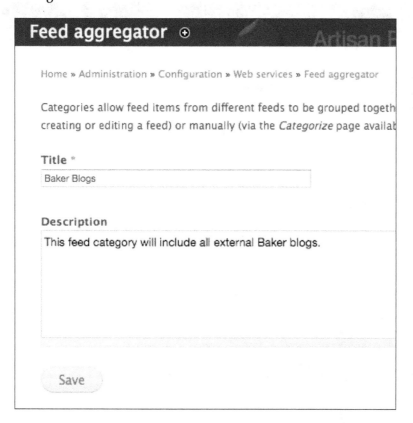

5. After you have created your categories, you can edit them by clicking on the **LIST** tab.

6. To add a new feed to the **Feed aggregator,** click on the **Add feed** link. Drupal will display a form where you can enter the URL for the feed, as well as additional information for the feed, as shown in the following screenshot:

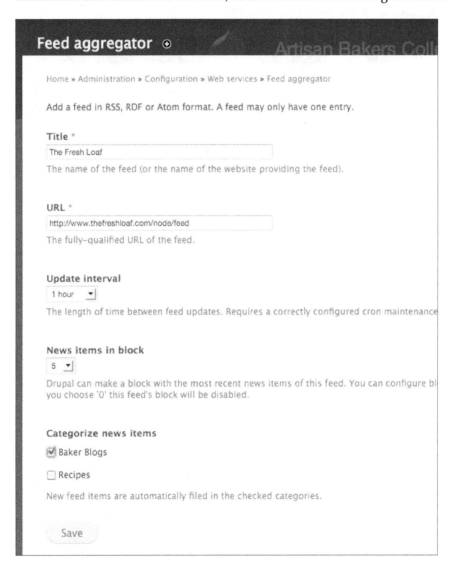

7. Let's go ahead and add the Fresh Loaf website feed. This is a Drupal-powered website for amateur bakers and contains a wealth of information and includes blog posts by users. First locate the feed URL on the Fresh Loaf site and then copy and paste this URL into the URL field on the Add feed form. The URL we're adding is: http://www.thefreshloaf.com/node/feed.

8. To reduce traffic on the site that you are receiving feeds from, you should try to set the **Update interval** in line with the frequency at which that site is updated. For example, there is no reason to poll a site every 15 minutes, if the site states that the feed is only updated once a day, or once a week. Let's leave this set to the default of **1 hour**. Also select the **Bakers Blogs** category.

9. After you are satisfied with your selections, click on the **Save** button.

10. After you create the feed, it will be displayed on the **List** page, as shown in the following screenshot:

11. As you can see, there are no **ITEMS** available for this feed, and it has never been updated. To update the feed manually, click the **update items** link. Once you click on the **update items** link, your feed from the Fresh Loaf site will update. You should now see that your feed contains 10 items and has a next update listed.

12. Click on the **feed** link to the Fresh Loaf and your site will launch the feed's page on your site. You'll see all of the Fresh Loaf content showing on your site in title and teaser format. If you click on the title links you'll be taken to the corresponding page on the Fresh Loaf site:

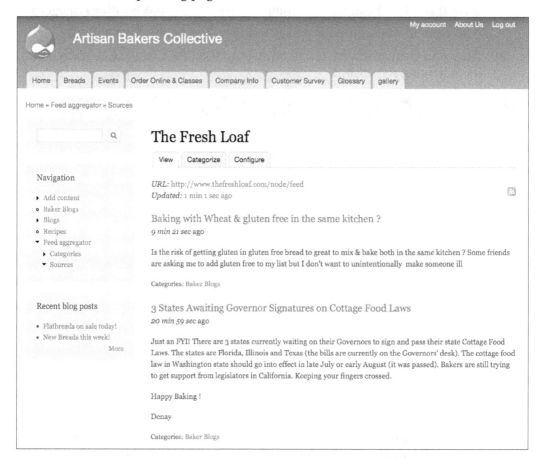

Viewing feeds

In this section, we'll display our feeds on our site so our users can access them.

Goal

Demonstrate how feeds will appear on the site.

Steps

In this section, we'll give permissions to our users so that they can view news feeds:

1. In order for a feed to be visible to users, you must update the user role permissions. Select **People** and then **Permissions**, from the toolbar menu.

2. Select the checkbox **View news feeds**, for each user role for which you want to see the feeds, as shown in the following screenshot:

3. If a user has permission to view news feeds, they will have a **Feed aggregator** menu item in the **Navigation** menu. This menu item can be either modified or disabled in the menu item, if you wish.

4. When a user clicks on the **Feed aggregator** link, a list of current posts will be displayed, as shown in the following screenshot:

5. The visitor can also display news items by category or by source. The **Categories** view is shown in the following screenshot:

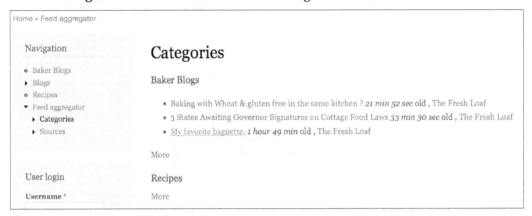

The **Sources** view is shown as follows:

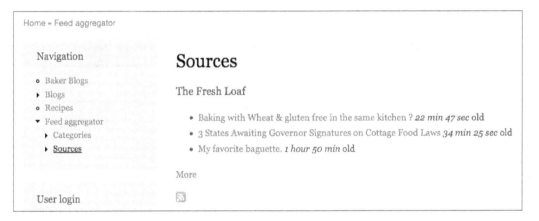

We can also add a block for the feeds, by using the block manager. There is a block for each category of news feed, in addition to a category for a specific feed. You can add these blocks to any section of the site that you want to, by changing the location and then saving the blocks. Go ahead and enable your **Baker Blogs** latest items block. You should see this in your sidebar region:

Baker Blogs

- Baking with Wheat & gluten free in the same kitchen ?
- 3 States Awaiting Governor Signatures on Cottage Food Laws
- My favorite baguette.
- Light Rye with Cumin and Orange
- Happy 50th "Chorleywood" Bread!

More

Automatically updating your feeds with cron jobs

In this section, we'll auto update our feeds using the Aggregator module and the `cron.php` script.

Goal

Set up a cron job to automatically read the news feeds at regular intervals and update the Aggregator categories and feeds on your site. Cron is a maintenance task and script that Drupal will activate to run on the site and server. This script will perform various tasks including indexing site content so it can be searched as well as running backups of your site if you're using a module such as Backup and Migrate. Cron basically automates many of the maintenance tasks on your website in Drupal.

Steps

We can manually update each feed by clicking the **update items** link in the **Feed Aggregator** manager. However, it can be time consuming and error prone to have to do this for each feed, once a day, or more frequently. Drupal allows you to automate the process of updating the feeds by using cron jobs.

A cron job is an automated task that runs at specific intervals. The cron job is activated by navigating to `http://yoursite.com/cron.php`. Each module that has been activated can run tasks every time the cron job is started. Even if you are not using the Aggregator, you should set up cron because Drupal uses the cron job for maintenance tasks, and many other modules use cron to perform maintenance.

You can also set up cron to run automatically in your Drupal 7 site without having to run cron.php manually. To do this go to **Configuration | Cron**. Here you can set how often to run cron on your Drupal site. Currently it's set to run every **3 hours**. You can also click on the **Run cron** button to run cron manually. Click on the **Save configuration** button once you configure your cron settings:

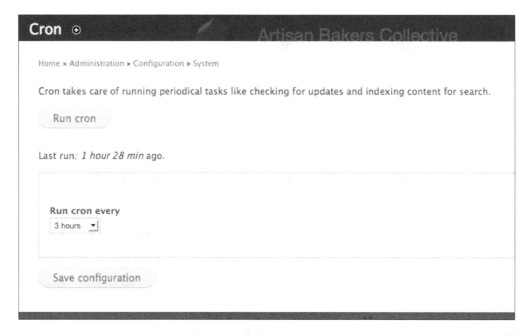

You can also configure cron to run on your server through a script. This is independent of Drupal but will specify your server configuration to run the Drupal cron script for your Drupal site. The method of setting up a cron job depends on the operating system that you are using. If you are running a control panel on your web server, such as cPanel or Plesk, you may be able to configure the cron job from within the control panel. In all cases, you will be instructing the operating system to automatically load the http://yoursite.com/cron.php page on your website at specific intervals.

Additional ways of setting up cron

The Drupal site has a wealth of information about setting up cron on various other systems, at: `http://drupal.org/cron`.

Summary

In this chapter, we have explored how to create a blog for your company, and how to incorporate news feeds from other websites into your site. Using blogs and other websites will help to keep your website content fresh, and will keep visitors and search engines interested in your site so that they visit frequently.

In the next chapter, we will work with several very useful modules to allow Baker James to create newsletters and a calendar of events to publicize current events at the Artisan Bakers Collective bakery.

6
Newsletters and Calendars

In this chapter, we will add new features which will allow Baker James to keep his customers informed of current events at Artisan Bakers Collective:

- We will provide two new means of communication. The first feature is a quarterly newsletter that customers can subscribe to. The newsletter will contain valuable information from Baker James including coupons, news, recipes, and more.

- The second feature is a calendar that will help customers learn about upcoming events at the Artisan Bakers Collective bakery.

Creating newsletters

A newsletter is a great way of keeping customers up-to-date without them needing to visit your website. Customers appreciate well-designed newsletters because they allow the customer to keep tabs on their favorite places without needing to check every website on a regular basis.

Creating a newsletter category

In this section, we'll install and configure the Simplenews module and configure our newsletter categories.

Goal

Create a new newsletter on the site, which will be content-relevant news about the bakery, and will be delivered quarterly to the subscribers.

Additional modules needed:

Simplenews (`http://drupal.org/project/simplenews`)

Steps

Newsletters are containers for individual issues. For example, you could have a newsletter called Artisan Bakers Collective newsletter, which would have four issues per year (summer, fall, winter, and spring). A customer subscribes to the newsletter and each issue is sent to them as it becomes available. The Simplenews module lets us create overall newsletters by using the core Drupal taxonomy module. Simplenews newsletters are categorized based on terms that you add to a Simplenews vocabulary in the taxonomy. Then you can add Simplenews issue by using the Simplenews content type form and select the tag or newsletter category that this specific issue node should be associated with.

1. Begin by installing and activating the **Simplenews** module, as shown in the following screenshot:

☑	Simplenews	7.x-1.0-alpha1	Send newsletters to subscribed email addresses. Requires: Taxonomy (enabled), Options (enabled), Field (enabled), Field SQ Required by: Simplenews action (disabled)
☐	Simplenews action	7.x-1.0-alpha1	Provide actions for Simplenews. Requires: Simplenews (enabled), Taxonomy (enabled), Options (enabled), F

 Note that Simplenews module is currently in alpha status for Drupal 7.x. (7.x-1.0-alpha1). The module also has a development version and both the alpha and development version could contain bugs and other issues. This process of testing the module will help the module developer, as we can report any issues or bugs back to the module's issue queue.

At this point, we only need to enable the **Simplenews** module, and the **Simplenews action** module can be left disabled. Save your module configuration.

2. Next, select **Content** and then click on the **NEWSLETTERS** tab, from the toolbar menu. Drupal will display an administration area showing you a table of all of your available newsletters as well as a search mechanism that allows for filtering of the newsletters:

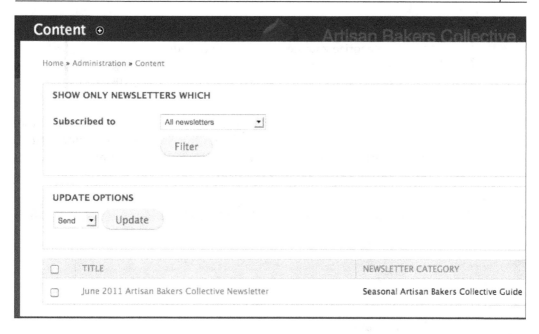

3. Currently, we have no available newsletters but the Simplenews module does add a default newsletter category called Artisan Bakers Collective newsletter. This is a term that's added to a taxonomy vocabulary that the module adds to our site called Newsletter. You can view this default vocabulary and associated term by going to your **Taxonomy** administration page:

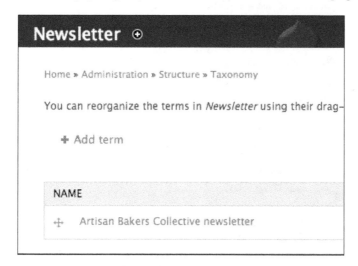

To categorize your newsletters, you can add new terms for each newsletter that you will end up adding newsletter issues for. We'll use this default term for now.

4. As the term is a newsletter category, you can add a specific description to the term if you want to specify more details about this specific newsletter. You can do this by editing the term by clicking on the **edit vocabulary** link next to the term in its associated vocabulary listing:

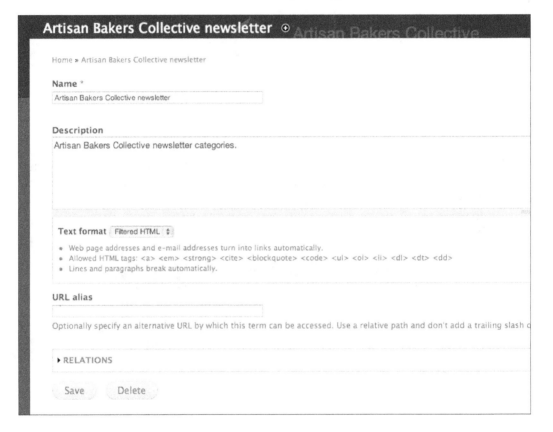

Viewing your newsletter categories

You can view all of your newsletter categories by going to **Structure | Newsletters**. This will show you all of your existing newsletter categories, allow you to add a newsletter category, and edit an existing category:

To add a new newsletter category click on the **Add newsletter category** link. This will launch a form where you can specify the settings for your newsletter. Follow the ensuing steps to add a newsletter:

1. Add a **Name** for the newsletter. We'll call our newsletter `Seasonal Artisan Bakers Collective Guide`.

2. Add a **Description** of the newsletter.

3. Select the **SUBSCRIPTION SETTINGS**. If you want users to subscribe through the user account registration page, make sure to set **Subscribe new account** to **Default on**.

4. Leave the **Opt-in/out method** set to **Double**.

5. Leave the **Subscription block** checked. This will add a subscription block to your site.

6. Set the **Email priority** to its default of **none**.

7. You can specify the **SENDER INFORMATION** including **From name** and **From email address** for your newsletter.

8. You can add a **NEWSLETTER SUBJECT**. Your form should look similar to the following screenshot:

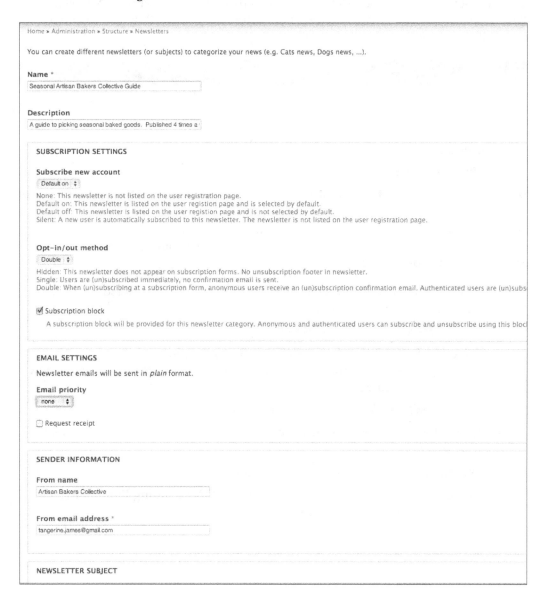

Home » Administration » Structure » Newsletters

You can create different newsletters (or subjects) to categorize your news (e.g. Cats news, Dogs news, ...).

Name *

Seasonal Artisan Bakers Collective Guide

Description

A guide to picking seasonal baked goods. Published 4 times a

SUBSCRIPTION SETTINGS

Subscribe new account

Default on ⬍

None: This newsletter is not listed on the user registration page.
Default on: This newsletter is listed on the user registion page and is selected by default.
Default off: This newsletter is listed on the user registion page and is not selected by default.
Silent: A new user is automatically subscribed to this newsletter. The newsletter is not listed on the user registration page.

Opt-in/out method

Double ⬍

Hidden: This newsletter does not appear on subscription forms. No unsubscription footer in newsletter.
Single: Users are (un)subscribed immediately, no confirmation email is sent.
Double: When (un)subscribing at a subscription form, anonymous users receive an (un)subscription confirmation email. Authenticated users are (un)subs

☑ Subscription block

A subscription block will be provided for this newsletter category. Anonymous and authenticated users can subscribe and unsubscribe using this bloc

EMAIL SETTINGS

Newsletter emails will be sent in *plain* format.

Email priority

none ⬍

☐ Request receipt

SENDER INFORMATION

From name

Artisan Bakers Collective

From email address *

tangerine.james@gmail.com

NEWSLETTER SUBJECT

9. Click on the **Save** button. You now will see the new newsletter in your **Newsletters** table:

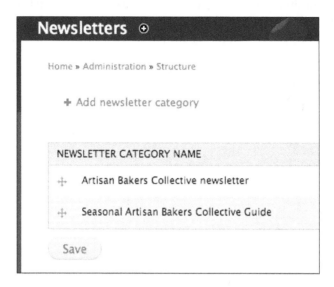

Adding newsletters

Let's go ahead and add a newsletter to our site. The Simplenews module adds a new content type to our site called Simplenews newsletter. As it's a content type it behaves like all of our other content types on our Drupal 7 site and can be extended by adding fields to it. To add a newsletter, follow the ensuing steps:

1. Click on the **Add content** link and then click on the **Simplenews newsletter** link. Drupal will display a standard form where we can enter the name, description, and relative importance (relative importance weight) of the newsletter.

2. Click on the **Save** button to save the newsletter. It will now appear in the list of the available newsletters.

Simplenews module settings

The Simplenews module provides general configuration options that you can tweak per your requirements. To access the settings, launch your **Configuration** screen and then look for the **Simplenews** table, as shown in the following screenshot:

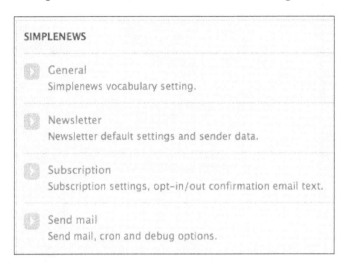

General and newsletter configuration

1. Click on the **General** link. This will launch a screen showing you the vocabulary that is being used for your newsletters. You'll also see the machine readable field name for your vocabulary term field.

2. Click on the **Newsletter** link, and this will launch your newsletter configuration form. Here you can set your default newsletter options including whether to send a plaintext or HTML formatted version of your newsletter.

3. To utilize an HTML formatted version of Simplenews, you need to install either the Mime Mail or the HTML Mail modules first. This is a requirement before setting the Simplenews formatter to HTML. Mime Mail and HTML Mail modules are available at:

    ○   http://drupal.org/project/mimemail
    ○   http://drupal.org/project/htmlmail

    i.   Install the module like you install all contributed modules and enable it.

    ii.   Mime Mail and HTML Mail depend on the Mail System module so you also need to install Mail System. You can find it here: `http://drupal.org/project/mailsystem`:

MAIL			
ENABLED	**NAME**	**VERSION**	**DESCRIPTION**
☑	HTML Mail	7.x-2.55	Enables HTML in system emails. Requires: Mail System (disabled), Filter (enabled)
☑	Mail System	7.x-2.25	Provides a user interface for per-module and site-wide mail_system selection. Requires: Filter (enabled) Required by: HTML Mail (disabled), Mime Mail (disabled), Mime Mail Action (disabled), Mime Mail CSS Compressor (disabled)
☑	Mime Mail	7.x-1.x-dev	Send MIME-encoded emails with embedded images and attachments. Requires: Mail System (disabled), Filter (enabled) Required by: Mime Mail Action (disabled), Mime Mail CSS Compressor (disabled)
☐	Mime Mail Action	7.x-1.x-dev	Provide actions for Mime Mail. Requires: Mime Mail (disabled), Mail System (disabled), Filter (enabled), Trigger (enabled)
☐	Mime Mail CSS Compressor	7.x-1.x-dev	Converts CSS to inline styles in an HTML message. (Requires the PHP DOM extension.) Requires: Mime Mail (disabled), Mail System (disabled), Filter (enabled)

4. Once the modules are enabled, go back to the main Simplenews configuration screen and click on the **Newsletter** link. This will launch a form where you can set your newsletter **Format** to **HTML**.

5. You can set e-mail **Priority**, and **Request receipt**. You can also specify that you want to **Send one test version of the newsletter to a test address** before the newsletter is pushed out to your entire e-mail list of addresses. This is the recommended setting.

   In the next section, you can set a test e-mail address for yourself. It's highly recommended that you send a test newsletter before you send it to the entire subscription list to prevent errors in the final newsletter. The test address defaults to the administration e-mail address for your site. You can also check the box here to override the test address per newsletter. This way you can specify a different test address to use on your actual newsletter form when you're creating it and adding its node content to the site.

6. In the **SENDER INFORMATION** section, you can specify the **From name** and **From email address** to use as the defaults for all of your e-newsletters. This setting can be overridden per specific newsletters. You should now see a screen that looks similar to the following screenshot:

7. Click on the **Save configuration** button.

Subscription and Send mail configuration

Let's go back to our main Simplenews configuration screen and click on the **Subscription** settings link. Here you can specify the default subscription settings to use for your newsletters. To subscribe and configure e-mail, follow these steps:

1. Leave the **Synchronize with account** checkbox checked. This will allow for all subscriptions to be synched automatically with the user account of the subscriber.

2. The **CONFIGURATION EMAILS** section allows you to configure specific content for your confirmation subject and body text elements.

3. Finally, you can specify a node on your site to use as the page subscribers and get redirected to after confirming their newsletter subscription. By default, they will be redirected to the site's home page. You should now see a screen that looks similar to the following screenshot:

4. Click on the **Save configuration** button.

5. The last configuration screen is your **Send mail** options. Here you can specify the **Mail system** to use on your server. By default, you can leave this set to **Default** in your localhost environment. You may need to change this depending on the mail system your server is using.

6. Leave the **Use cron to send newsletters** checkbox ticked.

7. You can leave the **Cron throttle** and **Mail spool expiration** set to their defaults.

8. You can also choose to **Log emails** if you want e-mails logged to your log entries when e-mails are sent through Simplenews. Now your screen should look similar to the following screenshot:

9. Click on the **Save configuration** button.

We're now ready to create a new issue of our newsletter and send it out.

Creating a new issue of the newsletter

In this section, we'll create a new HTML-based issue of our newsletter.

Goal

Build a new issue of the Seasonal Artisan Bakers Collective newsletter in preparation for it to be sent to newsletter subscribers.

Steps

In this section, we'll be adding a new newsletter issue to our site. In order to create a new issue of the newsletter, follow the ensuing steps:

1. Creating a new newsletter issue is similar to creating any other page within Drupal. We will begin by clicking on **Add content** and then on **Simplenews newsletter**:

Simplenews newsletter

A newsletter issue to be sent to subscribed email addresses.

2. This will display a form where you can select the newsletter for which you want to create an issue, and can enter information about that issue, as shown in the following screenshot:

3. You can select **Full HTML** as the **Text format** as we'll be sending the newsletter as an HTML newsletter. Any links, lists of images you add to the newsletter content will be rendered correctly as **Full HTML** when you send out the newletter.

4. As you are adding content, you can also specify whether to add the newsletter to your Drupal menu system, specify a path alias, **Comment settings**, and also tweak the **Publishing options** of your newsletter.

5. When you are satisfied with your issue, click on the **Save** button. The newsletter node will publish to your site and you'll see your newsletter node immediately. Drupal will tell you that the newsletter has been created successfully:

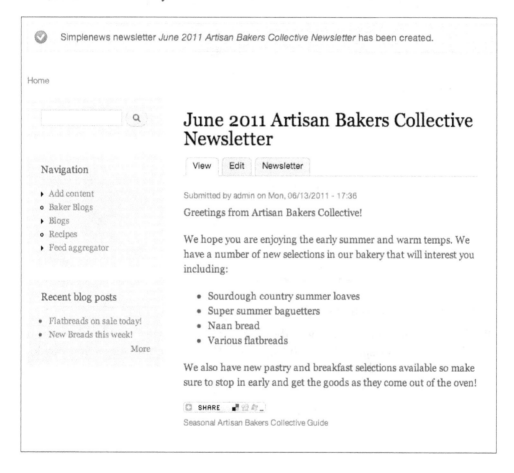

6. Now you can test sending it. To send a test to your test newsletter address, click on the **Newsletter** tab just above the newsletter node. On the **SEND NEWSLETTER** screen, make sure that the **Send one test newsletter to the test address** radio button is selected. Here, you can also override the **Test email addresses**. You can add multiple e-mail addresses separated by a comma:

7. Click on the **Send test** button.

8. You can tell immediately whether the test e-mails were sent by checking your **Recent log messages** through **Reports | Recent log messages**. In your log table you'll see that the Simplenews type log entries and the status message will be listed. If you click on the message, you'll see the log for the send:

9. After you have sent a test e-mail and checked that it was delivered correctly, you can send the newsletter to the full list of subscribers by changing the **Send newsletter** options to **Send newsletter**. Click on the **Save and send** button:

10. Once the newsletter has been scheduled, it will be sent to a portion of the subscriber list each time that cron is run. This is done to avoid flooding the network. You can configure the number of e-mails that are sent each time that cron is called by editing the **Send mail** settings for the Newsletter, which is accessed by selecting **Site Configuration** and then **Simplenews**. The available settings are shown in the following screenshot:

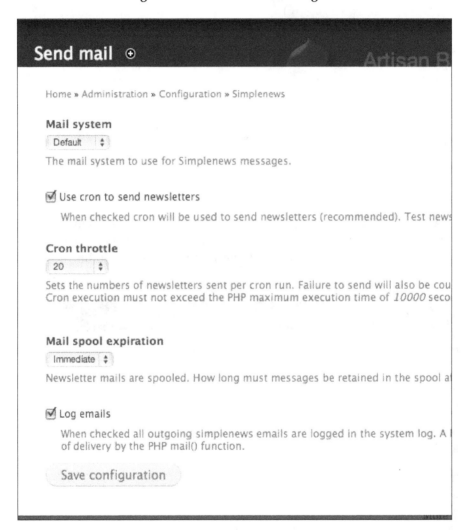

By default, only twenty e-mails are sent each time that cron is run. This is fine, if you are running cron frequently, but if you are running it less frequently, you may want to increase the number of e-mails that are sent each time. Some web hosting companies only allow a specific number of e-mails to be sent every hour, to help prevent spammers from utilizing their servers. Before sending newsletters to large mailing lists, you should check with your host to ensure that you comply with their policies.

Allowing users to sign up for the newsletter

In this section, we'll allow users of the site to sign up for the newsletters through a **sign up** block.

Goal

Demonstrate how registered and unregistered users can sign up for a newsletter, and configure the registration process. The Simplenews module provides a subscription block for each newsletter you create on the site.

Steps

In this section, we'll allow our site's users to subscribe to the newsletter:

1. To allow customers to sign up for the newsletter, we will begin by adding a block to the site.

2. Go to **Structure | Blocks** from the toolbar menu. Look for the Newsletter block in your disabled blocks section. Enable the block for the newsletter that you want to allow customers to subscribe to, as shown in the following screenshot:

Sidebar second

✛   Newsletter: Seasonal Artisan Bakers Collective Guide*

3. Save your block's configuration. You can also click on the **configure** link next to the newsletter block. This will open up the specific block configuration form. Here you can specify a **Block message**, **Subcription interface**, a link to previous issues of the newsletter, how many issues to show, and whether to display an RSS icon. We'll leave all the defaults set here:

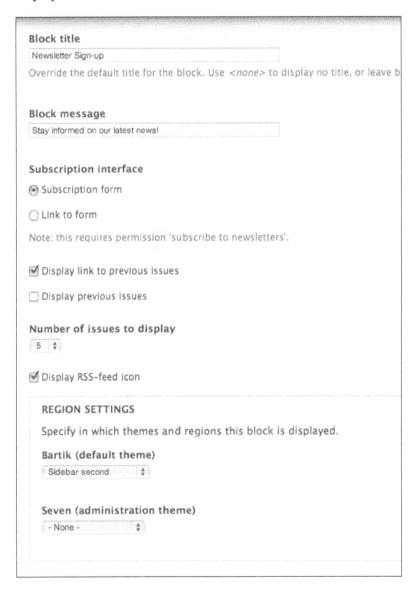

4. We will now need to give users permission to subscribe to newsletters by selecting **People** and then **Permissions**, from the toolbar menu. We will give all users permissions to subscribe to newsletters as shown in the following screenshot:

5. Now you can log out of the site and you'll see the subscription block in the right sidebar, or the specific region you placed it. Your block should look similar to the following screenshot:

6. To subscribe to the newsletter, the customer will simply type in their e-mail address and then click on the **Subscribe** button. Once subscribed, the user will need to check their e-mail for a confirmation e-mail message that will ask them to confirm their subscription. The user will click on the confirmation URL in the e-mail they receive and be redirected to the website. They will see a page that looks similar to the following screenshot:

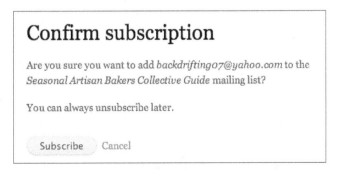

When they click on the **Subscribe** button, their e-mail address will be added to the newsletter subscription list.

7. Clicking on the **Previous Issues** link will launch a page showing all previous issues of the newsletter. You'll notice that this list will appear as a taxonomy URL path. For example: `/taxonomy/term/19`, as the newsletters are being categorized by term. Finally, the block contains an RSS icon link that will launch a specific RSS feed for the previous issues of the newsletter.

Managing sign ups

In this section, we will learn how administrative users can manage subscribers to our newsletters.

Goal

Generate a list of all the users who have signed up for a newsletter, and demonstrate how to remove suspicious users.

Steps

In order to manage subscribers to our newsletters, follow the ensuing steps. After customers have begun to sign up for your newsletter:

1. You can view a list of all existing subscriptions by selecting **People** and then clicking on the **NEWSLETTER SUBSCRIPTIONS** tab from the **People** administration screen.

2. You will see a screen that shows all the current subscribers, a method of filtering by newsletter, and updating subscription options:

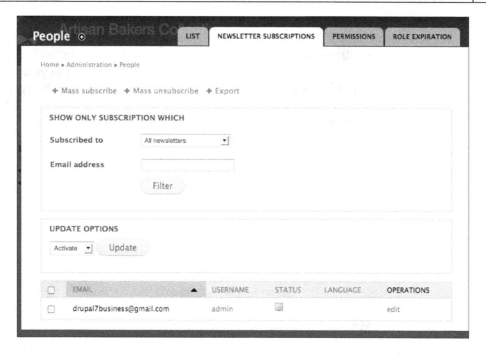

3. You can filter the display, to list only specific newsletters, or to list only those newsletters that a specific customer has subscribed to. To edit individual subscriptions, click on the **edit** link. This will display a page similar to the following screenshot where you can uncheck or check to select the newsletters you want to allow the user to have access to:

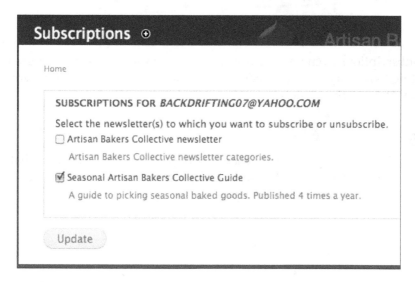

4. You can also activate, deactivate, or delete subscriptions by selecting the subscription you want to modify, selecting the appropriate action in the **Update options** drop-down list, and then clicking on the **Update** button. This allows you to remove malicious users who have subscribed to your newsletters. You can deactivate or delete the user's subscription entirely. If you receive a significant number of invalid sign ups, you may want to add a CAPTCHA to the sign-up form:

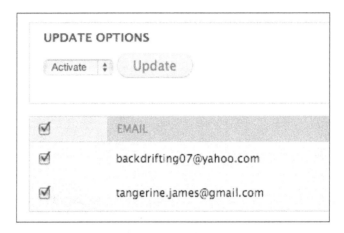

Importing and exporting subscriptions

In this section, we will import e-mail addresses from an external list into our Simplenews subscriber list, and also show how we can export all of our lists.

Goal

Import subscriptions from another list management system that was in use prior to you starting to manage your newsletter, by using Simplenews or export your current subscriber list from Simplenews.

Steps

If you already have a large list of subscribers to your newsletter, you probably wouldn't want to throw this list away because a good contact list takes time to build and can be very lucrative for you.

1. You can import a comma-delimited list of e-mail addresses by clicking on the **Mass subscribe** link from the **NEWSLETTER SUBSCRIPTIONS** admin page. This will display a page similar to the following screenshot:

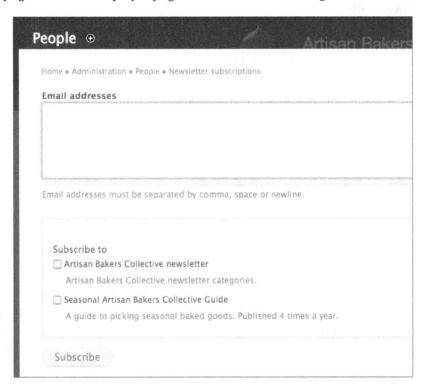

2. Simply copy and paste the list of e-mail addresses from your current management system and then click on the **Subscribe** button. Drupal will display a list of addresses that were added.

3. If you want to export your current Simplenews subscriber list, you can click on the **Export** link from the **NEWSLETTER SUBSCRIPTIONS** screen. Here you can specify the status of the user, whether they are subscribed and what specific newsletters you want to include. Click on the **Export** button. After clicking on the **Export** button, you'll see your **Export results**. You can simply copy the list from here, and paste it into a CSV file.

Adding a calendar

A calendar is a fantastic way of keeping customers coming back to your site and business at regular intervals, so that they can take advantage of specials, sales, and other time-limited events.

We will create a basic visual event calendar, which displays information about musical concerts, special events, and more, for the Artisan Bakers Collective bakery. The calendar will show a month grid view with events posted as clickable event title links. The event titles will click to a full node in Drupal.

Tweaking our date and time settings

In this section, we'll configure our Date and Time zone settings on our Drupal site.

Goal

Create an event that will be displayed on the calendar.

Additional modules needed

Date (`http://drupal.org/project/date`). The current version of the Date module is: 7.x-2.0-alpha4.

Steps

In this section, we will install and configure the Drupal Date module:

1. Before we add events to our site, we need to be sure that we have the Date module installed. The Date module will handle all specific date and time settings on our Drupal site. Install the Date module like you install all contribute modules. Then enable the suite of Date modules on your **Modules** administration screen and save your configuration:

	ENABLED	NAME	VERSION	DESCRIPTION
▼ DATE/TIME				
	✓	Date	7.x-2.0-alpha3	Defines date/time fields and widgets. Requires: Date API (enabled) Required by: Date Tools (enabled)
	✓	Date API	7.x-2.0-alpha3	A Date API that can be used by other modules. Required by: Date (enabled), Date Popup (enabled), Date Repeat API (enabled), Date Tools (enabled), Date Views (enabled)
	✓	Date Popup	7.x-2.0-alpha3	Enables jquery popup calendars and time entry widgets for selecting dates and times. Requires: Date API (enabled)
	✓	Date Repeat API	7.x-2.0-alpha3	A Date Repeat API to calculate repeating dates and times from iCal rules. Requires: Date API (enabled)
	✓	Date Tools	7.x-2.0-alpha3	Tools to import and auto-create dates and calendars. Requires: Date (enabled), Date API (enabled)
	✓	Date Views	7.x-2.0-alpha3	Views integration for date fields and date functionality. Requires: Date API (enabled), Views (enabled), Chaos tools (enabled)

2. To modify the **Date and time** settings, select **Configuration**, then **Date and time**. Drupal will display a page similar to the following screenshot, where you can choose the default format for your date and time displays:

3. Choose the format that you want to use on the site and then click on the **Save configuration** button.

4. You'll also want to set the default time zone for the site. This is done by selecting **Configuration** and then **Regional settings**. Here you can specify the **Default country**, **First day of the week**, and **Default time zone** to use for your site. We'll leave this set to the **America/New York** timezone as the bakery is located on the east coast in the eastern time zone:

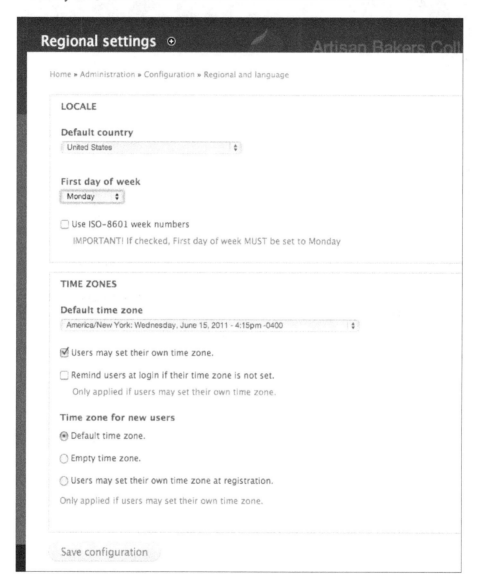

5. Click on the **Save configuration** button to save your changes.

Adding an event content type and custom date/time field

In this section, we'll add an Event content type to our Drupal site to post event nodes. We can then leverage this when we display our event nodes in a Calendar view.

Goal

Build events using Drupal's core content types and the Date module.

Steps

Depending on your site, it may be more convenient to use the core Drupal content types and the Date field to build events. This strategy also gives you additional control over what information is included in the event and in the display. In order to add an event content type and custom date/time field, follow the ensuing steps:

1. Go to **Structure** | **Content types** from the toolbar menu.

2. Click on the **Add content type** link to begin creating your new event type. We will call this type Event. Add a **Description** and then configure specific settings for your content type. For now we'll leave most of the default type settings configured:

Content types ⊕   Artisan Bakers Collective

Home » Administration » Structure » Content types

Individual content types can have different fields, behaviors, and permissions assigned to them.

Name *

Event   Machine name: event [Edit]

The human-readable name of this content type. This text will be displayed as part of the list on the *Add new content p unique.

Description

This content type is used to post events to the site.

Describe this content type. The text will be displayed on the *Add new content* page.

Submission form settings Title of Event	**Title field label** * Title of Event
Publishing options Published , Promoted to front page	**Preview before submitting** ⦿ Disabled
Display settings Display author and date information.	○ Optional
Addthis settings	○ Required
Comment settings Open, Threading , 50 comments per page	**Explanation or submission guidelines**
Menu settings	

This text will be displayed at the top of the page when creating or edit

Save content type   Save and add fields

3. After you are satisfied with the information for the new content type, click on the **Save content type** button to create the new event type.

4. We now need to add a field to store the date and time of the event. Click on the **manage fields** link to begin the process.

5. We will call the field `Event Date` add a machine-readable field name of `event_date` and make the type a **Date** field so that we can enter both the day on which the event occurs and the time of day at which it starts. For widget type, let's make this field a **Text Field with Date Pop-up calendar**:

6. Click on the **Save** button to save the new field. This will launch a screen where you can modify various settings related to how the `Date` field is displayed. Here you can specify a **To date**, the date and time **Granularity**, and the **Time zone handling**. Let's leave these set to their defaults for now.

7. Click on the **Save field settings** button. Your screen should look similar to the following screenshot:

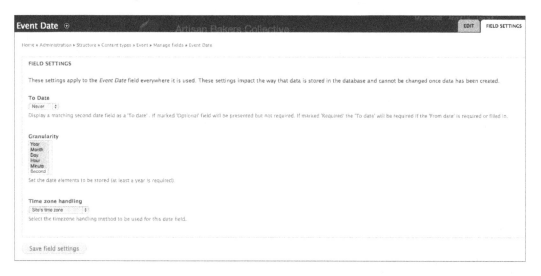

8. On the next screen, you can configure the specific **EVENT DATE FIELD SETTINGS**. Specify the **Default Display** format for your date, a **Default value** if any, the **Input format, Years back and forward**, and **Time increment**. You should have a form that looks similar to the following screenshot:

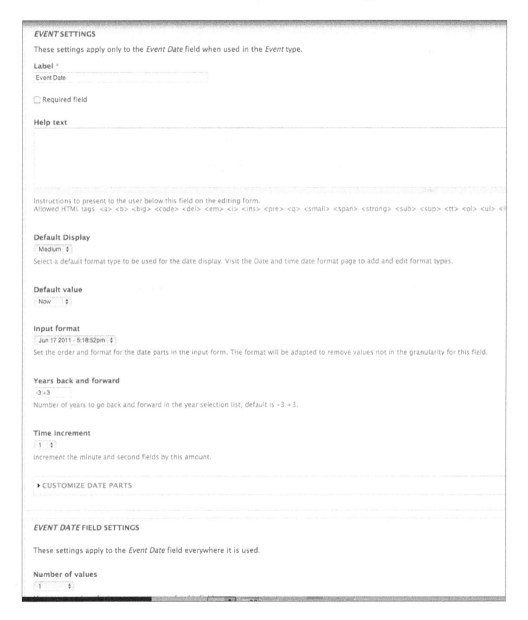

9. Save your field settings. We're now ready to post events to our site.

Adding events to the site

In this section, we'll add events to our site using our new Event content type.

Goal

With our new content type and custom date field, we'll add some events to our site.

Steps

Now that we have our new Event content type and our custom date field, we can start posting events to the website. To do this, follow the ensuing steps:

1. Go to your Add content screen (`node/add`) and then click on the Event link (`node/add/event`) to add an event to the site.
2. Select the Event content type and you'll load the Create Event form.
3. Give the event a **Title**, description in the **Body** field, and an Event Date using the `Event Date` field that we added as a custom field. You'll notice that when you click in the `Event Date` field, the field will pop out a calendar widget that allows you to click on a date and select it:

4. Once you select a date, you can click on the `Time` field and specify a time for the event.
5. Click on the **Save** button to save your event node.

6. When you view your node, you'll see the `Event Date` field's data output on your new Event node:

7. Go ahead and post some additional events. Post events for different dates and times.

8. Now we're ready to display our events in a Calendar view.

Displaying events on a calendar

In this section we'll add a calendar to our site.

Goal

Display a calendar that will present our events in a nicely designed visual calendar layout. The overall goal here is to have a calendar presented in a visual monthly grid layout.

Additional modules needed

- Calendar (`http://drupal.org/project/calendar`)
- Views (`http://drupal.org/project/views`)
- Date API (`http://drupal.org/project/date`)

The Calendar module will allow us to create a visual monthly, weekly, and yearly grid layout-based calendar. The Date API module will allow us to integrate dated and timed events with our calendar. The Views module will help to build the actual visual grid layout of our calendar.

Steps

Now that we can create events, we need to display them on the site. We will begin by creating a page where visitors can browse all of the upcoming events using a convenient calendar. To display events on a calender, follow the ensuing steps:

1. Begin by installing and activating the Views and Calendar modules if you have not done so already.

2. Once you've installed the Calendar module, go ahead and enable the **Calendar**, **Calendar iCal**, and **Calendar Multiday** modules as shown in the following screenshot:

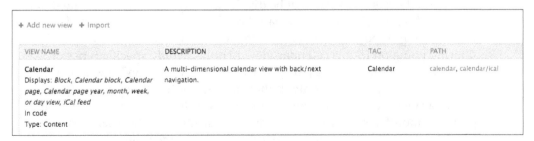

3. Save your module configuration. You have now installed and enabled the Calendar and Views modules.

4. Calendar module installs a default view into the Views module interface that you can use. To see this go to **Structure | Views**. You'll see the Calendar view listed at the top of your core Views listing:

VIEW NAME	DESCRIPTION	TAG	PATH
Calendar Displays: *Block, Calendar block, Calendar page, Calendar page year, month, week, or day view, iCal feed* In code Type: Content	A multi-dimensional calendar view with back/next navigation.	Calendar	calendar, calendar/ical

5. You can view the current core Calendar by clicking on the hyperlinked calendar URL in the path column of your default view. You can also just browse to your calendar URL path. Doing so you'll see a visual calendar with your events and other dated nodes displayed as shown in the following screenshot:

6. This default Calendar view will be displaying any content on the site that is associated with a Date and time based on the custom field we added to the Event content type, or based on a node's author date. There is no specific filtering going on to this calendar view to only display specific types of content. But as this is a Drupal view we can easily edit the View to make tweaks to its display and content filtering. Also notice that your default Calendar view contains a pager that allows you to navigate to the next and previous months in the calendar. You can also click on the **Year**, **Month**, **Week**, or **Day** link to change the display layout of the calendar. If you click on the actual event on a specific day it will launch the event's page.

If you do not want to tweak your default core Calendar view, you can clone it so you can easily make any edits or changes to a cloned copy of the calendar. The easiest way to build new views using the calendar is to clone the default Calendar view and customize it to meet your needs.

7. To clone the View, select the **clone** link from the **OPERATIONS** drop down links labeled — **edit**, **disable**, **clone**, and **export**:

8. Click on the **clone** link to make a copy of the calendar. Drupal will allow you to change the name of the view. Change the name to Event Calendar and then click on the **Continue** button to edit the view:

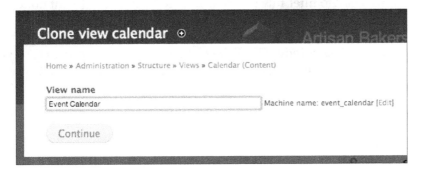

The default settings for the view are shown in the following screenshot. We will edit several settings for our purposes:

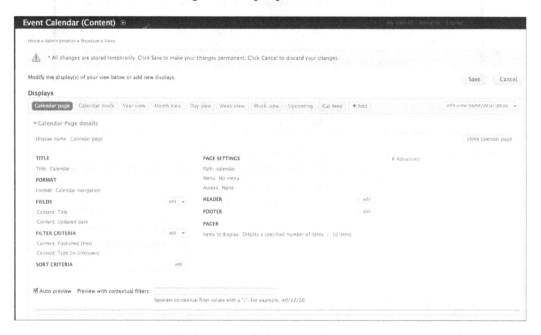

9. First, we want to filter this calendar to only include our Event nodes. To make this change we need to click on the **Content: Type (in Unknown)** hyperlink that sits in the **Filter Criteria** section. Click on this link. This will open up a modal window that allows you to select the content type you want to filter to. Leave the **Operator** set to **Is one of** and then check the **Event** type:

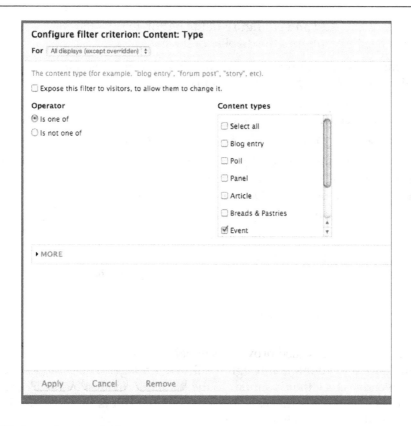

10. Click on the **Apply** button.

11. When the new tweak is active you should see the preview Calendar view update in real time and now it should only be showing you the Event content type nodes.

12. The next change we need to make is to modify the fields by selecting **Content: Updated date**. We want to add our custom date field and not use the default Updated date field. Click on the **Content: Updated date** link.

13. Click on the **Remove** button to remove this field from the view.

14. Click on the **Add** next to the **Fields** label to add a new field.

15. Enable the **Content: Event Date** checkbox for the new field to be added, as shown in the following screenshot:

16. Click on the **Add and configure fields** button to save the changes. You will now need to configure the display of the field.

    In most cases, including this one, the defaults are acceptable. So we will just click on the **Apply** button to continue.

17. The final change that we need to make to the view is in the **Contextual Filters** section. First expand the **Advanced** section of your View and then click on the **Date:Date (node) (Content: Updated date)** link in the **Arguments** section.

18. Drupal will display a list of parameters that you can use to customize the arguments. We will need to change this to use our Content Event time fields, and then click on the **Update** button to save the changes.

19. Now that all of the required changes have been made, click on the **Save** button to finish building the view.

20. We can now return to the list of all views by clicking on the **List** link, and disable the default calendar view by selecting the **Disable** link for the default Calendar view.

21. Now that our view has been completely set up, we can use it to browse our events.

22. The calendar view also provides several block displays that can be activated and added to your site through the **Block Manager**. These blocks include a Calendar block that is similar to the display provided by the Event block, and a Legend block that can be used to allow visitors to understand the information in the calendar more easily.

Summary

Congratulations! You have now added newsletters and events to your sites. These will provide valuable ways of communicating with your customers to ensure that they keep coming back to your website, and more importantly, to your business.

In the next chapter, we will leverage sites such as YouTube, Flickr, and Google to provide advanced functionality to Baker James Artisan Bakers Collective website.

7
Sharing and Consuming with YouTube, Flickr, Google Maps, and Twitter

Now that we are comfortable with building content, we will begin to add more content that is developed and maintained on other websites. Some of this content will be contributed by you, while some may be created by other people in your community, or even across the world.

In this chapter we'll integrate content from popular social web sharing sites including YouTube, Flickr, Google Maps, and Twitter with our website. We'll do this by:

- Integrating YouTube videos using a YouTube filter on our Drupal site
- Adding images to our site via our Flickr photo sets
- Integrating the Google Maps API with our website so we can embed maps into our site's content
- Posting content from our Drupal site directly to our Twitter feed

Integrating your site with other web content

You may wonder why you would want to store content on another site that you don't have control over, especially when we have shown that it is so easy to build content with Drupal.

Although, you do give up some control, there are several great reasons to use some of these resources:

- Bandwidth can be expensive. If your site is popular and makes heavy use of large pictures, or videos, you can easily exceed your monthly bandwidth limits. By storing the pictures and video on someone else's server (possibly for free), you avoid overhead charges.

- Their servers are better than yours. The servers that are used to store and serve the pictures and videos are typically best-in-class servers. Because they are used to store data from many different people, the actual cost is spread out, so you don't have to pay the full cost.

- You can leverage the work of other community members to help you build and maintain the content. This is especially important if you have a lot of content that regularly changes or you want to collect content that other people have created. For example, if you want to offer pictures of your town, you can use Flickr to store the pictures, and also link to pictures that other people have taken and posted on Flickr. Please make sure that you have permission to use the images before linking to them, though! This can be as easy as contacting the original photographer via their Flickr account and asking them if you can share their photos via your Drupal website.

Online baking class

In this section, we will add video content from YouTube that demonstrates various baking techniques used at the bakery.

Embedding a YouTube video with a filter

In this section we'll use the Media module to configure a field that will allow us to embed a YouTube video.

Goal

Add videos that are stored on YouTube to an existing page.

Additional modules needed

- Media (`http://drupal.org/project/media`).
- Media: YouTube (`http://drupal.org/project/media_youtube`)
- File Entity: `http://drupal.org/project/file_entity`.

Steps

YouTube (www.youtube.com) is a popular video sharing site where you can view videos that have been created and submitted by people across the globe. YouTube allows you to link to videos stored on their site so that you can share them with your own visitors, without incurring bandwidth charges. In fact, you can even earn revenue from the videos if you have a Google AdSense account.

To insert a YouTube video into a Drupal node, we'll first install and configure the **Media and Media: YouTube** modules so we can easily embed a YouTube video into our site. Let's go ahead and get started:

1. First, we need to install and activate the **Media**, and **Media: YouTube** modules. Install the modules using the same process for installing contributed modules on your site. Make sure to use the development version of the Media module (*7.x-2.x-dev*) as its version currently supports the integration with YouTube. You will also need the **File Entity** module since this is a dependency of the **Media** module.

2. Once installed enable all of the **Media** modules and the **File Entity** module:

▼ MEDIA			
ENABLED	NAME	VERSION	DESCRIPTION
✓	File Entity	7.x-1.x-dev	Extends Drupal file entities to be fieldable and viewable. Requires: Field (enabled), Field SQL storage (enabled), Chaos tools (enabled) Required by: Media (enabled), Media Internet Sources (enabled), Media: YouTu
✓	Media	7.x-2.x-dev	Provides the core Media API Requires: File Entity (enabled), Field (enabled), Field SQL storage (enabled), Ch Required by: Media Internet Sources (enabled), Media: YouTube (enabled)
✓	Media Internet Sources	7.x-2.x-dev	Provides an API for accessing media on various internet services Requires: Media (enabled), File Entity (enabled), Field (enabled), Field SQL stor Required by: Media: YouTube (enabled)
✓	Media: YouTube	7.x-1.0-alpha5	Provides YouTube support to the Media module. Requires: Media Internet Sources (enabled), Media (enabled), File Entity (enabl File (enabled)

3. Now, we need to add the media file field to our content type so we can embed a YouTube video. You can add brand new content type to your site just to handle your video content, or you can simply add a Media file field to an existing content type. Let's add a Media field to one of our existing content types.

4. Manage fields on your existing Article content type and add a new field called `Video`. Let's give the field a machine name of: `field_youtube_video`.

5. Select **File** as the field type.

6. Select **Media file selector** as the widget type.

7. Save your field.

8. On the next screen you can specify your **FIELD SETTINGS**. This includes whether to enable the display field, and whether files are displayed by default. Leave both of these set to their unchecked defaults. You can also specify the upload destination for your video files. We want all of our site visitors to view the videos so leave the default **Public files** radio button selected:

9. Click the **Save field settings** to move to the next screen.

10. In the **FIELD SETTINGS** be sure to allow **Video** as a media type and also check the YouTube URI scheme as an allowed URI scheme. This will allow you to embed YouTube URLs.

11. Save your settings.

12. You can manage your field display settings and hide the label display. Click on the **Manage Display** tab. You want to tweak the display of the **Video** file since Drupal will give it a format of **Generic file** by default. In order for the YouTube videos to display correctly we need to make them display the rendered file as the format and the original view mode as the **View mode** settings.

13. Select **Rendered File** as the format, and then select **Original** as the **View mode**:

14. Now, we also need to tweak the main **Media** module configuration to reference our new custom Video field and assign the correct display mode to it.

15. Go to **Configuration | Media | File Types**.

16. Select the manage fields option next to the Video file type. Now add your existing custom video field.

17. Now click on the Manage File Display tab. This will allow you to select the YouTube Video as your enabled display. Selecting YouTube Video will open up a width and height dimension box where you can specify width and height dimensions for your embedded YouTube videos. You should see a screen that looks like the following:

18. Save your configuration.

Let's go ahead and embed a YouTube video now that we've configured our Media field and content type:

1. First we need to add content so click on your **Add content** link and add an **Article** node. Give the node a title and tag it. Baker James wants to add a new Peter Reinhart How To video that is accessible via YouTube. Peter Reinhart is a famous artisan baker and this will add some dynamic video content to the bakery site for marketing purposes. First, we need to locate the URL of the video on YouTube. The Peter Reinhart video is here: `http://www.youtube.com/watch?v=TtCu9hYGhOU`.

2. On our **Add article** form we can click on the **Select media** button to choose our video.

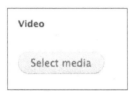

3. Once you click on **Select media** click on the **Web** tab and then paste in the YouTube URL to the video. Click the **Submit** button:

4. Now you should see the video appear in your form. Click the **Save** button. Go to your site's home page, and you should see the video appear in the teaser mode of the article on your home page.

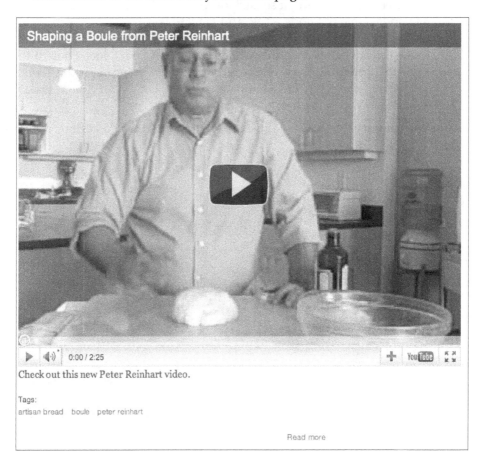

Creating a YouTube playlist and display a random video

In this section we'll tweak our YouTube filter to play an entire list of videos.

Goal

Enhance the YouTube filter to play from a list of videos, and explore other features of the Video Filter module.

Additional modules needed

Video Filter (`http://drupal.org/project.video_filter`)

Steps

Now that you can add a single video to your page, you may want to add more videos that are displayed in random order, automatically start the video when the page loads, or control the size of the video. All of this is possible by using the Video Filter.

1. First, let's install the Video Filter module. Enable the **Video Filter** module:

This is a filter, so we're going to use it in the body of our node and add it directly into our body text box.

2. Before we add the filter code, we need to make sure to configure our text formats to be allowed to use the new video filter format. To do this go to **Configuration | Text Formats**. Then click on the **Configure** link next to the **Full HTML** and/or **Filtered HTML** formats.

3. Check the box next to **Video filter** under your enabled filters.

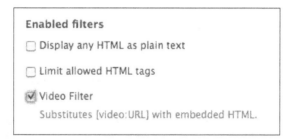

4. Scroll down and you can set the default width and height settings for your video filter; apply an autoplay setting and configure whether to use HTML5, as shown in the following screenshot.

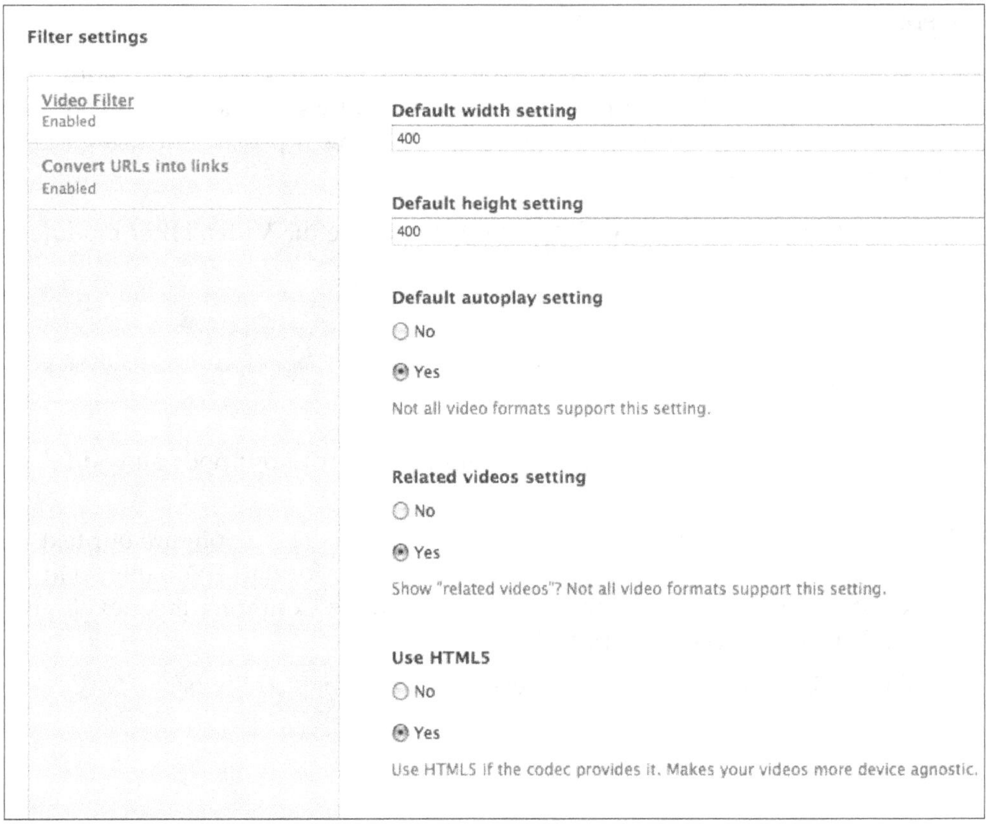

Filter settings

Video Filter
Enabled

Convert URLs into links
Enabled

Default width setting

400

Default height setting

400

Default autoplay setting

○ No

⦿ Yes

Not all video formats support this setting.

Related videos setting

○ No

⦿ Yes

Show "related videos"? Not all video formats support this setting.

Use HTML5

○ No

⦿ Yes

Use HTML5 if the codec provides it. Makes your videos more device agnostic.

5. Save your configuration. Now, let's add a video to our site using the new **Video filter**.

6. To do this create a new **Article**. To add one YouTube video using the Video filter add this code to your body text box in the following format:

`[video:url]`

7. So, we'll add the following to reference one of the Peter Reinhart videos:
`video:http://www.youtube.com/watch?v=1timJlCT3PM`.

8. Choose the correct text format of Full HTML. Then save your node. You should see the video embedded on your site:

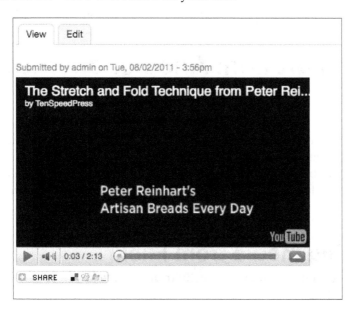

9. To add multiple random videos to a filter, you just need to add multiple videos separated by commas. For example, you could enter the video URLs in the following format:

```
[video:url,url,url]
```

```
video:http://www.youtube.com/watch?v=0Q2aPi9ZEgs, http://
www.youtube.com/watch?v=dTDVKDzVOcg,http://www.youtube.com/
watch?v=eV__oOckAPM
```

Remember here that all three videos in this case will not show up at the same time on the Web page. They will still play as single videos but they will show randomly each time you refresh the web page.

10. If you do not want a video to start automatically, you can set the **Default autoplay** setting to **No** in the video format configuration.

11. To resize your video, you will need to enter the width and height of the video in the default width and height setting of your video format configuration. You can also override this setting on a specific node by adding the width and height dimensions within the format code in the following format:

```
[video:urlwidth:Xheight:Y]
```

```
video:http://www.youtube.com/watch?v=BYhrHdvI6m8 width:240
height:160
```

12. You can also control the alignment and autoplay configuration on a specific node using the same code formatting:

```
[video:urlwidth:Xheight:Yalign:left/right autoplay:1/0]
```

Flickr integration: Another alternative for images and slideshows

This is another alternative for images and slideshows. Flickr is an extremely popular website that allows you to post and share pictures with people around the world. You can either upload your own pictures to Flickr and use it for storage, or embed images that other people have taken into your own site. Of course, you need to check the license for all of the images that you want to embed before using them on your site.

Embedding media from Flickr

In this section we'll embed images directly from our Flickr photo set using the Media:Flickr module.

Goal

Add images to our site from the Flickr photo sharing website.

Additional modules needed

- Media (http://drupal.org/project/media).
- Media Flickr (http://drupal.org/project/media_flickr)

Steps

We have previously used the Media module to display YouTube movies on our site. In this step, we will also use it to display images from Flickr. We'll add a plugin module for the main Media module called **Media: Flickr**. This will allow us to integrate Flickr images in our site.

1. If you have not already installed and activated the Media module, do so now. We also need to install and activate the **Media: Flickr** module, which will allow Flickr integration.

☑	**Media: Flickr**	7.x–1.x–dev	Integrates Flickr.com photos and photosets with Media. Requires: Media (enabled), File entity (enabled), Field (enabled), Fie (enabled)

2. Before we can add content from Flickr, we will need to apply for a Flickr API Key. You can request an API key at `http://www.flickr.com/services/api/keys`. You can sign into Flickr with your Google or Yahoo account. If you do not already have a Yahoo or Google account, you will be prompted to create one.

3. After you sign into your Yahoo and Flickr accounts, you'll be logged into the Flickr API section of the Flickr site. Here you'll see any API keys you already have active on a website or you can apply for an API key by accepting the terms of service.

4. You will need to specify whether the key is for commercial or non-commercial use, enter the name of the app you are building, and a description.

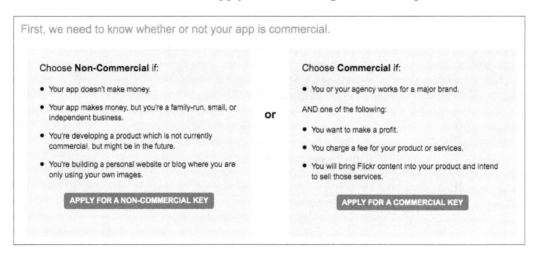

Then, you agree to Flickr's terms of service, and enter your name and e-mail account. When the sign-up is complete, you will receive a long key for use with Flickr. You should store this key in a safe place.

Tell us about your app:

Owner	amblentdrupal
	▢ This app will be associated with your **amblentdrupal** account. You will not be able to change this after you submit your application.
What's the name of your app?	
What are you building?	
(And trust us when we say you can't be detailed enough)	

▢ I acknowledge that Flickr members own all rights to their content, and that it's my responsibility to make sure that my project does not contravene those rights.

▢ I agree to comply with the Flickr API Terms of Use.

SUBMIT or Cancel

5. Once you have your API key, you can enter the Flickr key in your Drupal
    site on the Media Flickr configuration page. To do this go to **Configuration |
    Media | Flickr settings**. Expand the **FLICKR API** fieldset which appears as
    follows, and enter your key:

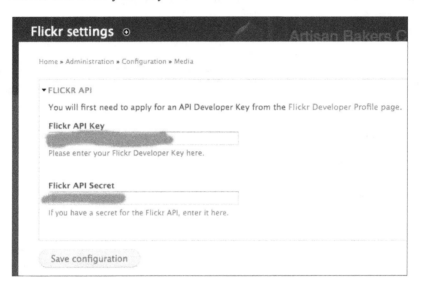

6. Now, we need to add a Media Flickr upload field to our content type. Go to
    Structure | Content types and click on **Manage fields** for the **Article type**.

7. In the **Add new** field section add a **Flickr Image** field with a machine
    name of `flickr_image`. Select the **File** field type and a widget of **Media
    file selector**.

8. On the configuration form allow the Image media type, and allowed URI
    schemes of `flickr://`(**Flickr photos**). Save your new field.

9. Now go to **Manage display** and choose the display options for our new Flickr image. We want to show the label above the image but you could choose to hide it. Also select the format as **Rendered file**.

10. Click **Save** to complete the new field definition.

11. We can now either create a new article, edit one that we created previously, or add an image using our new Flickr field.

    In either case, the field will appear as follows on our Article content type form:

12. Click the **Select Media** button. This will launch a modal window giving you some select options. Click on the **Web** tab in the modal window. This will launch a screen asking you to embed an URL path to an image via your Flickr set.

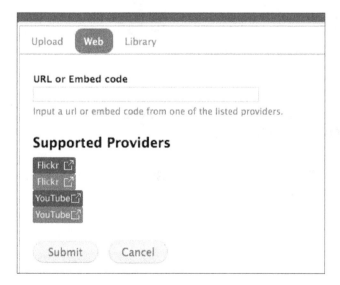

13. I've uploaded a bunch of bread photos to my Flickr account. So I'm going to reference an URL path to one of my bread images in the URL or Embed code field.

14. Add the URL to your image on Flickr and then click the Submit button.

Once you click Submit you should see the image appear in a thumbnail version on your form:

Save your Article and you should see a larger version of your Flickr-based image on your page.

Using the Flickr module to insert photos using a filter

In this section we're going to insert Flickr photos and photosets using another Drupal module called Flickr. This module not only lets you insert individual photos but entire Flickr photosets.

Goal

Add photos from your Flickr photosets to an existing block or piece of content in Drupal using a filter format.

Additional modules needed

Flickr module (http://drupal.org/project/flickr)

Steps

Although the **Media:Flickr** is very convenient for adding pictures as a field, there may be times when you want to display an image within a block of text; or when you want to display an entire photoset or collection of Flickr images on your Drupal site. To do this, we will use the **Flickr** module.

1. Begin by installing and activating the Flickr module. At the time of this book's writing the current version of the Flickr module is in development. The version we'll use is *.7.x-1.x-dev*.

2. After installing the module go to your module's administration page and enable the entire suite of Flickr modules as shown in this screen:

	ENABLED	NAME	VERSION	DESCRIPTION
▼ FLICKR				
	☑	Flickr	7.x-1.x-dev	Flickr and Drupal integration. Required by: Flickr Block (disabled), Flickr Filter (disabled), Flickr Sets (disabled), Flickr Tags (disabled), Flickrfield (disabled)
	☑	Flickr Block	7.x-1.x-dev	Adds capability to display Flickr photos and sets into blocks. Requires: Flickr (disabled)
	☑	Flickr Filter	7.x-1.x-dev	Adds a filter to insert Flickr photos and sets into content. Requires: Flickr (disabled)
	☑	Flickr Sets	7.x-1.x-dev	Adds photoset capability to the Flickr module. Requires: Flickr (disabled)
	☑	Flickr Tags	7.x-1.x-dev	Adds tags capability to Flickr module. Requires: Flickr (disabled)

3. This includes the following modules:

    ◦ **Flickr**
    ◦ **Flickr Block**
    ◦ **Flickr Filter**
    ◦ **Flickr Sets**
    ◦ **Flickr Tags**

Save your module's page configuration. Now we can begin configuring the Flickr module. The main configuration screens are located at **Configuration | Flickr** in the Media table:

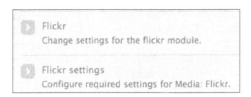

4. Previously, we configured the Flickr settings for the **Media: Flickr** module. Now, we'll configure the settings for the **Flickr** module. Let's first click on the Flickr link to set up our initial Flickr module configuration.

5. Like we did in the preceding section with the **Media:Flickr** module, we need to enter our Flickr API key on the Flickr configuration screen. You can enter the same API key that you signed up for in the preceding section since we're going to be using this key on the same website and with the same Flickr account. Go ahead and type your **API Key, API Shared Secret** into the fields. You can also enter your **Flickr User Id** here though it's not a required field. This field is more important if you have multiple users on your site using their own Flickr accounts to load photos and you want to make one account the default site account.

6. You can also select an **Update interval** on this screen. This is how often the Drupal site will check your Flickr account for new photo content. If you do not update your site often with new photos you may want to leave this set to a higher number. Let's leave it set to the default of **1 hour**.

7. Finally you can set the number of photos you want to show in each photoset when it's fed to your site from Flickr. Let's leave this set to the default of **30**.

Home » Administration » Configuration » Media

API Key *

API Key from Flickr

API Shared Secret *

API key's secret from Flickr.

Default Flickr User Id

An, optional, default Flickr username or user id. This will be used when no user is specified.Disabled

Update interval

| 1 hour | ⬍ |

The refresh interval indicating how often you want to check cached Flickr API calls are up to date.

Number of photos per photoset

| 30 | ⬍ |

The number indicates how many photos of a photoset display in your nodes. After saving the config

Save configuration

8. After you have entered this information, click on **Save configuration**.

9. We can now build an input format that allows us to embed Flickr images into content, by clicking on **Configuration** and then **Text** formats, from the **Toolbar** menu.

10. Next, click **Add Text** format to begin building the new format.

11. We will call the **Input format** Flickr, and enable only the **Flickr linker** filter by selecting its checkbox:

☑ Flickr linker

Allows you to insert Flickr images: [flickr-photo:id=230452326,size=s] or [flickr-photoset:id=72157594262419167,size=m]

12. Click **Save configuration** to finish building the input format.

13. We can now use the new input format in a new page or in an existing page. Let's add a new article for our Flickr images using the article content type. Let's call this article Featured Breads for November.

14. We will modify the description to include a Flickr image first. To do this we'll use the following code to specify the image we want to add. You will need to locate the Flickr ID of the photo from your photoset and swap it into this line of code:

```
[flickr-photo:id=6329116106,size=m]
```

15. Change the **Text format** to **Flickr**, as shown in the following screenshot:

16. You can also specify a size to use in the formatter line of code as per the following sizes:

   ° s - small square 75x75

   ° t - thumbnail, 100 on longest side

   ° m - small, 240 on longest side

   ° - - medium, 500 on longest side

- ° b - large, 1024 on longest side
- ° o - original image

17. I've set my individual image to show at `medium (m) size:`. On saving, the resulting page appears as follows:

18. You can get the photoset id from the Flickr URL of your photoset main page. For example I have the following photoset which is visible via this URL: `http://www.flickr.com/photos/59625319@N02/sets/72157627964821413/with/6329116106/`.

    So my photoset ID that I'll add to my Drupal Flickr filter is this: `72157627964821413`.

On Flickr, my set looks like the following:

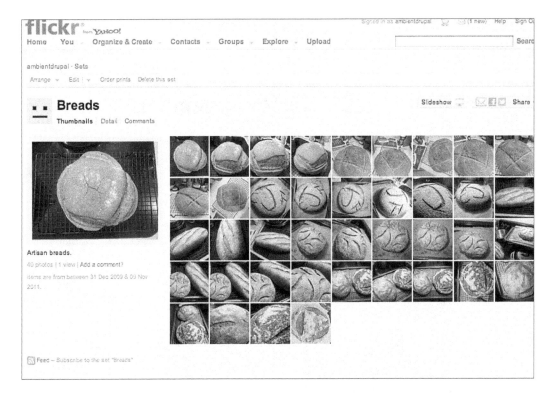

Adding the photoset code to my article page and then saving gives me this on my Drupal site. You should see all of the images from your photoset stacked on top of each other on your Drupal page:

Featured Breads for November

View | Edit

Submitted by admin on Thu, 11/17/2011 - 10:14pm

Now, if you remove the blocks from the page that you've inserted the photoset in you can get a nicer arrangement and design of your images. You can also try using a different size. For example if I remove the blocks from both of the sidebar regions on my Flickr photo gallery page I can fit more images per row of my display. This allows me to set up a photo gallery display of my photoset images on my site:

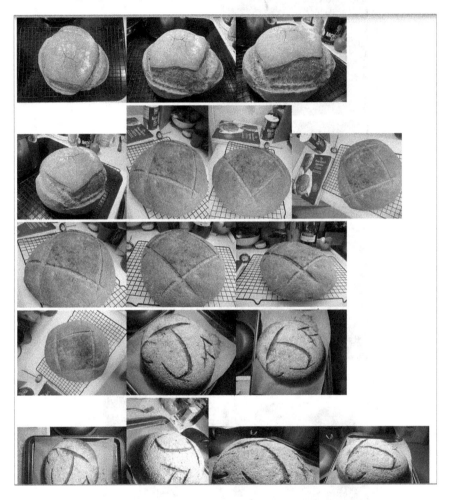

To change the size of the photos in the display all we have to do is change our filter code to reflect the new size. Let's change our display to thumbnail size. Our filter code will now look like the following:

```
[flickr-photoset:id=72157627964821413,size=t].
```

Now, if we save our page and refresh it our images will appear in thumbnail size and look pretty close to what our photoset looks like on Flickr:

Flickr module blocks

The Flickr module adds a set of blocks to our Drupal blocks administration page that we can try out on our site. The following blocks are added by the module and I've added a brief description of each block and what it does. For each of these blocks you can specify the number of photos to feed into the block and the size of the photos in square, thumbnail, small and medium dimensions. Here are the block descriptions:

- **Flickr group photos**—This block will show a specified number of photos from a Flickr Group pool based on the Group's ID.

- **Flickr random photo from photoset**—This block allows you to show a specified number of random photos from one of your photosets based on the photoset ID.

- **Flickr random photos**—This block allows you to show a specified number of random photos from a Flickr User ID.

- **Flickr recent photos**—This block allows you to show a specified number of recently uploaded photos from a Flickr User ID.

- **Flickr recent photosets**—This block allows you to show a specified number of recent photosets from a Flickr User ID.

- Flickr user page photosets, random photos, and recent photos —These blocks allow you to show a specified number of photosets, random photos, and recent photos from a user's Flickr account on their user page if you are allowing your site's users to add Flickr images.

  On your blocks administration page you will see this in your disabled block section:

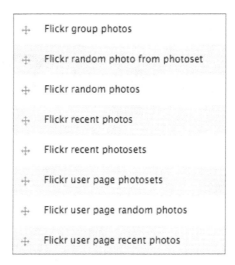

Let's go ahead and enable a couple of these blocks to show what they do. First let's enable the Flickr group photos block. Before we enable it click on the **Configure** link next to the block on the blocks administration page so we can set specific settings for our Flickr group photos block.

When we click **Configure** we can do the following:

1. Give the block a title—let's title it `Sourdough Fan Club`

2. Now, let's add a Group ID to the **Show photos from this Group ID**. Here, we can add a group ID from the Flickr Website as long as the photos are shared publicly on Flickr. The group ID we'll use here for this example is from the Sourdough Companion group on Flickr. The group URL is: `http://www.flickr.com/groups/sourdoughbread/`.

3. To get the **Group ID** for this public group we can use a website called **idGettr** which allows you to paste the URL of a Flickr group and then the site will return the Group ID. This is the site's home page with the Sourdough Companion URL, as shown in the following screenshot:

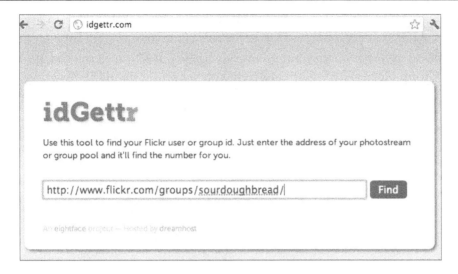

4. Click the Find button. The page will refresh and show you the Group id. In this case the id that gets returned is: `id: 906935@N25`

5. Now paste that Group ID into the block's **Show photos from this Group ID** field.

6. Specify the number of photos you want to show from the group. Let's show 10 photos.

7. Now set the size of the photos. We'll use the **75x75 pixel square** size. You should now see this on your block administration form:

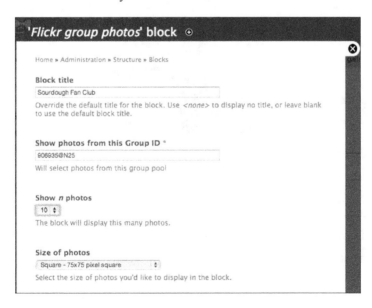

8. Click the **Save Block** button. Now, we need to enable our block. Let's enable the Flickr group photos block in the sidebar second region. Save your blocks.

9. Now refresh your site and go to your home page. You should see the Flickr Group block showing in your right sidebar and it should be showing 10 photos from the group. If you click on any of the photos they will link to the corresponding Flickr page with the full size photo.

10. Now let's go ahead and implement one more of the Flickr module blocks.

11. Configure the **Flickr random photos** block.

12. Give it a block title of **Our Sourdough Breads**.

13. Now add your Flickr user ID to the user ID field

14. Use the **idGettr** site to locate your Flickr user ID by adding the URL of your Flickr photostream. My photostream URL is: `http://www.flickr.com/photos/59625319@N02/`.

15. You'll notice the user ID is also shown in the photostream URL. My ID is: `59625319@N02`

16. Specify how many random photos you want to show. I'll show the default of **4** photos.

17. I'll select thumbnail as the size of the photos.

18. Save your block

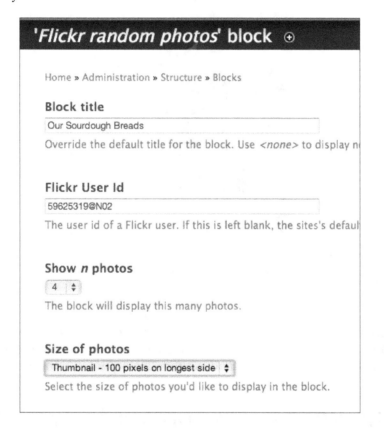

19. Go ahead and enable this block in your right region. Now take a look at your home page and the block. It should be feeding in four random photos from your photostream. Additionally if you refresh your home page the block's four images should change and be 4 new random images from your Flickr account.

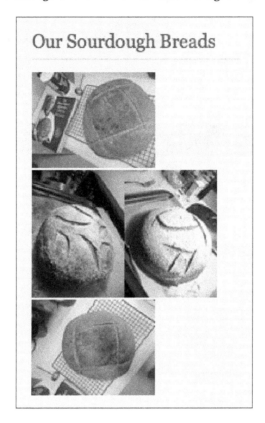

You've successfully added photos to your site via your Flickr account using the Flickr module. We added a page of photos and also enabled a couple of the Flickr module blocks to show both group and random Flickr photos on our site.

Posting your site's content to Twitter

After you have built high quality content for your website, you need to make sure that everyone knows about it. One of the best ways to do this is by adding an announcement about your site's content to the popular micro-blogging site Twitter

Twitter when you post

In this section we'll post a notification to Twitter when we add a node to our Drupal site.

Goal

Provide Twitter notifications each time content is posted or updated on our site to ensure that customers always stay up-to-date.

Additional modules needed

- Twitter (`http://drupal.org/project/twitter`)
- OAuth Common (`http://drupal.org/project/oauth`)

Steps

Twitter is a popular micro-blogging Web application that allows users to post very brief messages at frequent intervals, so that other people can remain updated on what they are doing. You can subscribe to a person to follow everything they do, or search for specific posts.

In order for the Twitter module integration with the Twitter site to work, you're going to first need to move your localhost website to a production site environment on a hosted server solution. In this example I'll be using the same Artisan Bakers Collective site demo that we've been working on, but hosting it here from my `variantcube.com` web hosting. This way the site will be able to communicate with the Twitter application API via OAuth. So if you haven't moved your site and database to a production server and you want to try out these examples you should do that migration first.

Let's first install and enable the module as we have all of our other contributed modules. The current stable version of the Twitter module is: *.7.x-3.0-beta3*.

You will also need to install and enable the required OAuth module. This is a dependency. The latest version of OAuth is *7.x-3.0-alpha2.*.

1. Enable the following modules once you have installed them:
   - OAuth
   - OAuth Provided UI
   - Twitter
   - Twitter Post
   - Twitter Sign in

2. The Twitter settings can be accessed by clicking on the **Twitter** link in the **WEB SERVICES** table on your **Configuration** screen:

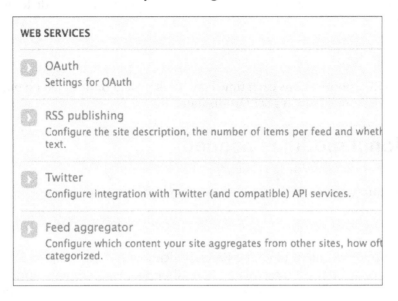

3. The Twitter configuration page will first ask you to enter your OAuth settings. This is the OAuth API access for integration with the Twitter module. If you do not have an OAuth account yet you can register your application here: `https://dev.twitter.com/apps/new`.

4. You'll be asked to log in with your Twitter account into the Twitter developer's site, so if you do not have a Twitter account you can sign up for one now if you want to be able to test out this module.

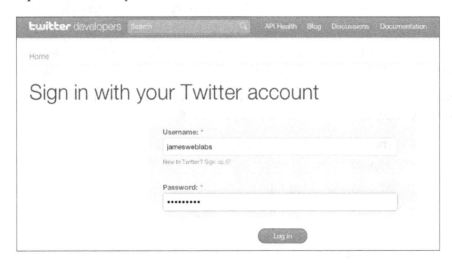

5. When you log in you'll be prompted to create an application. Give your application a name, description, website URL, and also a callback URL. The callback URL will be given to you by Drupal on the Twitter module settings page. My callback URL in this example is: `http://variantcube.com/artisanbakers/twitter/oauth/`. Make sure the callback URL uses a forward slash just after the `/oauth/`. That slash is required. Also, make sure you grant your application read and write access. You should see a screen that looks like the following:

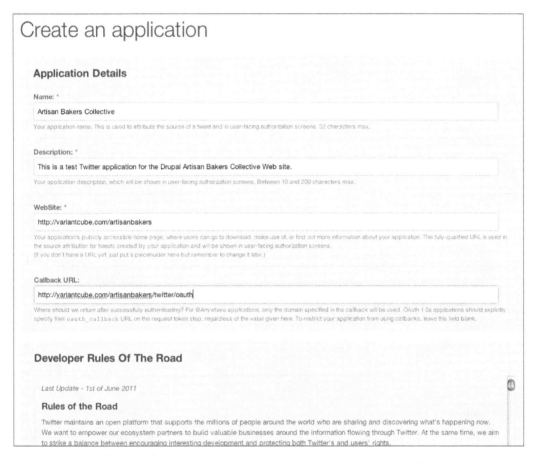

6. Agree to the developer rules of the road and then enter the CAPTCHA and click on the **Create your Twitter application** button.

7. Upon creating your application you should see the next screen that loads will contain all of your application's **OAuth settings** including the **Consumer key** and **Consumer secret** that you can copy and paste into the corresponding fields on the Twitter configuration form in your Drupal site.

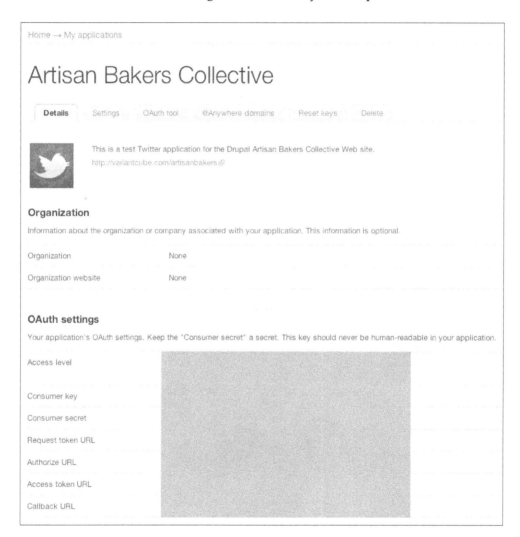

Go ahead and do this.

8. Save your Twitter module configuration. Now we're ready to test posting our node content over to our Twitter account profile page.

9. You can tell the Twitter module which content types you want to be able to post to Twitter by clicking on the **POST** tab on your **Twitter** module configuration page. I'll check the boxes next to **Article**, **Basic page** and **Blog entry**.

10. We'll leave the **Default format string** to the default string of: `New post: !title !tinyurl`. This is the actual string and link that will be posted to your Twitter account. The `!title` is a token placeholder for the page title on your Drupal site and the `!tinyurl` will replace the full Drupal node path with a tinyurl generated link:

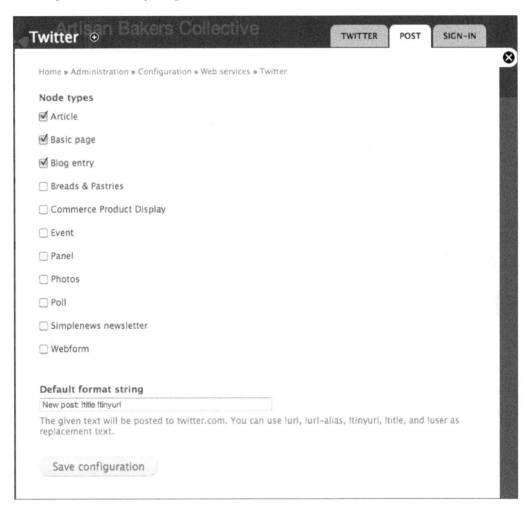

11. Save your module configuration.

Posting to Twitter

1. Since posting to Twitter is authentication based there's a final set of steps we need to complete before posting our site content over to our Twitter account.

   We need to authorize the account we're logged in as (currently the admin account) to post to our Twitter account. To do this:

2. Go to your Drupal account profile and edit it.

3. Click on the **Twitter accounts** tab

4. Click the **Add account** button

5. Now, you'll be asked to sign into your Twitter account to authorize that the Drupal site account can communicate with your Twitter account. Go ahead and do this:

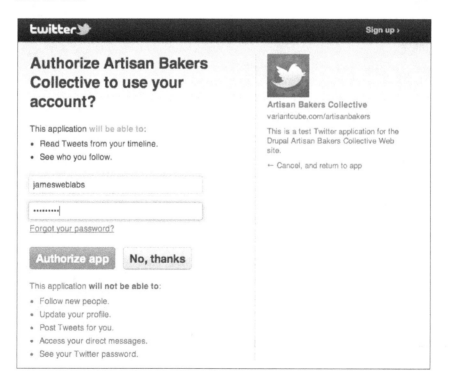

6. Click the **Authorize app** button. Once you do this you'll be redirected to your Drupal account's Twitter tab again but this time you'll see your Twitter account show up inside your Drupal account profile page:

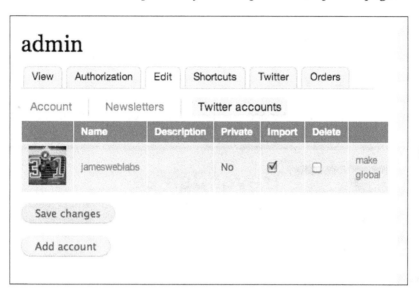

7. Now you have synched your Drupal admin account to your Twitter account and you're ready to post to it.

8. Let's go ahead and post an article on our site and test posting it over to our Twitter account. First, create the Article node by adding an article. I'm going to announce a test post for the purpose of this example. My node title will be "Test Twitter post". On the Article node form notice that you will now have a fieldset titled **POST TO TWITTER.COM** with a checkbox allowing you to **Announce this post on Twitter**. You'll see the field value formatter that you entered in your Twitter module post settings:

9. Check the box and then save the node. After you click **Save** you should see a message telling you that the post was successfully posted over to your Twitter account:

- Successfully posted to Twitter
- Article *Test Post to Twitter* has been updated.

If you view your Twitter account home page you should see the post:

10. Clicking on the tinyurl in the post on Twitter will direct you back to the node on your Drupal site.

Recall that we authorized our admin account to sync with our Twitter account by clicking on the **Twitter** tab on our user account edit form and adding our Twitter account authorization access. Now that you've added the authorization you can also view a table listing all your Twitter posts right in your Drupal account.

To do this open up your main admin account page and click on the Twitter tab. You should see something similar to the following screenshot:

Just be aware that the tweets will update in your tweet table based on how often you run cron on your site. So once you run cron this will flush out any old tweets that you have removed and also consume and display any new tweets that you have posted.

Summary

In this chapter, we have explored a number of ways to integrate your website with sites created by other developers and other companies around the world, either by including information from their sites into your site or by publishing information from your site to them.

Including content from other websites is an extremely powerful way of building new content for your website without having to dedicate hundreds and thousands of hours and precious resources on the development of functionalities that have already been created by other developers. This allows you to focus on your core business and on the development of functionalities that are critical to the success of your site.

In the next chapter, we will discuss various ways of providing free content to your visitors, as well as ways of transferring information to them via the download of menus, pictures, brochures, or other content.

8
Freebies and Downloads

In this chapter, we will explore various ways of adding downloads to your website to provide free content, or to deliver paid content to users. We will also discuss the automatic conversion of pages to PDF files, which your users can download to read or print.

Free content is a fantastic way of building customer loyalty. Depending on the content that you provide, you can also keep your brand in front of people. For example, a simple tastefully-done screen saver or desktop background can be used to always keep your logo on your customers' desktops. Of course, you need to make sure that the free content is of the highest possible quality to ensure that the customers will actually use the content.

Many visitors want to print content or save it to their computers for later use when they are not online or are not working on their computers. We will build PDF files automatically, to give your visitors this convenience

If you allow visitors to download content from your site, you need to be careful that your site security is solid, so that an unscrupulous user cannot download content that you don't want them to have access to. We will discuss how to protect your content in this chapter.

To summarize, in this chapter we will:

- Add file downloads to our site
- Allow the conversion of our Drupal pages to PDF

Adding downloads and PDFs to the website

In this section, we will discuss how to add downloads and PDFs to the website.

Controlling how files are downloaded

In this section we'll configure our Drupal file system.

Goal

Ensure that Drupal has full control over any files that are uploaded, so that we can specify who can download the files.

Additional modules needed

None

Steps

Drupal allows you to set downloads to either **Public** or **Private**. The public setting does not have any additional download security. The private setting allows Drupal to secure and manage the downloaded files.

You can control this functionality using the **File system** settings, which are available by selecting **Configuration** and then **File system**, from the **Toolbar** menu, as shown in the following screenshot:

On the **File system** configuration form we can specify the path to both the public and private file systems for our site. Drupal 7 allows us to serve both public and private file downloads which is an improvement over Drupal 6. Here, we can leave the default download method set to public, but then we can add specific private file upload fields to our content types to secure private files. So on this configuration screen let's specify a path to store our private files in:

1. We'll first create a folder at the root level of our MAMP install titled /private and make sure Drupal has write access to this folder. The /private folder will not be accessible directly via the web browser but will be writable by the Drupal website. This will provide an additional layer of authentication and security.

2. Create a /private folder in my /Applications/MAMP/ folder and then make sure it's read and writable by you, and writable by the admin and all the user accounts on your computer.

3. Leave the **Default download method** set to **Public files served by the webserver**. Notice that now that we have a /private path defined an additional private default download method will appear. You could select this if you wanted to make the default download method a secure method on your website. For now we'll leave ours set to Public. Your form should look like the following:

4. Once you have configured your file system settings click on the
Save configuration button.

You can also control where the public files are stored on the website, and also specify
a temporary location to be used while files are being transferred. In most cases, the
defaults are acceptable, in our case we want the public files to be stored in /sites/
default/files which will be our main public file folder. However, you may need
to customize the directories depending on how your server and site are configured.
If you are using the private download method, the **File system** path should not
be accessible via a web browser. To ensure that a directory is not available via a
web browser, you should choose a folder that is not located within the Drupal
installation. It should also not be located within your root web folder. On most
systems, the root web folder is named htdocs. If you are unsure what your root
web folder is, ask your webhost. Some hosting companies do not allow you to create
folders outside the root web folder. If this is the case, you can contact your host to see
if they can make an exception, or you will have to use the public download method.

Allowing files to be uploaded to the website

Goal

Allow authorized users to upload a file to the website.

Additional modules needed

None

Steps

In order to allow a user to download a file, you must first upload files to the website.
We will create a downloads page that stores all of the files that have been uploaded.
In Drupal 7 we can add a file upload field to any existing content type, or we can
define a brand new content type to use just for our uploads. This gives us a lot of
flexibility in how we attach files since we can attach files to existing content or create
a brand new content type. For the moment Baker James wants to keep things simple
and leverage his existing content types, so we're going to add a new file field upload
to the existing Basic page content type. In Drupal 6 you had to first enable the core
Upload module but in Drupal 7 all we need to do is add a new field to our content
type. The module is already enabled in core Drupal 7.

1. Begin by going to your **Structure | Content types | Basic page type** and
editing click on the **Manage fields** link.

2. We can now add a brand new field to our **Basic page type** for our file upload. We'll call this field `File upload`. Select the **File** as our field type and **File** as the widget type. You should see the following:

3. Click the **Save** button.

4. On the next **FIELD SETTINGS** screen, check the **Enable Display field** box, and make sure the **Upload destination** is set to **Public files**. The first file field will be used to upload files that we want public anonymous users to access such as the Bakery menu in PDF format. If you were going to be adding a private file here that you only wanted specific users and roles to access you would choose the **Private files** radio button. Here's where Drupal 7 gives you flexibility in whether you want your files to be publicly accessible or secure.

5. Click the **Save field settings** button.

6. On the **BASIC PAGE SETTINGS** form you can add a custom label, make the field required, and add some help text for your form user. You can also specify the types of file extensions you want to allow. Let's add the following file extensions to this field: `txtpdfdocdocx`. This will allow our users to upload PDF files and Word files. You can also add a folder name for the file directory location that the files will be uploaded to. Let's add `publicfiles` here as our directory name. You can specify a maximum upload size. This is important if you have space restrictions on your site and server. This will likely be determined by what the maximum file upload setting is in your PHP configuration. My PHP setting limits the maximum to 32MB so we'll make our max upload size `30 MB`, as shown in the following screenshot:

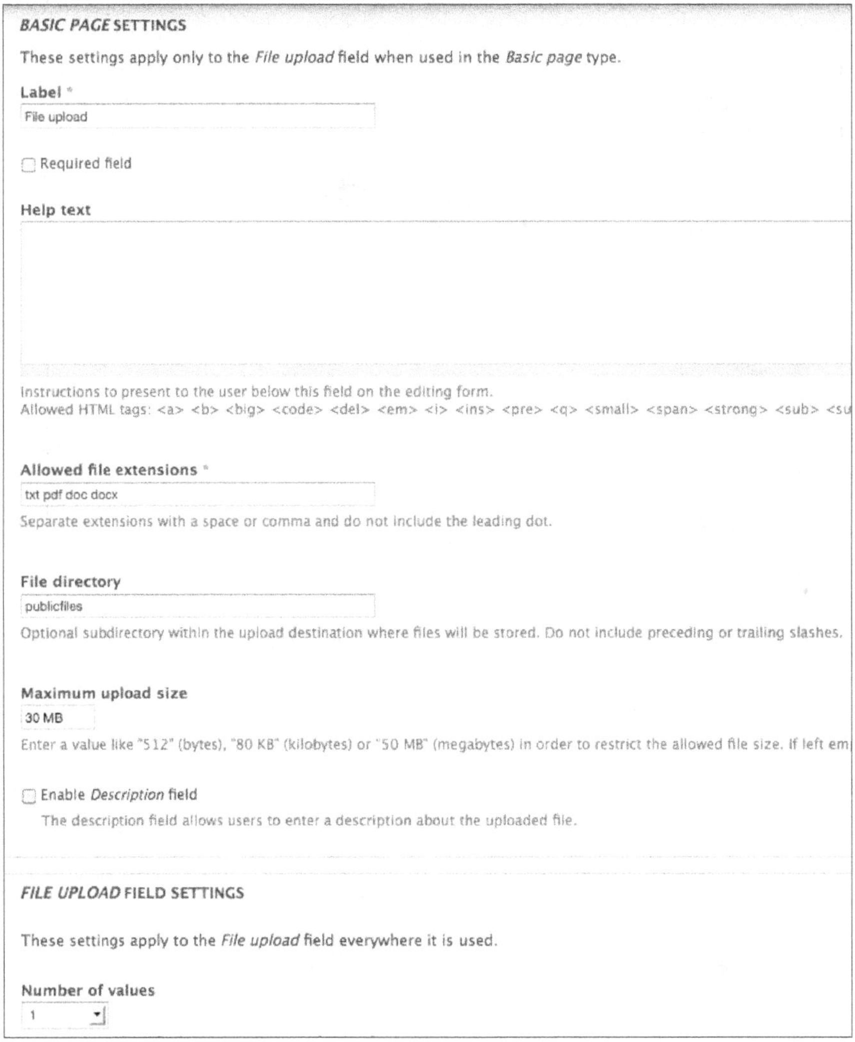

BASIC PAGE SETTINGS

These settings apply only to the *File upload* field when used in the *Basic page* type.

Label *

File upload

☐ Required field

Help text

Instructions to present to the user below this field on the editing form.
Allowed HTML tags: <a> <b> <big> <code> <del> <em> <i> <ins> <pre> <q> <small> <span> <strong> <sub> <su

Allowed file extensions *

txt pdf doc docx

Separate extensions with a space or comma and do not include the leading dot.

File directory

publicfiles

Optional subdirectory within the upload destination where files will be stored. Do not include preceding or trailing slashes.

Maximum upload size

30 MB

Enter a value like "512" (bytes), "80 KB" (kilobytes) or "50 MB" (megabytes) in order to restrict the allowed file size. If left em

☐ Enable *Description* field
　The description field allows users to enter a description about the uploaded file.

FILE UPLOAD FIELD SETTINGS

These settings apply to the *File upload* field everywhere it is used.

Number of values

1 ▾

---

7. Finally you can specify the number of files you'll allow to be uploaded per web page. So you can set the values to 4 for example if you want a user to be able to upload up to 4 files per page. Let's do that here. We'll leave **Enable Display field** checked and our **Upload destination** set to Public. Click your **Save settings** button.

   Now we're ready to upload a file to our site.

8. First click on **Add Content** and then the **Basic page** content type link. This will open up your Basic page form. Let's add a PDF formatted menu to our site.

9. Add a title and description to the form; then click on the **Browse** button under the **FILE UPLOAD** field and browse for a PDF. Click on the **Upload** button to attach your PDF file.

10. You will see the file attach along with a small PDF icon next to the file name. You should see the following:

11. At this point you can choose to override the default display of the file on your page if you want.

12. Click the **Save** button to save your webpage.

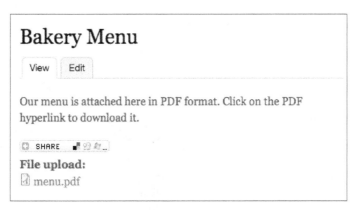

13. Your page will load and you should see a link to your PDF file. Click to open it. Notice that you will be asked to download and save or view the PDF file via your file browser. Go ahead and save, and open the PDF.

Configuring files for secure private download

Now there may be cases where you want to upload files that only your site's VIP role users can access and download. You may want to upload freebies or coupons to the site and only allow your VIP users access to download these files.

To do this you need to add a secure private file upload field to your content type or make the public field you added earlier a private secure field.

We're going to go ahead and add a private field to the **Basic page** content type.

1. To do this go through the first three steps of the public field instructions given in the preceding text but when you see the **Upload destination** field select the **Private files** radio button. Additionally, I'm calling my private field **VIP Uploads**. You should see the following screenshot:

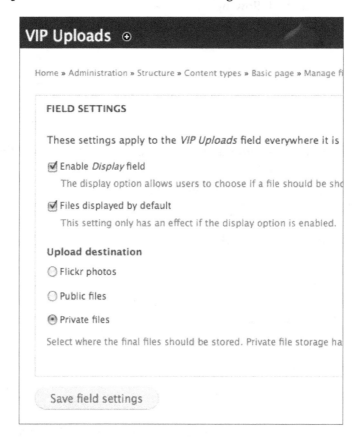

2. This time I'll specify a file directory specifically for these VIP role files called `private_vip`. This way I can keep my private files organized in a separate folder from my public files. Additionally Drupal will upload these private files into the main `/private` folder on our server that we created earlier since we're specifying that they need to be secure.

3. Go ahead and save your field settings.

4. Now go ahead and create a **Basic page** and this time upload a VIP file using the VIP Uploads field.

5. Once uploaded logout of the Website and try browsing directly to your private file via the URL path to the file. In my case the URL path is:`/sites/default/files/private/coupons_0.pdf`.

   I receive a Forbidden 403 error in the Web browser. Drupal is protecting the file via an HTACCESS file in the root of the `/private` folder. If you open up the htaccess file you'll see the following code:

   ```
   SetHandlerDrupal_Security_Do_Not_Remove_See_SA_2006_006
   Deny from all
   Options None
   Options +FollowSymLinks
   ```

6. Your files are now secure and protected and only accessible by users who have permissions to view those files when they login.

Sending the correct file types to a user

Goal

Ensure that the correct file type is sent to the browser so that the visitor's computer can accurately determine how to handle it.

Additional modules needed

File MIME (`http://drupal.org/project/filemime`).

Steps

As you add files to your site for download, it is important to make sure that a visitor's browser knows how to display the file. With websites, this is done by setting the MIME type for the file. Some common MIME types are:

* text/`html`: A standard web page
* text/`csv`: A comma-delimited file

- text/`plain`: Plain text with no formatting
- audio/`mpeg`: Audio mpeg1 and mpeg2 files
- audio/`mp4`: Audio mp4 files
- image/`jpeg`: JPEG encoded image files
- image/`gif`: GIF encoded images
- application/`pdf`: A PDF document
- application/`javascript`: A script file written in JavaScript

A full list of how Drupal handles each file type can be found at: `http://api.drupal.org/api/drupal/includes--file.inc/function/file_get_mimetype/7`.

It's important to know here that Drupal 7 comes with default MIME type support and display based on the core Drupal code. You can see the `mime_type` function code here on the Drupal documentation page specific to MIME types. `http://api.drupal.org/api/drupal/includes file.mimetypes.inc/function/file_default_mimetype_mapping/7` .There may be times you want to override this default mime type behavior. To do this you need to install the **File MIME** module. The **File MIME** module automatically detects the type of file based on the file extension, and sets the appropriate MIME type, which is returned to the browser.

To use the File MIME module, carry out the following steps:

1. Download, install, and activate the **File MIME** module. The module's project page is here: `http://drupal.org/project/filemime`.

2. Configure the module by selecting **Configuration** and then **File MIME**, from the **Toolbar** menu:

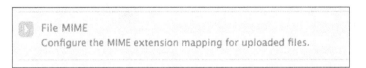

3. The module allows you to specify the location of the `mime.types` file, which is installed along with your web server. The Apache web server installs this file in the same directory in which your `httpd.conf` file is installed. On my MAMP install, the `mime.types` file is in `/Applications/MAMP/conf/apache/mime.types`.You can add this path to the **Local mime.types file path**.

4. You can also add additional custom mappings for specific file types. For example, you may want .csv files to be treated as Microsoft Excel files if you know that a significant number of your users are running Windows-based machines and want to download .csv files into Excel. You can do this by adding the following line to the settings, as shown in the following screenshot: application/vnd.ms-excel csvxls.

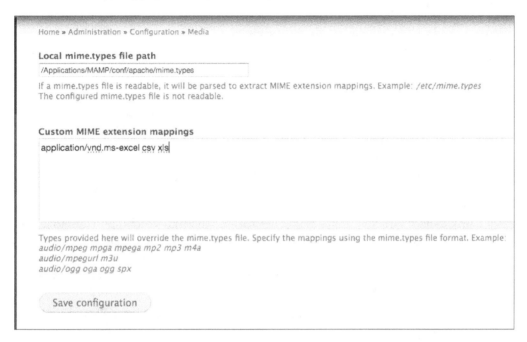

5. Click the **Save configuration** button. After the module has been properly configured, the module will automatically set the correct MIME types each time that a file is downloaded.

Forcing a file to be downloaded

Goal

Force a file to be downloaded even if it could be displayed within the browser.

Additional modules needed

File Force Download (`http://drupal.org/project/file_force`).

Steps

In the preceding section, we discussed setting the MIME type automatically so that the browser can handle the file correctly. However, in some cases, you may want the file to always be saved to the user's computer, even if it is a common file type that can be read by the browser. For example, you may want to have PDF files or pictures downloaded to the customer's computer even though all modern browsers can display these types of files in the browser.

1. To use the **File Force**d ownload module, download, install, and activate it.You can download the module from its project page here: `http://drupal.org/project/file_force`.

2. The **File Force** module does not require any configuration, so you can begin using it immediately. To use the File Force module, you simply need to prefix any link to downloadable content with the text `download`. So, if you have a link called: `/sites/default/files/song.mp3` that you want users to always download, you would replace the link with `/download/sites/default/files/song.mp3`. File Force will then modify the information returned to the browser to indicate that the file should be downloaded rather than be displayed or played.

3. So if we want to use the File Force download module on our Basic page content type file upload field we need to change the display field formatter from the default to a custom File Force download module provided formatter.To do this go to the **MANAGE DISPLAY** tab on your Basic page content type .Next choose the **File Force: Generic file formatter**.

4. Click the **Save** button. Now test downloading your PDF file.You should see the following path in the browser menu bar:

    `#overlay-context=download/sites/default/files/publicfiles/menu.pdf`.

Configuring Printer-friendly pages in Drupal

Goal

Add a printer-friendly link to our Drupal nodes that will allow our site users to print out HTML-only versions of our Web pages.

Additional modules needed

Printer, e-mail, and PDF (`http://drupal.org/project/print`).

Steps

As you continue to work on your website, you will find that many users want access to your content, even if they aren't online. With the **Printer, e-mail**, and **PDF** module, you can easily and automatically provide content in various formats for offline usage. The **Print module** allows you to configure printer-friendly versions of your Drupal nodes, e-mail options so your site users can easily e-mail an URL link of the Drupal page to a friend, and options to convert the pages into PDFs. We'll look specifically at the PDF options in this exercise.

1. To begin with, download and install the **Printer, e-mail**, and **PDF versions** module from its project page here: `http://drupal.org/project/print`. Once you have installed the module enable the **PDF version**, **Printer-friendly pages** and **Send by e-mail modules** as shown in the following screenshot:

ENABLED	NAME	VERSION	DESCRIPTION
☑	PDF version	7.x-1.0-alpha2	Adds the capability to export pages as PDF. Requires: Printer-friendly pages (disabled)
☑	Printer-friendly pages	7.x-1.0-alpha2	Adds a printer-friendly version link to content and administrative pages. Required by: Send by e-mail (disabled), PDF version (disabled)
☑	Send by e-mail	7.x-1.0-alpha2	Provides the capability to send the web page by e-mail Requires: Printer-friendly pages (disabled)

▼ PRINTER, E-MAIL AND PDF VERSIONS

2. You can now configure the basic options for the module by selecting **Site configuration** and then **Printer-friendly pages** from the **Administer** menu.

3. The general settings are accessed by clicking on the **Settings** tab. These settings are explained in the following text, and include options to style the printable pages, and to determine whether or not URLs and comments are displayed on the page. You can also control how the page is opened, and also which logos are displayed on it.

   By expanding the **Source URL** section, you can cause the URL of the page to be included on the printed output. You can also optionally add the date and time when the page was generated to the printed output.

   ○ The printable page (web page) configuration options include a variety of options to control how the links to the printable versions are displayed, as well as how the printable pages are displayed.

   ○ We have modified the **Printer-friendly** page link to be in the **Content corner** rather than in the **Links area**. You can also optionally display the printable page in a new window and automatically call the print function, as needed.

   ○ Opening the **Advanced link options** gives you additional options for how the link is displayed, and what pages it should be displayed on.

4. The **Robots META tags** section allows you to prevent search engines from indexing your printable version, which will help to ensure that visitors are directed only to your online content. This can also help prevent duplicate content penalties being imposed by search engines.

Automatically generating PDF files for a page

In this section we'll enable the PDF module so we can automatically convert our Drupal nodes to PDF format.

Goal

Generate PDF files of our pages so that the users can automatically download the pages for printing, or for offline usage.

Steps

If you visit your status report after enabling the PDF version module you'll see a warning message that looks like the following:

To create PDFs, we need to install a third-party tool to handle the conversion. First click on the **PDF settings page** to see the configuration options available to you. You will see the following error message telling you:

No PDF generation tool found! Please download a supported PHP PDF generation tool. Check this module's INSTALL.txt for more details.

So let's open the module's INSTALL.txt file to get more information on what PDF tool plugins we can use.

Here is the INSTALL.txt information that explains the various PDF tools at our disposal:

1. The print_pdf module requires the use of an external PDF generation tool. The currently supported tools are **dompdf**, **TCPDF** and **wkhtmltopdf**. Please note that any errors/bugs in those tools need to be reported and fixed by their maintainers. DO NOT report bugs in those tools in the print module's issue queue at Drupal.org.

2. Supported paths are as follows:
   ◦ print module lib directory (usually sites/all/modules/print/lib)
   ◦ libraries directory (sites/all/libraries)

3. dompdf support:
   ◦ The dompdf tool produces results that are more faithful to the HTML printer-friendly page. Good support of CSS 2.1 and partially CSS3.
   ◦ Download dompdf from http://code.google.com/p/dompdf/downloads/list
   ◦ Extract the contents of the downloaded package into one of the supported paths.
   ◦ Check if dompdf_config.inc.php fits your installation. In 99% of cases, no changes are necessary, so just try to use it and only edit anything if the PDF generation fails.
   ◦ Grant write access to the lib/fonts directory to your webserver user.
   ◦ If you're using dompdf-0.5.1, delete the dompdf.php file as it contains a security vulnerability.

- If you're using `dompdf-0.6` or later, you can try to enable the Unicodesupport, but you'll need to add some Unicode fonts. See `http://groups.google.com/group/dompdf/browse_thread/thread/9f7bc0162b04d5cf` for further information on this.

- Also, check `http://code.google.com/p/dompdf/` for further information.

4. TCPDF support:

- TCPDF's support for CSS is considerably worse than the other tools.

- Unicode is supported (use of Unicode fonts result in HUGE files). Page header and footer are supported. This module requires TCPDF >= 5.9.012.

- Download TCPDF from `http://sourceforge.net/projects/tcpdf/`.

- Extract the contents of the downloaded package into one of the supported paths. There is no need to modify the `config/tcpdf_config.php file`, as the module self-configures TCPDF.

- Grant write access to the cache and images directories to your webserver user.

- Check `http://tcpdf.sourceforge.net/` for further information.

5. wkhtmltopdf support:

- wkhtmltopdf is a webkit-based tool that actually is a browser in order to generate the PDF. Resource hungry: expect to need some 30Mb+ of RAM and several seconds of CPU power. The static binaries may need additional libraries in your site, which may present problems in shared hosting environments. However, it is the best if you can run it.

- Download wkhtmltopdf from: `http://code.google.com/p/wkhtmltopdf/downloads/list`. You can choose to download the source and compile it or simply download the static binary which doesn't require you to compile anything.

- Place the wkhtmltopdf executable into one of the supported paths (usually `sites/all/modules/print/lib`). You can also place a symbolic link to the executable.

- Check `http://code.google.com/p/wkhtmltopdf/` for further information.

6. You can choose from either TCPDF, dompdf, or wkhtmltopdf, which are available to download from the following URLs:

    ○ TCPDF: `http://sourceforge.net/projects/tcpdf/`

    ○ dompdf: `http://code.google.com/p/dompdf/downloads/list`

    ○ wkhtmltopdf: `http://code.google.com/p/wkhtmltopdf/downloads/list`

    You can install and use any of these. You can also install both of them and switch between the two, while you evaluate which one will meet the needs of your site best.

7. Let's install the dompdf tool plugin. Follow the install instructions for dompdf from the `INSTALL.txt` in the preceding text. Be sure to download the beta-2 version of the tool: `dompdf_0-6-0_beta2.tar.gz`.

8. Once extracted the tool will create a folder titled `dompdf`. I'll copy that folder into my Print module's `/lib` folder. So paste it into `/sites/all/modules/print/lib`.

9. After you instal `ldompdf`, you can access the PDF tabbed page in the Printer-friendly pages configuration or by going here:`/admin/config/user-interface/print/pdf`.

10. The PDF generation options are similar to the printable web page options, but with a few additions. To begin with, you need to select which generation tool is to be used, as shown in the following screenshot. If you have only installed one PDF generation tool then that will be the only option visible:

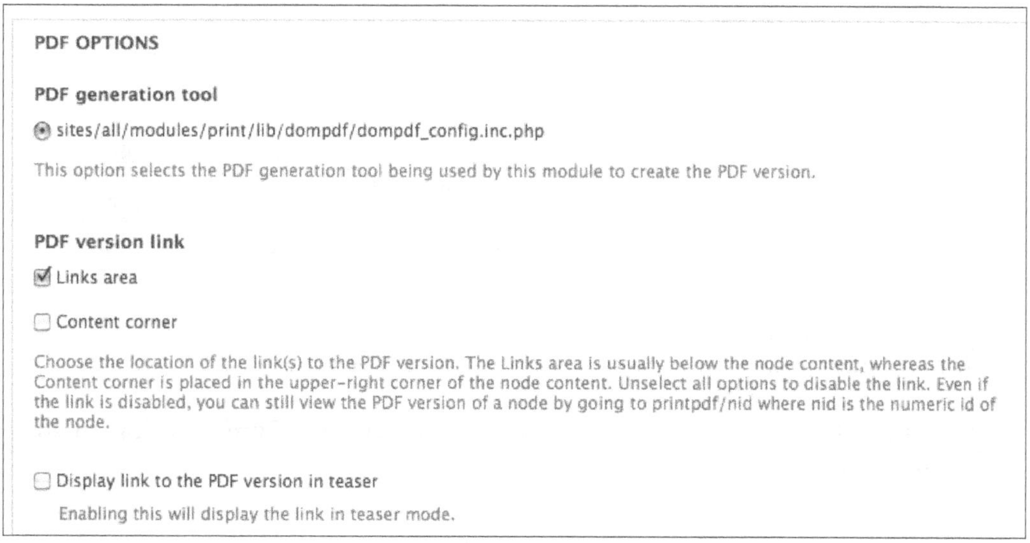

PDF OPTIONS

PDF generation tool

⦿ sites/all/modules/print/lib/dompdf/dompdf_config.inc.php

This option selects the PDF generation tool being used by this module to create the PDF version.

PDF version link

☑ Links area

☐ Content corner

Choose the location of the link(s) to the PDF version. The Links area is usually below the node content, whereas the Content corner is placed in the upper-right corner of the node content. Unselect all options to disable the link. Even if the link is disabled, you can still view the PDF version of a node by going to printpdf/nid where nid is the numeric id of the node.

☐ Display link to the PDF version in teaser

Enabling this will display the link in teaser mode.

11. You can also control how the PDF will be opened, in the same browser window or a new window; the paper size and orientation to be used in the PDF, as well as font sizes, and whether the PDF should be displayed after it is created, as shown in the following screenshot:

12. After all of the options have been updated, click **Save Configuration** on your settings page.

13. If you load one of your site's nodes now you should see a PDF icon in the content corner or links area of your node. It should look like this:

14. If the user clicks on the **PDF icon**, a PDF will be generated, and either displayed to the user or saved to the user's hard drive, as shown in the following screenshot:

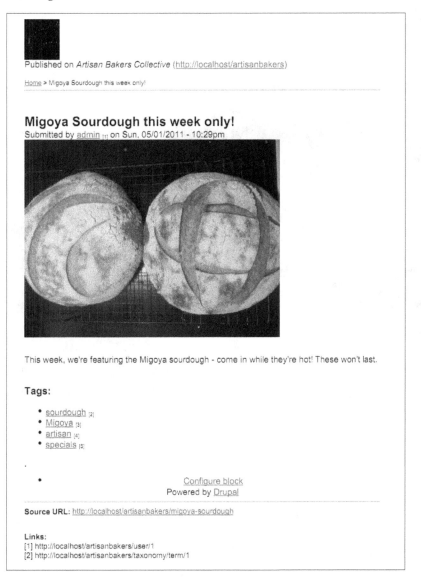

Your site user can download the PDF file using their browser's **Save as** functionality and then open the file directly as a PDF from their desktop. Here is the file opened in Preview on the Mac:

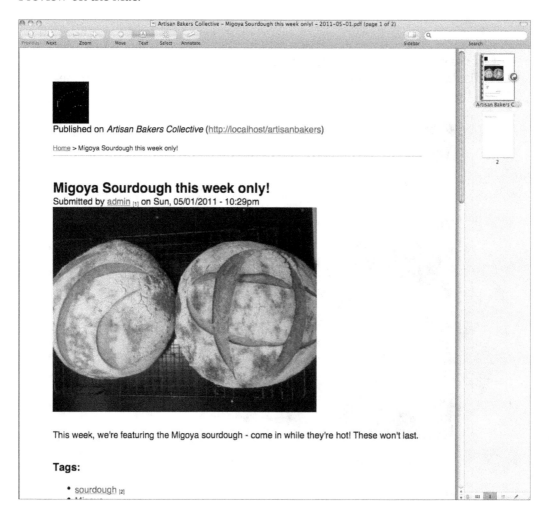

Summary

In this chapter, we reviewed some methods of making the most out of the downloadable content. As long as you provide high quality downloadable content, your customers will appreciate getting something useful from you. In return, you receive the opportunity to market to your customers.

The amount of downloadable content for a site will vary depending on the goal of the website, as well as the requirements of the visitors to the site.

We have also discussed automatic creation of PDF files for offline use as well as for printing. This is a great way of allowing your users to make use of the site even when they are not actively browsing the site online.

In the next chapter, we will create a take-out menu that our customers can order from and then pay for their orders online.

Online Orders and Payments

A common goal for many business websites is to integrate their website with their store, take reservations, and accept payments.

For example, a retail store may allow customers to browse their store inventory and then purchase items either for delivery or for pick-up at the store. A salon may allow patrons to view appointment times that are available, select a time for their appointment, and optionally pre-pay for their appointment online.

For the Artisan Bakers Collective site, we will do the following:

- Allow customers to view online products in our case Breads for sale on the website
- Select products that they want to purchase
- Pay for the order online
- After an order has been submitted, the order will be sent via an e-mail to the bakery staff so that they can begin preparation of the order.
- The order will also be available for viewing online.

The Drupal Commerce module

We're going to install and configure a brand new e-commerce module for Drupal called Commerce.

The Commerce module is a new module for Drupal 7 that gives your site e-commerce ability and functionality while leveraging the new Drupal 7 fields API and fields configurations. This module looks to be the next major step in Drupal e-commerce integration; taking much of the Ubercart functionality and renovating it for Drupal 7's core content construction field's functionality.

The module has the same module developers behind it that contributed originally to Ubercart. This module may still have bugs and may also be a bit trickier to configure since it's a brand new module and does not have advanced documentation yet. In this section I'll guide you through installing and configuring the Commerce module.

Goal

Set up the Commerce module so you can add products and take online orders on your site using Commerce.

Additional modules needed

Commerce (http://drupal.org/project/commerce)

Address Field (http://drupal.org/project/addressfield)

Entity API (http://drupal.org/project/entity)

Download and install Commerce

First we need to download the latest version of the Commerce module. The version at the time of writing is *7.x-1.0*. It's a stable release of the module. Commerce has a lot of dependency modules most of which we've already installed and configured on our site. I'll review these instructions in the following text.

Go ahead and download and install the Commerce module, as you would any contributed Drupal module. The Commerce module's project page is here: http://drupal.org/project/commerce.

Drupal Commerce does have some dependency modules that you should install to be able to use all of the module's base configuration options. These modules include: CTools, Views, Entity API, Rules, and Address Field. We already have all of these modules installed besides the Address Field module. So let's download and install the Address Field module as well. That project page is here: http://drupal.org/project/addressfield.

Since Commerce depends significantly on the integration with Drupal's Rules, Views and Fields modules, the module developers have provided a base Kickstart installation profile that you can install on your site as a module. This profile will install a base starter Commerce configuration that you can use to get your e-commerce store initially configured in Drupal. To install this go to the Commerce Kickstart module project page and download and install the latest *7.x-1.0-rc5* version. That project page is here: http://drupal.org/project/commerce_kickstart.

The Kickstart profile can be used on a brand new Drupal site installation. If you install the profile, then when you go ahead and proceed to install Drupal, you will be able to select the Commerce profile. The profile gives you some test product content to work with. We're not going to install the profile since we already have all the required modules installed on our existing site.

So to summarize these are the modules we need to make sure we have installed and enabled:

- Commerce
- Commerce Kickstart
- Views
- Rules
- CTools
- Entity API
- Address Field

First, let's install the Commerce, and Address Field modules (assuming you have already installed the other dependencies. Go ahead and install these two modules like all other contrib modules into `/sites/all/modules`.

Now refresh your modules' administration page and you'll see a large section with all the **COMMERCE** modules; as well as a section with the **Address Field** module. This includes the following sub-modules:

- **Cart**
- **Checkout**
- **Commerce**
- **Commerce UI**
- **Customer**
- Customer UI
- Line Item
- Line Item UI
- Order
- Order UI
- Payment
- Payment UI
- Price
- Product
- Product Pricing

- Product Pricing UI
- Product Reference
- Product UI
- Tax
- Tax UI

Enable all the modules as per the following screenshots:

▼ COMMERCE				
ENABLED	**NAME**	**VERSION**	**DESCRIPTION**	**OPERATIONS**
☑	Cart	7.x–1.0	Implements the shopping cart system and add to cart features. Requires: Commerce (disabled), Entity API (enabled), Rules (enabled), Entity tokens (enabled), Checkout (disabled), Commerce UI (disabled), Order (disabled), Customer (disabled), Address Field (disabled), Chaos tools (enabled), Line Item (disabled), Price (disabled), Product (disabled), Product Pricing (disabled), Product Reference (disabled), Options (enabled), Field (enabled), Field SQL storage (enabled), Rules UI (disabled), Views (enabled)	
☑	Checkout	7.x–1.0	Enable checkout as a multi–step form with customizable checkout pages. Requires: Commerce (disabled), Entity API (enabled), Rules (enabled), Entity tokens (enabled), Commerce UI (disabled), Order (disabled), Customer (disabled), Address Field (disabled), Chaos tools (enabled), Line Item (disabled), Price (disabled) Required by: Cart (disabled)	
☑	Commerce	7.x–1.0	Defines features and functions common to the Commerce modules. Must be enabled to uninstall other Commerce modules. Requires: Entity API (enabled), Rules (enabled), Entity tokens (enabled) Required by: Commerce UI (disabled), Customer (disabled), Price (disabled), Line Item (disabled), Order (disabled), Checkout (disabled), Product (disabled), Product Reference (disabled), Product Pricing (disabled), Cart (disabled), Customer UI (disabled), Line Item UI (disabled), Order UI (disabled), Payment (disabled), Payment Method Example (disabled), Payment UI (disabled), Product Pricing UI (disabled), Product UI (disabled), Tax (disabled), Tax UI (disabled)	
☑	Commerce UI	7.x–1.0	Defines menu items common to the various Drupal Commerce UI modules. Requires: Commerce (disabled), Entity API (enabled), Rules (enabled), Entity tokens (enabled) Required by: Checkout (disabled), Cart (disabled), Customer UI (disabled), Line Item UI (disabled), Order UI (disabled), Payment UI (disabled), Product Pricing UI (disabled), Product UI (disabled), Tax UI (disabled)	
☑	Customer	7.x–1.0	Defines the Customer entity with Address Field integration. Requires: Address Field (disabled), Chaos tools (enabled), Commerce (disabled), Entity API (enabled), Rules (enabled), Entity tokens (enabled) Required by: Order (disabled), Checkout (disabled), Cart (disabled), Customer UI (disabled), Order UI (disabled), Payment (disabled), Payment Method Example	

FIELDS

ENABLED	NAME	VERSION	DESCRIPTION
☐	**Address Field**	7.x-1.0-beta2	Manage a flexible address field, implementing the xNAL standard. Requires: Chaos tools (enabled) Required by: Customer (disabled), Order (disabled), Checkout (disabled), C Payment Method Example (disabled), Payment UI (disabled)

Save your module's administration page. You may receive a message to enable the Rules UI module in order to use the Tax UI module. Go ahead and do this.

Setting up your Store with Commerce

The first thing we need to do is configure our product type in Commerce. To add our Commerce product type click on the Commerce Store menu link in your top admin toolbar menu. Make sure you're clicking to the following URL which is Commerce module-specific:

`/user/1#overlay=admin/commerce`

Now, click on the **Products** link as shown in the following screenshot:

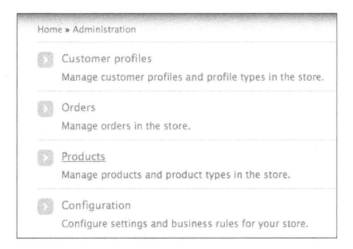

That will load the **Products** configuration screen. You'll see a link to **Add a product** and also a tab for **PRODUCT TYPES**. Click on the **PRODUCT TYPES** tab. By default the core Commerce module will add a Product content type to your Drupal site. This may work for you if you just want to sell one type of product. However, if your needs are more specific you can (similarly to Ubercart) set up custom product types:

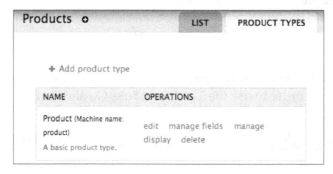

So let's do this. We'll add a product type just for our Breads. Click on the **Add product type** link.

On the product type form add a Breads product type by filling in the **Name**, **Description** and, **Explanation or submissions guidelines fields**. Save the product type by clicking on the **Save and add fields** button:

Now, on the next screen we can add specific fields to our type to collect additional information.

By default the Commerce module will add the following fields to your product type:

- **Product SKU**
- **Title**
- **Price**
- **Status**

These are the core product fields that ship with the Commerce module. You can add additional fields using the **Add new field** area. I went ahead and created a new taxonomy vocabulary for Products and added a couple of tags (Baguette and Sourdough) to my vocab. I'll add a term reference field here on my **Product type | MANAGE FIELDS** screen.

Type `Product Tag` into the **Add new field** box. Type `commerce_product_tag` in the Name field; then select **Term reference** as the field type and **Select list** as the **WIDGET**. You should see something like the following on your screen:

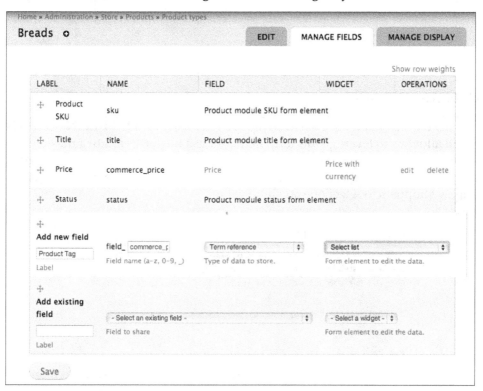

Click the **Save** button.

Next, you'll be asked to configure your term reference field. Select the **Products** vocab from the drop down select box. Then click the **Save field** button.

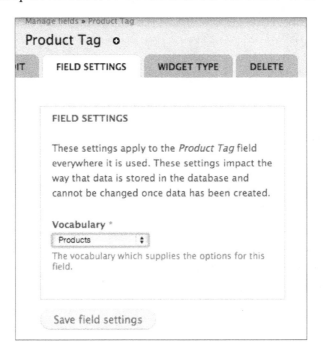

Click the **Save field settings** button.

On the next screen make sure to check the **ATTRIBUTE FIELD SETTINGS** checkbox. This will allow us to leverage this term field and use the terms as attributes of our product. So our users will be able to select a term to specify the type of bread they want to buy. Select the **Radio buttons** option as the **Attribute selection widget**. This will allow shoppers to select one attribute value:

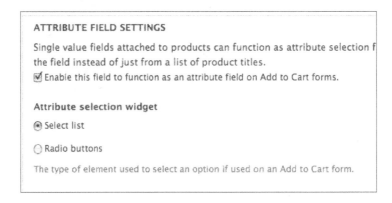

Click the **Save settings** button.

Now, click on the **MANAGE DISPLAY** tab on your **Breads** product type screen. This will launch the manage display screen and allow you to tweak any display settings for your specific fields. We'll leave these set to their defaults for now:

Click the **Save** button.

Adding a content type in Drupal to display our Commerce product types

Now, we need to add a content type in our Drupal site that will display all of our Commerce products that we add using the product type we just configured. This is an additional step that we need to complete before we can actually add products and see them displayed on our site. So let's add our product display content type.

Go to your **Drupal Structure | Content types** screen and click on the Add Content type link.

Name your type Commerce Product Display:

Content types ⚙

Individual content types can have different fields, behaviors, and permissions assigned to them.

Name *

Commerce Product Display   Machine name: commerce_product_display [Edit]

The human-readable name of this content type. This text will be displayed as part of the list on the *Add new content* page. It is recommended that this name begin with a capital letter and contain only letters, numbers, and spaces. This name must be unique.

Description

This type displays our Commerce products.

Describe this content type. The text will be displayed on the *Add new content* page.

Submission form settings	Title field label *
Title	Title

Publishing options
Published , Promoted to front page

Preview before submitting

Display settings
Display author and date information.

○ Disabled

Addthis settings

● Optional

○ Required

Comment settings
Open, Threading , 50 comments per page

Explanation or submission guidelines

Diff

Menu settings

Printer, e-mail and PDF versions

Save your content type.

Now click on the **MANAGE FIELDS** link of your new content type. We're now going to add a **Product Reference** field so that we can use our new content type to display all of our Breads product types. To do this type in a new field name called `Commerce Breads Product`. Make sure to select **Product Reference** as the field type. Select **Autocomplete text field** as the **WIDGET** type.

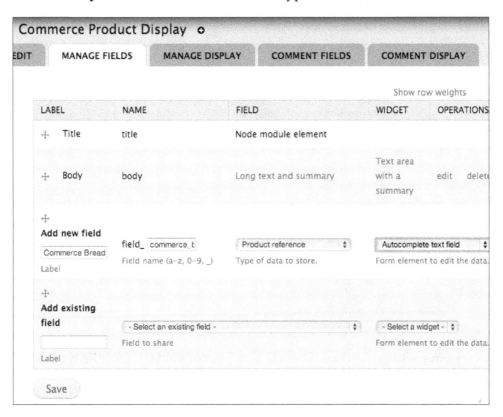

Click the **Save** button. On the configuration screen make sure to reference the product type by selecting the **Breads** and **Product** types here. Check both boxes. Leave the rest of the settings set to their default:

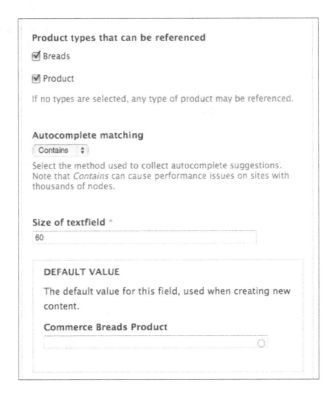

Click the **Save settings** button. Now, click on your **MANAGE DISPLAY** tab for your **Commerce Product Display** content type.

For your **Commerce Breads Product** product reference field make sure you have selected the **Add to Cart form** for your field format. Do this for your **Teaser** display as well.

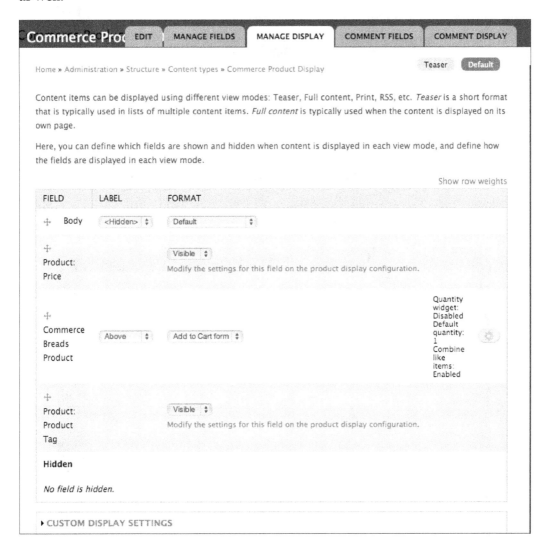

Click the **Save** button. We're now ready to add some products to our site.

Adding Products using Commerce

Go to your **Store | Products** screen and click on the **Add a product** link.

Now, click on the **Create Breads** product type link:

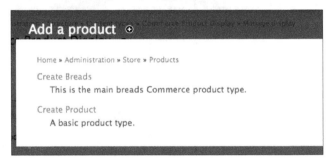

This will launch your product type form. Add a **Product SKU**, **Title**, **Price** , configure the **Status** to be set to **Active**, and select a **Product tag**:

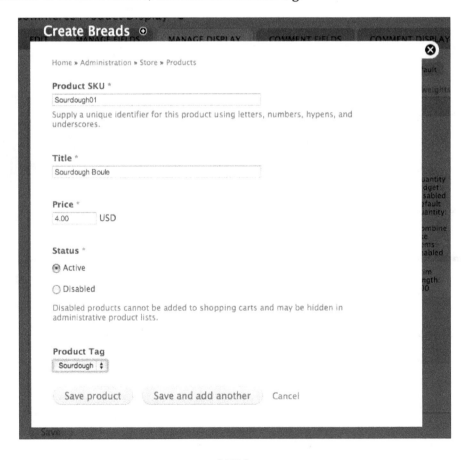

Click the **Save product** button. You will see your new product in your products table as follows:

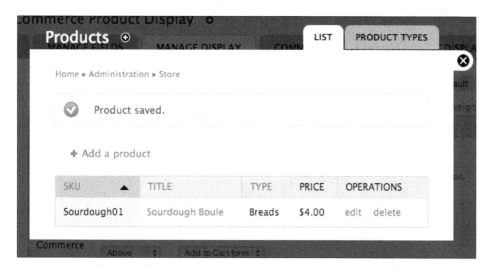

Now that we have added our product, we need to go back to the Drupal side of things and add a content node using the content type we created to actually display our product to our shopper. Drupal basically does two things for us here—we're adding products using the Commerce module—think of this as if we're adding products physically to our store's stock room. Now, we need to grab those products we've added and actually put them out on the display floor of our store so our shoppers can see them and buy them.

So, go to **Add content** and click on the **Commerce Product Display** link to use our new Drupal content type that we created earlier. That will launch our product display form.

Give the title of the node something like `Sourdough Boule`. Then add a description of your bread item in the **Body** box. Now, in your **Commerce Breads Product** autocomplete field start typing in the name of your **Sourdough Boule** product that you added in the last step. The SKU and title should appear as you begin to type. Select it in the field.

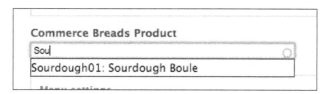

Click the **Save** button. Now, your node should load and you'll see your new Sourdough Boule product node along with the price displayed, an **Add to cart** button and the product tag. You should see something like the following:

If you load your site's home page you should also see the product displayed on your home page.

Go ahead and log out of your site and then click on the **Add to Cart** button on your home page's product. You should see a message telling you that the Sourdough Boule has been added to your cart. Click on your cart's hyperlink to actually load the shopping cart.

The cart should show in a table with the product and quantity. Here you can tweak the quantity if you want to add additional quantities of the item. You can also click the **Update cart** button once you make these changes. I'll tweak my cart to 2 items. You should see the following:

Now, we need to enable the shopping checkout functionality so our shoppers can go ahead and checkout via their shopping cart. The easiest way to do this is first to enable your Commerce module shopping cart block.

To do this you'll have to enable the Commerce shopping cart block via your block's administration page. Enable the **Shopping Cart** block to show in one of your sidebars.

Save your block's configuration.

Before your shoppers can see the Checkout link in their shopping cart you should also check your Commerce module permissions to make sure that anonymous users have permissions to view the Checkout link. To do this load your User permissions screen in Drupal and then look for the Checkout section of the permissions screen. In that section make sure you have checked the **Access Checkout** link:

Now, log out of the site again and add the Sourdough Boule to your cart. Now, you should see a checkout link in your shopping cart:

Click on the checkout link and the checkout form should load. This form will look similar to Ubercart's. It will ask you for your e-mail address and billing address. Fill this out and then click on the **Continue to next step** button. Commerce has greatly improved the user interface for the checkout process by splitting up the checkout form into multi-steps.

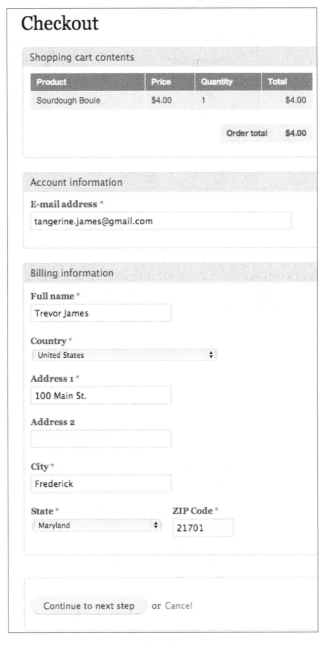

The next screen will show you a review display of your order form and allow you to enter payment information. Commerce automatically defaults to an example payment method for when you are testing out your transaction and checkout process. It will ask you to enter a name for your example payment. Go ahead and do this. I'll enter `Payment 1234`. This is just for testing purposes.

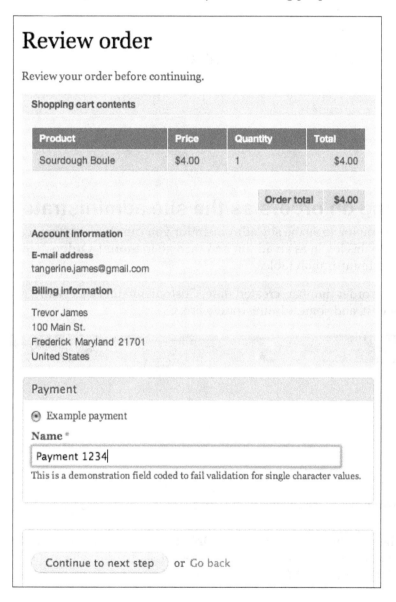

Click the **Continue to next step** button. If you've used a user account e-mail that's already had an account on your site the transaction should process and the order will be tied to that user account. If the shopper does not have an account the user will have the option to create a new account now when they are purchasing (similar to Ubercart's process). Once you complete the purchase you should see a success page that looks like the following:

Checking on orders as the site administrator

Now when you log in as the site administrator you can check on your customer's orders. To do this log in as an admin and then go to **Store | Orders**. This will load the **Orders** administration table.

You'll see the order number, created date, Customer name, user name, order status, total order cost, and some administrative links:

Click on the **view** link under **OPERATIONS** to view the order details. The order detail screen will load showing you all of the detailed order information as well as an **EDIT** tab, and a **PAYMENT** tab:

Click on the **EDIT** tab. This will allow you to edit the order and also update its order status. So currently the order is pending. You can select the next status such as Processing; and then click the **Save order** button.

There are a lot more administrative options here and you can go ahead and play around with your order editing to see what some of the other tabs do such as **User information** and **Order history**. Click **Save order** when you are done.

Click on the **PAYMENT** tab. This screen will show you the payment status table and allow you to both **EDIT** the payment and also **view** the payment via the **OPERATIONS** links:

Clicking on the **view** link will show the entire transaction history for the payment as follows:

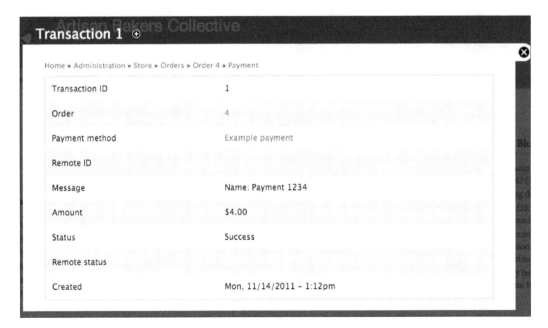

Commerce Store Configuration

There are many more configuration options for your Commerce Store that you can tweak. Go to **Store | Configuration** and you'll see the following options:

- Checkout settings
- Currency settings
- Line item types
- Order settings
- Payment methods
- Product pricing rules
- Taxes

You can explore each of these sections in more detail. For example if you want to add **Paymentmethods**, click on that link. We've been using the core testing example Payment method that Commerce ships with. Before you launch your site you'll want to add a new payment method such as PayPal, so you can run all of your transactions via PayPal Website Payments Pro for example. So to enable the Payment method click on the Payment methods link and that will launch a Payment methods screen. You'll see the Example Payment method in your enabled rules. Click on the **Add a payment method rule** to add a custom method for example for PayPal:

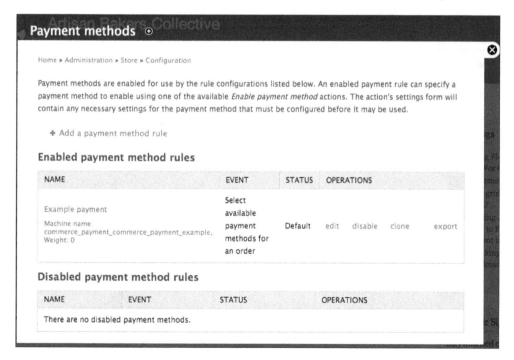

There's much more you can do with the Commerce module. Explore the module and tweak some of its configuration to make it work on your site per your specific site requirements. This module stands to be the next big e-commerce solution for Drupal and it has definite benefits over using Ubercart both from its ease of use and user interface improvements. There's also a lot of configuration that is provided by default in the module's core.

Summary

In this chapter, we have truly integrated the website into our business by allowing users to order from our menu and place orders from the site. You can apply many of the same techniques to your own site to make the most of your website. We installed and configured the Commerce module.

In the next chapter, we will discuss essential tasks for administering your website and ensuring that your site stays up-to-date. We will cover backups, installing updates to Drupal, and third party modules, along with moderating content.

10
Image Galleries and Slideshows

In this chapter we're going to extend the use of images on our site by adding photo gallery pages and jQuery powered slideshows. The image slideshows will allow automatic animation of one image to the next as well as user controlled manual image navigation. We're also going to install and configure the Views module to set up and configure pages that display all of our images. We'll build an online image gallery that will look very similar to how Flickr or many online photo applications display photos.

Additionally, we'll use the Lightbox module to add an animated slideshow component to our gallery and to allow our images to be clicked to larger versions that appear in modal windows above our main site's content. This will give the viewer of the site a rich and dynamic method of viewing our photos.

Before we get started make sure you have a good collection of about 20-30 photos to use during this chapter's exercises. We're going to be uploading photos into our site and building a large image gallery, so get a good selection of photos to use in your gallery. I have about 20 photos of various breads that I'll be uploading.

In this chapter we will do the following:

- Install and configure the Views module
- Build a photo gallery using Views
- Add the Lightbox module to enhance our photo gallery with a slideshow component

Using Views to build image galleries

Baker James wants to display photos of the bakery's breads in an image gallery design on the Website. He has about 20 images he would like to display on the page and he wants to grow this gallery over time and add more photos. To set this up we're going to use the Views module. First, we'll install and configure the Views module and get introduced to the power of using Views to create lists and displays of content including photos. By building an image gallery for the website you'll learn how to use the Views module.

Installing and Configuring the Views module

The Views module lets you build lists of content including text and images and display these in visually compelling galleries, tables, bulleted lists, and more. Views enables you to filter to specific types of content on your site and exclude types of content. For example if we're building an image gallery we can tell the View to only display the Photo content type content, and only content tagged with the "bread" tag. Then we can display just the image field component of our content and so our View display will only be made up of photos. Views makes it easy to construct complicated database queries of your Drupal site's content without having to write a line of code.

Goal

Install Views module and build an image gallery.

Additional modules needed

Views (http://drupal.org/project/views), CTools (http://drupal.org/project/ctools).

Steps

To get started with **Views** we need to:

1. Download the most recent version of the module which is currently *7.x.-3.0-rc1*. You can download Views from its project page here: http://drupal.org/project/views. Views requires the CTools module so also make sure to download and install CTools: http://drupal.org/project/ctools.

2. Since we'll be building our slideshows using the Views slideshow module you can also install this. The Views slideshow module is available from its project page here: http://drupal.org/project/views_slideshow. Install the *7.x-3.0-alpha1* version.

This version requires the Libraries module. You can download and install Libraries from here: `http://drupal.org/project/libraries`.

3. Once you install Views go to the main modules administration screen and enable all the **Views** modules as shown in the following screenshot:

4. Next, let's add a new content type for our Photos that we'll be including in our image gallery. We'll tag our photos as we add them so we can set up categorized image galleries and slideshows. So follow these steps to set up and configure the content type we'll be using. This should all be reviewed based on work we've done in the previous chapters.

5. Add a new content type called **Photo**.

6. Add a new taxonomy vocbulary for your slideshows called **Slideshows** and add the following tags to that taxonomy vocabulary: Breads, Pastries, and Bakery.

7. To the Photo content type add an image upload field. This field should have the following configuration settings: Label = `Photo`; field Name = `field_ photo`; Image field and using an Image widget type. Save your image field and leave the **Upload destination** set to **Public files**. Click the **Save field settings** button.

8. On the Widget settings make sure to set the **Number of values** to **Unlimited**. This will let us upload multiple photos to one Photo page and then cycle all of them into our **Slideshow**. Save your field settings.

9. Now, add a **Term Reference** field that references the Slideshow's taxonomy vocabulary we created earlier.

10. Now, you have your content type and vocab of terms configured and ready to go.

Add some photos

Let's go ahead and create a page of our Bread photos. This will be a page that will show a bunch of our bread photos. We'll then create our View display of this page's photo content.

To do this:

1. Add content and then select your new Photos content type.
2. Add a title to the Photos page and then start uploading your photos.
3. Add as many as you want to this one single Photos node. Tag the **PHOTO** page with the "Breads" tag. You should see something similar to this on your Photos form once you add the photos and before you save your node:

4. Save your node. I've uploaded 20 photos to my **PHOTO** page. I've uploaded the largest quality photos from my local desktop so these images are all about 3+ MB each. In the next section we'll set up some imagecaching so we can tell Drupal how we want to size and scale our images in our gallery display.

5. If you view your Photos page now you'll see that all of your photos have published at their highest resolution. In our gallery we're not going to want the images to be so large. So we're going to set up a series of **imagecache** scale and crop sizes that our images will be given automatically by Drupal when they are rendered in the View based image gallery. Let's set up those imagecache settings next.

Configuring Imagecache

To set up your imagecache presets:

1. Go to **Configuration | Media | Image styles**. This will open up a default **Image styles** screen with some default Drupal image styles. Let's add two image styles for our new image gallery. We want to show our images in a smaller thumbnail size on the main gallery page so we'll choose a scale and crop of 200x200 pixels. Then, those thumbnails will be clickable to a larger scaled size of our image. That larger scaled and cropped size will be set to 600x600 pixels.

2. Click **Add Style**. Give a Style name of gallery_thumb:

3. Click the **Create new style** button.

4. The next screen will show you a preview of what your image style preset will look like. Let's add the actual effect to our style first. Click the **Select a new effect drop down box** and choose **Scale and crop**. Then click **Add**:

5. Set the **Width** and **Height** pixel dimensions to **200** px each. Click **Add effect**:

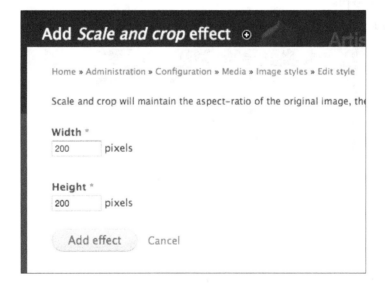

6. Now the preview screen will show you a preview of your new `gallery_` `thumb` preset image style. Let's add another image style for our 600x600.

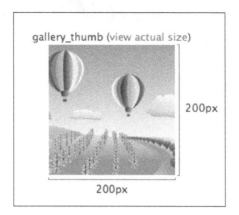

7. Go back to your main Image styles screen and add a new style. Call this one `gallery_large`. Add a **Scale and crop** effect to it and set the scale to 600x600 pixels. Great! We now have our two image styles configured. We're now ready to build our View gallery page.

Configuring Image Galleries with Views

To build the View for our gallery:

1. Go to **Structure | Views**. This will launch the main Views administration screen. Click on the **Add View** link. Give our view a name of `Photo Gallery`. Drupal will automatically give the View a machine name and a path based on this name.

2. We want to show content from the Photos type so select **Photos** in the type select box. We'll leave the sort set to **Newest first**.

3. Leave the **Create a page** box checked. Leave the page title set to `Photo Gallery`. The path should be photo-gallery. **Display Format** should be set to **Grid** and we'll do a **Grid of fields** since we want to add our photo image field.

4. At this point you should have the following screen:

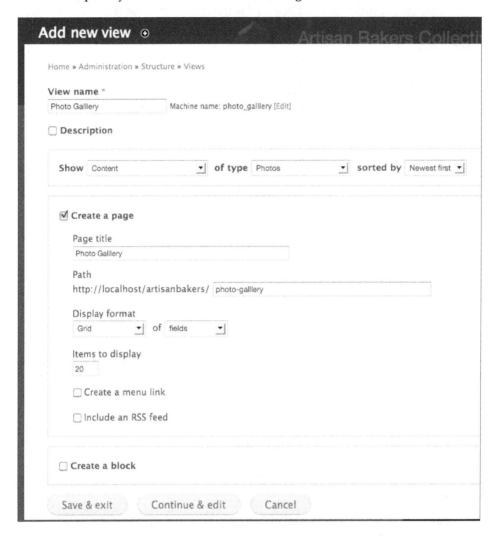

5. Items to display can be set to 20. Leave the rest of the defaults in place and then click **Continue & edit**. Our first step in setting up the View is complete. Now we need to add the specific image field to our View.

6. The next screen that loads will be the main Photo Gallery View configuration screen. The top of the screen will show our configuration and the bottom will show us a preview of our View. In the **Fields** section of your View configuration click the **Add** link. Filter to Content and then check the **Content: Photo** field. Click the Add and configure fields button.

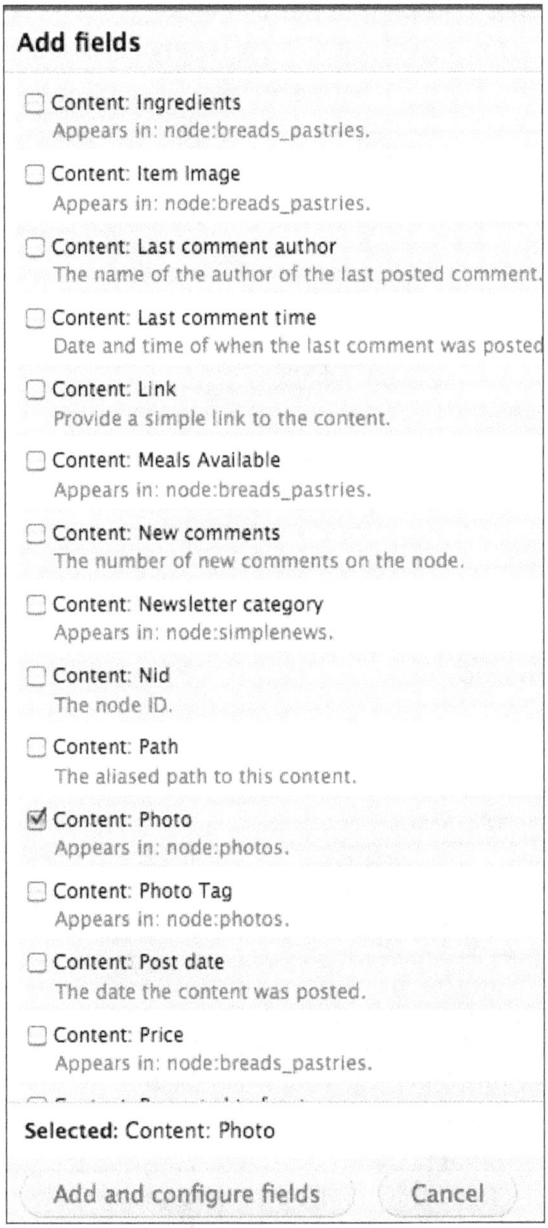

Add fields

☐ Content: Ingredients
Appears in: node:breads_pastries.

☐ Content: Item Image
Appears in: node:breads_pastries.

☐ Content: Last comment author
The name of the author of the last posted comment.

☐ Content: Last comment time
Date and time of when the last comment was posted

☐ Content: Link
Provide a simple link to the content.

☐ Content: Meals Available
Appears in: node:breads_pastries.

☐ Content: New comments
The number of new comments on the node.

☐ Content: Newsletter category
Appears in: node:simplenews.

☐ Content: Nid
The node ID.

☐ Content: Path
The aliased path to this content.

☑ Content: Photo
Appears in: node:photos.

☐ Content: Photo Tag
Appears in: node:photos.

☐ Content: Post date
The date the content was posted.

☐ Content: Price
Appears in: node:breads_pastries.

Selected: Content: Photo

(Add and configure fields)   (Cancel)

7.   Uncheck the **Create a label** box. Leave the formatter set to Image and then set the Image style to `gallery_thumb`. Set the **Link image to File**.

8. Expand the **MULTIPLE FIELD SETTINGS** and uncheck the **Display all values in the same row** box. Click the **Apply** (all displays) button to save your configuration.

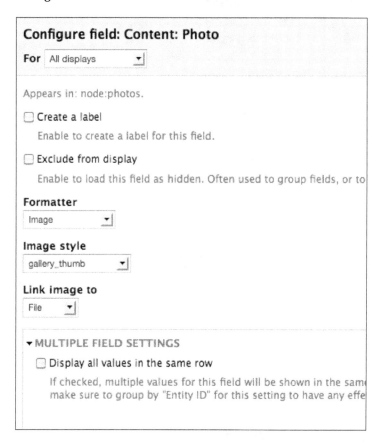

9. When you main View screen reloads you should immediately see thumbnail photos start to load in your preview. Notice that all your photos now show up in the View preview area. You'll also see that the node title of the Photos page is showing up above the photo.

10. We want to hide that node title so it won't appear above every photo on our gallery page, so to do this scroll back up to your Views configuration and click on the **Content:Title** link in the Fields section. Then click the **Remove** button.

11. Now scroll back to your preview and you'll see all the thumbnail images without a node title above them. It should look like the following in your preview mode:

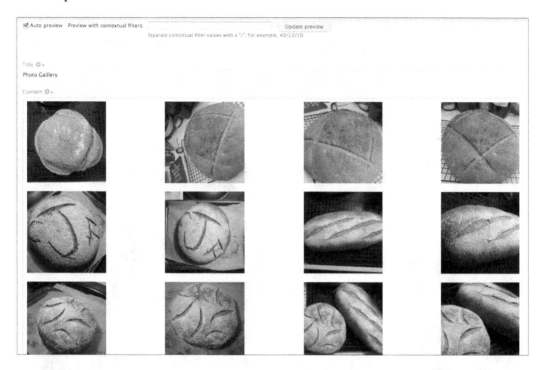

At this point we have configured our main Gallery View and we're ready to test it out on the site. In order to save our View and its configuration make sure at this point to click the big Save button on the top right of your View configuration page. This will save your Gallery view to the site. Once saved you can visit the path of your View page which is `yoursite.com/photo-gallery`.

When you load the photo-gallery page you may see blocks that are showing up above your gallery View. Go to your blocks administration screen and make sure to hide these blocks from your specific photo-gallery page by configuring each block to not show on that path.

Once you do this log out of your site and then go to your /photo-gallery path. You should see your photo gallery:

Photo Gallery

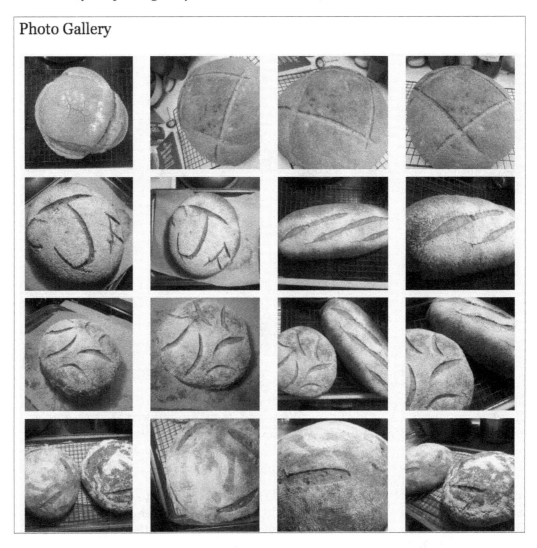

Go ahead and click on one of the thumbnail images. Notice that it will open up the original file in the same browser window. So, if the site visitor wants to see the larger version of the file they can just click on the thumbnail.

Congratulations! You've successfully built an image gallery using the Views module. In the next section we'll add a slideshow mechanism to our gallery using the Lightbox module.

Setting up slideshows with Lightbox and Views

In this section we will install the Lightbox module to add slideshow functionality to our Views powered photo gallery.

Goal

Install the Lightbox2 module and configure it to add slideshow displays to our View gallery.

Additional modules needed

Lightbox2 (http://drupal.org/project/lightbox2)

Steps

1. We can add a slideshow animation to our image gallery using the Lightbox module. Lightbox will allow our site visitors to click on one of the gallery thumbnail images and open up the larger scaled image in a Lightbox modal window.

2. This Lightbox window will allow you to navigate from one image to the next automatically and manually using a fade animation or transition. So to set this up the first thing we need to do is install the Lightbox 2 module for Drupal 7.

3. Go to the Lightbox 2 project page here and download the latest 7.*x* version of the module and install into your /sites/all/modules directory: http://drupal.org/project/lightbox2.

4. Once installed enable the module via the modules administration page:

ENABLED	NAME	VERSION	DESCRIPTION
☑	Lightbox2	7.x-1.0-beta1	Enables Lightbox2 for Drupal

(▾ USER INTERFACE)

5. Configure Lightbox 2 by selecting **Site Configuration** and then **Lightbox 2**, from the **Administer** menu. Lightbox 2 has a large number of settings, divided into four sections. Let's explore each of these.

General settings

The **general settings** page contains a variety of settings used to control the display of the Lightbox. These settings are

- **Use Lightbox2Lite**: Enabling this setting will greatly limit the functionality of Lightbox2. All controls will be removed, so the visitor will not be able to navigate from image to image. This may be desirable if your site gets a large amount of traffic, or if you want to ensure that only one image is displayed at a time.

- **Use Alternative Layout**: In the normal Lightbox layout, the **next** and **previous** buttons are overlaid on the image and display only when the mouse passes over the link. When the alternative layout is active, the links are always displayed and they are placed below the image, alongside the caption. I personally prefer to have this option enabled because it is much more user-friendly to always show the navigation to the user rather than make them search for the controls.

- **Force visibility of navigation links**: Enabling this setting causes Lightbox 2 to always display navigation controls.

- **ImageCount Text** and **PageCount Text**: These settings allow you to customize the text that is displayed in the caption.

- **DisableZoomFeature**: This setting will prevent the user from resizing the image if the image is larger than the page. Disabling the zoom may make for a cleaner Lightbox.

- **VideoSettings**: This setting allows you to display videos within the Lightbox.

- **Page Specific Lightbox 2 Settings**: This setting gives you the ability to prevent specific pages from displaying a Lightbox. This is useful if you are using custom modules that the Lightbox module detects and automatically attempts to display a Lightbox.

- **Advanced settings**: The **Advanced settings** section offers a variety of settings that allow you to fine-tune how the Lightbox is displayed on the page. Using these options, you can control colors of the Lightbox, how long each transition between images lasts, and whether or not the user can see your website beneath the Lightbox.

Slideshow settings

The **Slideshow settings** page provides various settings that control the functionality of the slideshow. This includes how long each picture is displayed, what should happen when the slideshow finishes, and what happens when the user clicks on the **Next** or **PreviousImage** buttons. These options are all well-documented on the settings page itself.

HTML content settings

The **HTMLContentsettings** control how large the Lightbox will be if it is displaying HTML content. These settings also control whether or not a border is displayed on the Lightbox.

Automatic image handling settings

The **Automatic image handling settings** are used to control how Lightbox2 automatically inserts itself into the images within your site. If used correctly, this functionality will save you a great deal of time because you don't need to manually add links to each image and ensure that you have all the settings correct.

In most cases, you can leave these settings with their default values as they are all set to sensible values. However, there are a few settings that you should take note of:

- **Image trigger size** (in **Image node settings**): This setting controls which sizes of image will trigger the Lightbox to be displayed. If you have added new custom sizes, you should review this setting to ensure that each new size is set correctly. For example, we will add the **Menu Item List** as a trigger for the Lightbox.

- **Custom image trigger classes** (in **CustomClassImages**): If you are using <img>tags, you can also use the custom image trigger classes to automatically display the Lightbox, which simplifies page creation and maintenance.

Adding a Lightbox slideshow to our Photo gallery

To add our Lightbox slideshow let's go back and edit our Photo gallery view.

1. Go to your **Structure | Views** administration page and click to edit your Photo Gallery view.

2. Once you load the configuration screen click on your **Content:Photofields** link, we're going to change our formatter to a Lightbox-specific formatter. Scroll down until you see a **Lightbox2:lightshow:gallery_thumb-|gallery_large** formatter. Select this one. This means that we want the field to show the thumb nail and be clickable to the larger scaled version in a Lightbox modal window.

3. Click the **Apply to all Displays** button. Your preview should look the same.

4. Save your View.

Now go back to your /photo-gallery page. So far everything looks the same. The thumbnail images still show up. But now if we click on a thumbnail it will open up the 600x600 scaled version of our image in a Lightbox modal window above our page. Additionally we'll have an automatic slideshow start as soon as we open up our modal Lightbox powered image. If you sit back you can watch the slideshow play through all the images.

You can also pause the slideshow by clicking the pause icon. You can close the modal Lightbox window by clicking the **X** icon. If you hover your mouse cursor over the large image you'll see navigation arrow icons appear that will let you go back and forward from one image to the next. So you also have manual control over the slideshow.

Additional topics

The Lightbox2 module provides a lot of power, and displaying slideshows is just the beginning of what it can do. You can use Lightbox2 to display nearly any type of content, including HTML pages, video, Flickr photos, and much more.

The Drupal site contains a wealth of information about the Lightbox2 module. The documentation begins at: `http://drupal.org/node/144469`.

Summary

In this chapter, we learned how to use the Views module to create a dynamic image gallery display. We also installed the Lightbox2 module and added a modal window-powered slideshow to our Photo gallery.

Our photo gallery now allows site visitors to click on the smaller photo and view the larger scale image in the Lightbox2 modal window above our site. They can then watch an automatic transitioning slideshow of our images.

In the next chapter we will learn best practice methods for maintaining and taking care of our Drupal Website. This will include running backups and maintaining our Drupal MySQL database.

11
Maintaining and Optimizing your Drupal Site

Now that we have built our site and integrated it into our business, we need to ensure that our site stays clean and up-to-date. In this chapter, we will explore various maintenance tasks to keep our site operating at peak performance.

We will begin by discussing how to back up our website and then restore it again, to protect it against hardware failures or malicious users. Next, we will discuss performance tuning to ensure that your site can meet any level of traffic demand. Finally, we will review managing and moderating content.

At the end of this chapter, you will be prepared to publish your website to the world, knowing that you are prepared for anything.

To summarize, in this chapter we will:

- Backup our Drupal site files
- Backup our MySQL database
- Install and configure the Backup and Migrate module
- Maintain and optimize our database
- Learn about how to optimize and tweak performance settings on our Drupal site

Website backups

A strong backup plan is critical for any successful website. A good backup plan will protect against hardware failure, allow you to transfer your website to another host, and allow you to recover from malicious hacking into your website.

When you create a backup plan, you should also test the restoration from this backup to make sure that the backup works correctly.

In this section, we will explore ways of performing backups regardless of the host that you are using. Your hosting provider may also offer a solution that will back up files and databases either one time, or on a recurring basis. If your host does provide backup capabilities, you should review them to see if they suit your needs completely, or if you want to augment them or replace them with the techniques in this section.

Manually backing up a site

In this section we learn how to back up our site's files, Drupal directory, and MySQL database.

Goal

Back up the website without using a custom backup module.

Steps

If you do not want to use a dedicated Drupal module to perform your backups, you can manually download the files and the database information that make up the site. However, this can be more time-intensive and error-prone than using a custom backup module.

A manual backup has two steps, in which you must first back up the files that make up the site and then back up the database information.

To back up the files for the website, use the following procedure:

1. Begin by opening the utility that you use to transfer files to the website. This could be an FTP client, or an online file manager. My favorite FTP client is **FileZilla**, which is a freely-available open source client. The FileZilla client can be downloaded from `http://filezilla-project.org/`.

2. Select the backup location on your local computer to which you want to copy the files, and select the root directory of your web server as the remote directory. You may want to date the backup folder so that you can maintain a history of the site.

3. Next, download the files to your local directory. If you want, you can compress the files into a ZIP file or a compressed archive.

4. To reduce the amount of data that you need to download, you should be able to download just the `sites` directory, because that folder contains all of the custom files, pictures, themes, and modules that you have added to the site, assuming that you have followed all of the guidelines in this book.

5. Here's a screenshot of our local Drupal site files that we are backing up. Since I'm running my local site via MAMP I can simply copy the entire site folder and then paste that copy into another location on my computer.

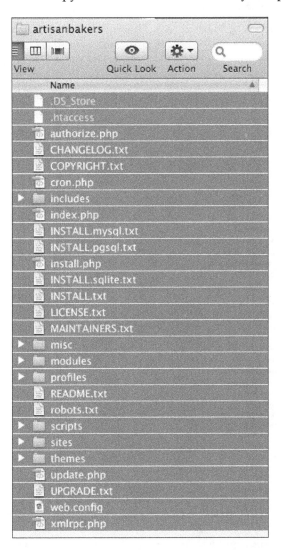

To back up the site's database information, you can use your website provider's database management utility. Many hosts provide **phpMyAdmin** for this purpose. If you are unsure whether or not your host gives you access to phpMyAdmin, you can contact their customer support group to check. We'll practice the following process on our localhost desktop via the MAMP phpMyAdmin interface:

1. Begin by opening **phpMyAdmin** and selecting the database that has your site information within it. To open up phpMyAdmin via your MAMP application open up the MAMP start screen and then click on **Open Start Screen** or **Web Start** if you're using MAMP Pro. Then click on the **phpMyAdmin** tab on the MAMP start screen. Now, select your site's database, in this example's case the database is called drupal7. Click on the database via the left hand menu in phpMyAdmin

   The following database screen should load and look similar to the following:

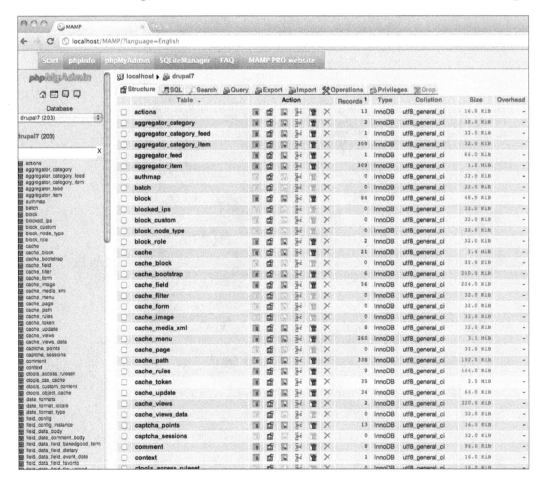

2. If you have multiple databases available on the host, you may need to select the database that you want to work with in the drop-down list at the upper left corner of the screen.

3. Next, select the **Export** tab at the top of the screen. PhpMyAdmin will prompt you to select the tables that you want to download and the format that you want to download in, as shown in the following screenshot. All the tables should be selected by default. Make sure to check the **Save as file** checkbox.

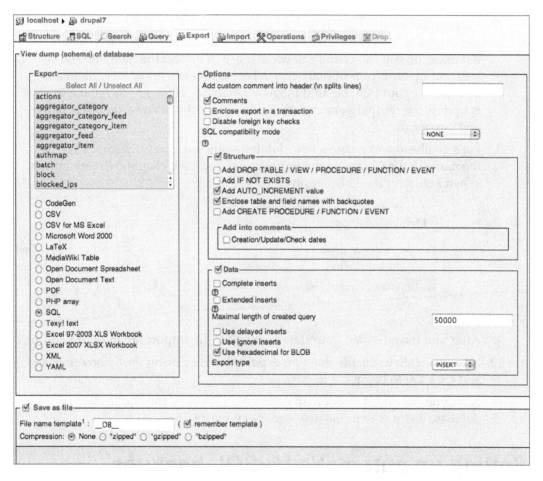

4. If you want to be able to rebuild the database at a later time, you should export all the tables in SQL format. The SQL format should be selected by default

5. Next, you will need to specify the name of the file to download to. You can use the default __DB__ as the database name.

   You may want to zip the file to reduce storage space.

6. Then click **Go** to begin the download process. You will be prompted for the location to which you want to save the exported data.

   When you are ready to restore the website from backup, you simply reverse the process.

7. You should always import into a blank database, to avoid conflicts with existing data. You can either drop or delete all of the titles in the existing database, or you can create a new database to import the data into. To be safe and in terms of best practice, it's best to create a brand new database and import your SQL file into the new database. Then all you'll have to do is update the Drupal settings.php file to reflect your new database name and password.

8. Let's go ahead and create a new database called drupal7backup. Type in the name in the **Create new database** field and then click the **Create** button. When I create it it will be empty:

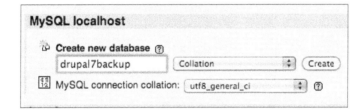

9. After you have created your database, select the **Import** tab in phpMyAdmin.

10. Now navigate to the file that you exported earlier using the Choose button, and click **Go** to begin the import.

11. Now you may need to open up your settings.php file and update the database settings with the new name of your database.

Setting up automatic MySQL backups

In this section we'll be setting up automatic MySQL backups using the Backup and Migrate module.

Goal

Back up a website so that it can be stored for easy recovery.

Additional modules needed

Backup and Migrate (`http://drupal.org/project/backup_migrate`).

Steps

Although you can manually back up your files and database, this process can be time-consuming and error prone. Luckily, the **Backup and Migrate** module makes this process easier, and optimizes the backups to exclude unnecessary data.

1. Begin by downloading and installing the **Backup** and **Migrate** module.

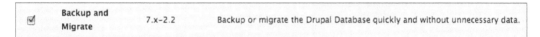

You can now back up your data by going to **Configuration** and in the System table select the **Backup and Migrate** link:

2. The **Backup and Migrate** module allows you to fully customize the backup files that are created. You can control which tables are included in the backup, and whether or not the data in the table is backed up. By default, the **Backup and Migrate** module does not back up cache information, session information, or watchdog information, because data in these tables is temporary and can be easily be re-created.

3. There are a variety of other options that you can choose from, which control how the resulting file is named, how it is compressed, and where it is compressed to.

   You can choose to do a **QUICK BACKUP** first and back up from the **Default Database** to either a download location on your local desktop or to a file directory for backup files that the module will create on your site. Let's first choose to back up to **Download.**

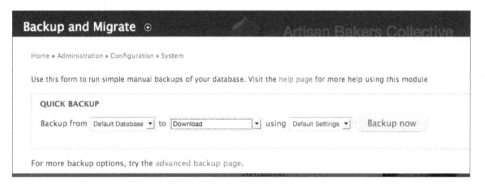

4. Click the **Backup Now** button to begin the backup process. If you have selected the **Download** option, the file will be sent to your computer so that you can store it. If you select the **Save to Files Directory** option, the backup file will be saved onto the server so that you can download it later, either directly from the server or using the **RESTORE** tab.

5. If you select to backup to the Files directory you should receive a screen that looks like the following once you run the backup, telling you that the file has been saved on your site in a **Manual Backups Directory**:

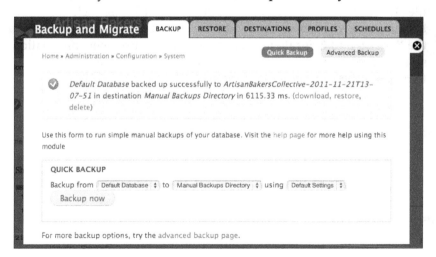

Clicking on the **RESTORE** tab will allow you to browse for one of your downloaded backup files, or to click on a link that shows the backups that you have saved to your backup directory on the site. The restore screen is as follows:

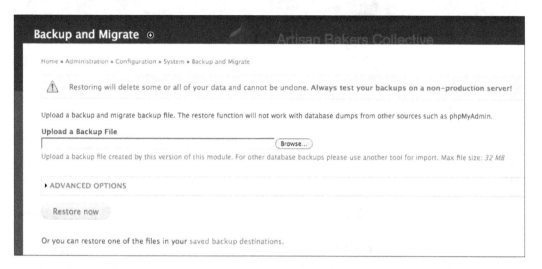

6. If you click on the saved backup destinations link you will load a screen that shows you your Manual and Scheduled Backup directories that are on your site. You can then click on the list files link to view any backup files that you want to restore from.

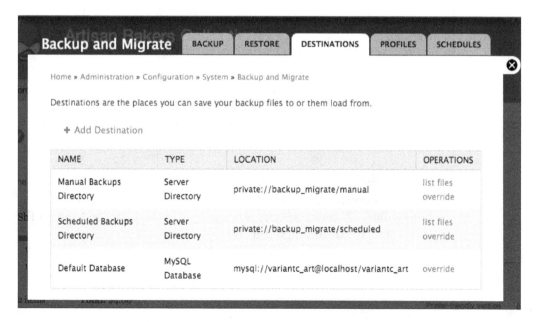

7. Clicking on **list files** I can then see the backup that I just ran to my **Manual Backups Directory**. To restore I can click the **restore** link. I can also download or delete the file:

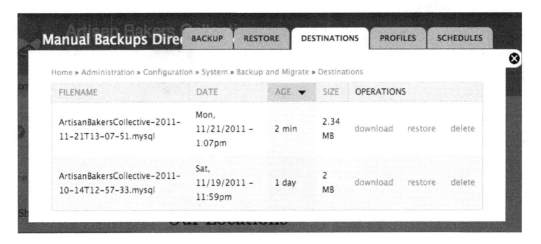

8. If you would like the **Backup and Migrate** module to back up your database automatically on a regular basis, you can schedule the back up to occur at specified intervals by clicking on the **Schedules** tab.

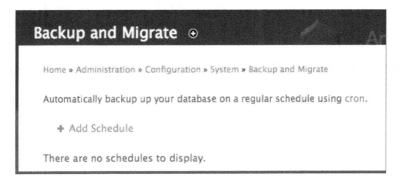

9. Now:

   ° Click on the **Add Schedule** link.

   ° Add a **Schedule Name**, and then add your backup frequency in hours, days or weeks, specify a number of backup files to keep and then select the destination directory.

10. I will back up once per day and keep seven backups at a time. This will give me a week's worth of backups.

11. Click **Save schedule**.

12. Now your backups will run on this schedule based on your Cron task schedule. So the backup will fire on schedule during your next cron run.

Please note that the backups created by the **Backup and Migrate** module do not include the files from the site, so you will still need to back up these files independently. You can minimize the backup file size by only backing up the files that the users can upload. These files are typically stored in the `files` directory. The process for backing up files is identical to the process used in the section on manual backups

Restoring a site from a backup

In this section we'll learn how to restore our database from a backup file.

Goal

Restore information from a backup file created by the Backup and Migrate module.

Additional modules needed

Backup and Migrate (`http://drupal.org/project/backup_migrate`).

Steps

Restoring a backup created by the **Backup and Migrate** module is a simple process. Before you run a restore make sure you always have a new backup of your site just in case the restore process causes issues. You'll only want to restore from backup if your site is having major issues.

1. Navigate to the **Backup and Migrate manager** by selecting **Configuration** and then **Backup and Migrate**, from the **Administer** menu.
2. Next, click on the **Restore** tab.
3. Navigate to the location of your backup file.
4. After you have selected the backup file, click on **Restore Database** to begin the restore process. Please read all displayed warnings carefully, and make sure that you test the import on a test installation for your site before running it on your production site. If you are sure that you want to proceed with the import, agree to the confirmation and click **restore**.
5. You may also need to import any saved files, if the server file system is not fully up-to-date. We discussed this previously in the section on manual backups.

Optimizing your Drupal site and its database

If your website has a moderate to large number of visitors, you should tune your website for maximum performance. This will ensure that all your visitors have a positive experience, and are not frustrated by delays in loading pages or accessing the website.

We will discuss ways to optimize both the backend database, and the frontend of the website that displays the information to the visitor.

Optimizing the database tables

In this section we'll optimize our MySQL database tables using the DB Maintenance module.

Goal

Optimize the database where your site content is stored, to ensure the best possible performance.

Additional modules needed

DB Maintenance (`http://drupal.org/project/db_maintenance`)

Steps

When a database is used as frequently as the Drupal database is, it can become less optimized over time, because having a large number of records inserted and deleted from each table can result in the database having wasted space. All databases will allow you to run an optimization process that removes unused space and rebuilds the indexes to make the search for information faster.

The **DB Maintenance** module can automatically perform the optimization process for you when cron is run. This can be done as follows:

1. Begin by downloading and installing the **DB Maintenance** module.

2. You can edit the settings for the **DB maintenance** module by selecting **Configuration** and then **DB maintenance**, from the **Administer** menu.

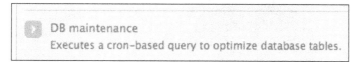

3. The settings allow you to control several options, including:

   ° Whether or not to write to the log when each optimization is performed. If you want to write to the log make sure to check the **Log OPTIMIZE queries** box.

- How often the tables are optimized, with options from hourly to bi-monthly, or at each cron run.

- Finally, you can control which tables are optimized. This allows you to not optimize tables that do not change frequently, which will allow the maintenance task to complete faster.

Once you have configured the settings properly, you simply save the settings, and the **DB maintenance** module will automatically perform the optimization at the specified intervals.

Let's go ahead and run our optimization process. First we go to **Status report** and click on the **run cron manually** link. When cron runs the optimization process will begin. Depending on how many MySQL tables you selected the process can take a few minutes to run. Once it runs you can see the results by visiting your **Recent log messages** table. Here's a screenshot of my results:

TYPE	DATE	MESSAGE
cron	10/14/2011 – 3:17pm	Cron run completed.
db_maintenance	10/14/2011 – 3:17pm	Optimized tables in drupal7 database: actions,...
db_maintenance	10/14/2011 – 3:17pm	Optimized webform_submitted_data table in drupal7...
db_maintenance	10/14/2011 – 3:17pm	Optimized webform_submissions table in drupal7 database.
db_maintenance	10/14/2011 – 3:17pm	Optimized webform_roles table in drupal7 database.
db_maintenance	10/14/2011 – 3:17pm	Optimized webform_emails table in drupal7 database.
db_maintenance	10/14/2011 – 3:17pm	Optimized webform_component table in drupal7 database.
db_maintenance	10/14/2011 – 3:17pm	Optimized webform table in drupal7 database.
db_maintenance	10/14/2011 – 3:17pm	Optimized watchdog table in drupal7 database.
db_maintenance	10/14/2011 – 3:17pm	Optimized votingapi_vote table in drupal7 database.
db_maintenance	10/14/2011 – 3:17pm	Optimized votingapi_cache table in drupal7 database.
db_maintenance	10/14/2011 – 3:17pm	Optimized views_view table in drupal7 database.
db_maintenance	10/14/2011 – 3:17pm	Optimized views_display table in drupal7 database.
db_maintenance	10/14/2011 – 3:17pm	Optimized variable table in drupal7 database.
db_maintenance	10/14/2011 – 3:17pm	Optimized users_roles table in drupal7 database.
db_maintenance	10/14/2011 – 3:17pm	Optimized users table in drupal7 database.
db_maintenance	10/14/2011 – 3:17pm	Optimized url_alias table in drupal7 database.
db_maintenance	10/14/2011 – 3:17pm	Optimized uc_zones table in drupal7 database.
db_maintenance	10/14/2011 – 3:17pm	Optimized uc_taxes table in drupal7 database.
db_maintenance	10/14/2011 – 3:17pm	Optimized uc_taxed_product_types table in drupal7...
db_maintenance	10/14/2011 – 3:17pm	Optimized uc_taxed_line_items table in drupal7 database.
db_maintenance	10/14/2011 – 3:17pm	Optimized uc_roles_products table in drupal7 database.
db_maintenance	10/14/2011 – 3:17pm	Optimized uc_roles_expirations table in drupal7...

Each table in the database will be optimized and you'll see a report for each specific table's results in your logs.

Using caching to improve performance

In this section we'll enable caching on our Drupal site and help boost core performance for our anonymous users.

Goal

Use caching to improve the performance of content display.

Additional modules needed

None

Steps

Because dynamically generated pages, such as those created with Drupal, can be time-consuming and resource-intensive to generate Drupal uses a sophisticated caching mechanism to pre-load sections of content for display to users.

To set up the Drupal cache, carry out the following steps:

1. Access the settings for the Drupal cache by selecting **Configuration** and then **Performance**, from the **Development** section.

2. The first section of settings relate to the **Page cache**, which is used to cache entire pages of data. The **Page cache** system will only cache pages for anonymous users, to prevent personal data for one user being made visible to other users, and also because it is simpler to ensure that the pages are successfully cached only if anonymous users are served cached content.

3. You can click the **Clear all caches** button to immediately flush the Drupal cache tables. You can also select **Cache pages for anonymous users** and **Cache blocks**.

4. If your site is exceptionally busy, you may want to enforce a minimum cache lifetime, which is the minimum amount of time that Drupal will wait for, before rebuilding cached pages. If your site receives infrequent updates, you may see a performance benefit by increasing this number to match your update schedule. You can also set the expiration of cached pages here.

5. Drupal also provides a **Block cache**, which caches just the content of the blocks rather than the entire page. Unlike the page cache, the block cache works for both anonymous users as well as users who have logged into the site.

6. The final type of optimization provided by Drupal relates to minimizing the amount of content that is sent to the user, by aggregating the CSS files and JavaScript files created by each module into a single CSS file and a single JavaScript file, which can be downloaded once by the user. These options are disabled if you are using the private filesystem. If you want to make use of these options, you will need to use the public filesystem on your site.

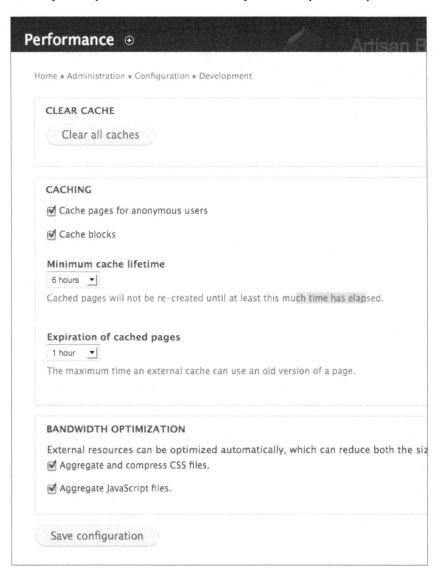

7. Although Drupal caching makes your site faster and gives users a better experience; it can interfere with your development of the website because the cache may prevent you from seeing the most recent changes to your site. If this is the case, you can clear the cached data by clicking on the **Clear cached data** button.

Creating content workflows and revisions

As you continue to add content to your website, you will need to ensure that your content is properly moderated, that old content is removed, and that changes to website content are tracked.

Creating content revisions

In this section we'll create revisions of our Drupal site content using the core revision functionality.

Goal

Create revisions of content to ensure that you have a complete record of changes to your website's content.

Additional modules needed

None.

Steps

Throughout this book, we have simply updated our pages as necessary to add new functionality and content. However, if you have many editors, content that changes frequently, a need to view the history of a page, or need the ability to easily return to an old version of a page, you will want to store multiple revisions of your pages.

To do this, carry out the following steps:

1. Edit the content for which you want to create a new revision.

2. Make the changes as needed and before saving, expand the **Revision information** section.

3. Select the **Create new revision** option and enter a message describing the changes that you have made to the node.

4. When you save the content, you will see a new tab called **Revisions on the page**.

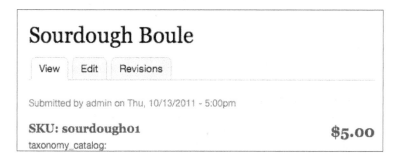

5. Clicking on this tab will show you a list of all of the revisions that have been created for the page.

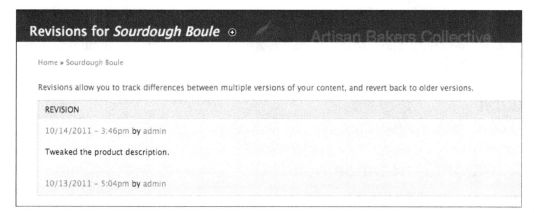

6. If you would like to return to an older version of the page, you can click the **revert** link. Or, if you want to remove an older revision, you can click the **delete** link to get rid of it permanently.

7. You can control which users have access to the revision system by using the **Permissions Manager**. Drupal allows you to control which users can: view revisions, revert revisions, and delete revisions.

8. If you want to force users to always create new revisions when editing content, edit the content type and then click on the **Publishing Options** tab.

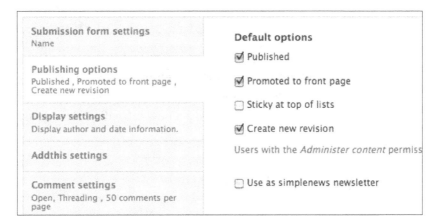

9. Change the default publishing options to add the **Create new revision** option. When editors change content, the **Create new revision** option will be selected by default, and they will not be able to change the option unless they have the administer nodes permission.

10. If you want to approve all revisions before publication, you can deselect the **Published** checkbox

Comparing content revisions

In this section we'll compare our content revisions using a contributed module called Diff.

Goal

Compare the text of two different revisions of a page

Additional modules needed

Diff (http://drupal.org/project/diff).

Steps

Although the built-in functionality for creating revisions in Drupal works perfectly well, it can be difficult to review the changes that were made in each revision. The **Diff** module makes comparing revisions very easy.

1. Begin by installing and activating the **Diff** module.

2. To use the **Diff** module, simply view the revisions for any page. You will notice that the **REVISION** list has changed to allow you to select the revisions to be compared.

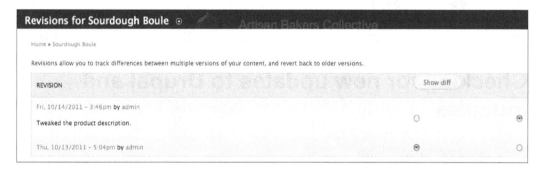

3. Select the revisions to compare and then click on the **Show diff** button. Drupal will then display information about the text that has been changed, added, or deleted.

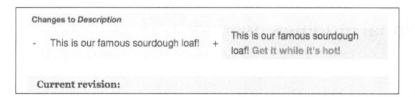

Upgrading to new versions of Drupal

One of the fantastic things about Drupal is that it is constantly evolving to offer new and improved functionalities. However, this requires you to regularly check for updates to Drupal and any contributed modules that are installed.

In this section, we will discuss how to find updates, test them, and install them onto your site.

There are two types of updates that you will encounter. Minor updates will correct security issues or problems found by users, and may have minimal functionality enhancements. A major update will typically have much more functionality, and may be incompatible with the previous versions.

The version number for Drupal contains two numbers separated by periods. For example, version 7.8 indicates major version 7 and minor version 8.

A custom module will begin with the version of Drupal it is compatible with, followed by a major and minor version for the module itself. If a module is compatible with all of the minor releases of a Drupal major release, the minor version will be represented by an x. For example, `version 7.x-1.5` indicates that the module is compatible with any version of Drupal 7, and that the major version of the module is 1 and its minor version is 5. A module may also indicate development versions by adding `−dev` to the end of the version, a beta version by adding `−beta1`, or a release candidate by adding `−rc1` after the version. Multiple beta and release candidates are indicated by incrementing the numbers after `beta` or `rc`, respectively.

Checking for new updates to Drupal and modules

In this section we'll learn how to check for and be notified about Drupal core and contributed module updates.

Goal

Ensure that we are using the latest versions of Drupal and the contributed modules that the site uses.

Additional modules needed

None (core).

Steps

Here are the steps to check for upgrades to your Drupal core and contributed modules:

1. Drupal 7 makes it easy to check for updates to Drupal and the modules that you have installed. By default, Drupal will check for updates to the system each time that cron is run.

2. You can check the current status of the system by selecting **Reports** and then **Available updates**, from the **Administer** menu. Drupal will also display a warning when you navigate to any administration page, if it has detected that Drupal, or some related content, is outdated.

If you want to, you can click on the **Check manually** link to ensure that all modules are up-to-date.

3. If any modules are outdated, they will be shown as follows.

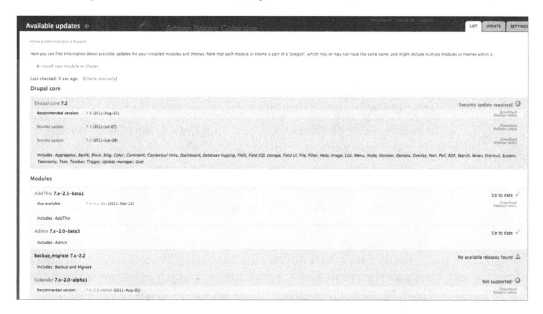

4. The display includes the version that you have currently installed, the recommended version that should be installed, a link to download a new version, and a link to the release notes for the new version. The **Release notes** will include a list of changes that have been made to the module. In the next few tasks, we will discuss upgrading your installation.

5. Notice here that we are being advised to upgrade our Drupal core install from version *7.2* to version *7.8*. There are also a number of contributed module upgrades we should perform.

Upgrading Drupal contributed modules

In this section we'll learn how to upgrade our contributed Drupal modules.

Goal

Upgrade between minor versions of Drupal 7 contributed modules

Additional modules needed

None (core).

Steps

When Drupal detects that a new version of one of your Drupal modules is available, it will inform you as mentioned earlier. On our site we have notifications that the **File Entity** and **Calendar** modules need to be upgraded. Drupal 7 allows you to upgrade directly via its Available updates administration screen. You can also do the updates manually.

1. Before you download and install the new version, you should read all of the release notes for the new version, to determine if there are any potential incompatibilities with the other modules that you have installed.

2. If you do not see any potential issues based on the release notes, you can begin testing the new version yourself.

3. Before installing the new version, make a complete backup of your site including all of the files and the database.

4. You should test the new version on a non-production test site, before installing it on your live site. If you do not have a test site set up yet, you can create a test site on your local computer, in a different location on your web host, or on another web host. If you choose to have the test website hosted at a web host, you should make sure that it is not publicly accessible to visitors. This will help to ensure that your visitors are not directed to the wrong version of your site through search engines.

5. If your test site is not available to the public, you do not need to worry about putting the site into **maintenance mode**.

6. Install the module into the test version of your site by copying the files to the server.

7. Or you can use the **Available updates** administration screen – check the modules you want to update and then click on the **Download these updates** button.

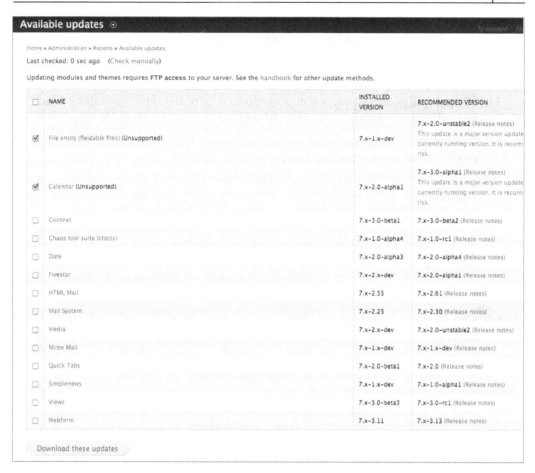

8. Once the updates are downloaded they will be installed. You'll get the
    following success message:

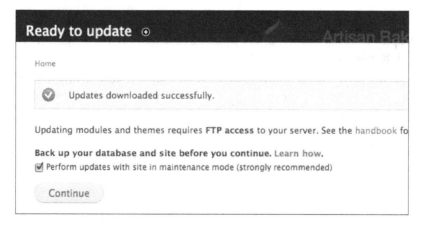

9. Click the **Continue** button to run the `update.php` script. This will update your database schema based on any module database table changes that occurred.

10. You can also run the update by going to `yoursite.com/update.php`

11. Drupal will then display a list of modules where the database tables need to be updated. By default, Drupal will select the correct version to upgrade to.

   In most cases, you will want to use the version that Drupal selects, but you can override the version selected if needed.

12. When you have selected the version you want to upgrade to, click the **Update** button.

13. You'll get a list of pending updates that will be applied:

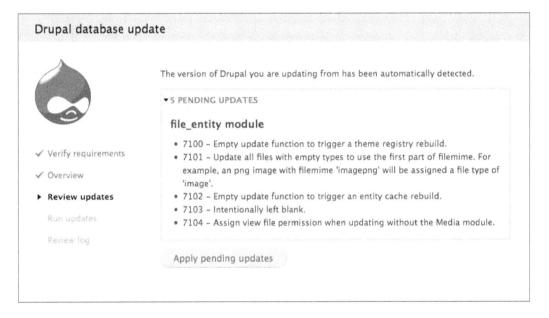

14. Drupal will now run all of the updates and display the results with links back to your site.

15. Once the installation is complete, you should test your website to ensure that it is still functioning correctly, and that all of the functionality related to the update is running properly.

16. Assuming that all functionality works correctly for you, and you do not detect any incompatibilities, you can use the same steps on your live site to install the updates in production. If you do detect any incompatibilities, please report the problems that you found on the Drupal site so that they can be corrected as quickly as possible. When reporting issues, make sure that you give a full description of the problem that you are having, the version it is related to, and, if appropriate, a list of the other modules installed on your site.

Upgrading to a new major or minor release of Drupal core

In this section we'll learn how to upgrade to a new major or minor release of Drupal core.

Goal

Upgrade to a new major or minor release of Drupal.

Additional modules needed

None (core).

Steps

The process of upgrading Drupal to a new release of Drupal core can be a non-trivial process, which you will want to undertake carefully.

1. If you are upgrading a live site, put your site into maintenance mode by selecting **Configuration** and then **Site maintenance**, from the **Administer** menu.

   Change the status to **Off-line** and then click the **Save configuration** button.

2. Make a complete backup of the files and the database tables that comprise your site.

3. Upload the new Drupal files to your site — the best method of doing this on your local MAMP install is to download the new version of Drupal, in our case Drupal 7.8 and replace all of your core Drupal files with the new versions.

4. Run the upgrade page at http://yoursite.com/update.php, as described in the previous task.

5. Test your site to ensure that all of the functionalities are working properly.

6. If your site is working properly, you can either repeat the steps on your live site, or copy the test site to the live site.

7. If any functionality is not working properly, you can try the upgrade process again using your backup, or contact the maintainers of the functionality that is not working, so that they can help you to resolve any issues.

Summary

In this chapter, we have reviewed a number of tasks that happen behind the scenes, in order to give your visitors the best possible experience, and to ensure that your website operates at peak performance even if you are confronted with hardware failures or other unforeseen events. We have also discussed ways of managing your content to ensure that your site is of the highest possible quality.

Although these tasks are not glamorous, they are essential to any professional website.

Index

Symbols

Mollom
  URL 153
Monthly Newsletter 9
multiple aliases
  creating 43, 44
MySQL 11
MySQL backups
  automatic setup 322
  automatic setup, steps 323-327
  modules 323
MySQL database 30

N

navigation
  setting up 52
navigation menu 54
newsletter category
  creating 171-174
  viewing 175, 176
newsletters
  adding 177
  categories, viewing 175, 177
  category, creating 171
  configuration 178-180
  creating 171-173
  creating, steps 172-174
  new issue, creating 183
  news issue, creating 184-189
  sender information section 180
  Send mail configuration 181-183
  sign ups, managing 192-194
  sign up, users allowing to 189, 191
  Simplenews configuration screen 181-183
  Simplenews module 171
  Subscription configuration 181-183
  subscriptions, exporting 194, 195
  subscriptions, importing 194, 195
newsreaders
  RSS feed, creating for 156, 157
new user comments notification
  email action, creating 114, 116
  modules, required 114
  new comments trigger, creating 117, 118
  setting up 114
node 30

node heading 37
notification, new user comments
  setting up 114

O

OAuth 243
Online baking class example
  about 212
  video content, adding from YouTube 212
online ordering 9
orders
  checking, as site administrator 294, 296

P

pages
  about 9
  adding, to menu 54-56
page alias
  about 43
  creating, automatically 45
Page Specific Lightbox 2 settings 312
path alias
  about 44
  using 43
PDF format
  Drupal nodes, converting 266-270
PDFs
  adding, to Drupal site 254
  auto-generating 266-272
People | Permissions screen 107
Permissions screen 89
permissions, content type
  controlling 89, 90
Peter Reinhart video
  URL 217
Photo gallery
  about 9
  Lightbox slideshow, adding to 313, 314
photos
  adding, to PHOTO page 302, 303
  inserting, Flickr module used 228-242
PHP 11
phpMyAdmin 320
Plesk 168

Thank you for buying
Drupal 7 Business Solutions

About Packt Publishing

Packt, pronounced 'packed', published its first book *"Mastering phpMyAdmin for Effective MySQL Management"* in April 2004 and subsequently continued to specialize in publishing highly focused books on specific technologies and solutions.

Our books and publications share the experiences of your fellow IT professionals in adapting and customizing today's systems, applications, and frameworks. Our solution based books give you the knowledge and power to customize the software and technologies you're using to get the job done. Packt books are more specific and less general than the IT books you have seen in the past. Our unique business model allows us to bring you more focused information, giving you more of what you need to know, and less of what you don't.

Packt is a modern, yet unique publishing company, which focuses on producing quality, cutting-edge books for communities of developers, administrators, and newbies alike. For more information, please visit our website: www.packtpub.com.

About Packt Open Source

In 2010, Packt launched two new brands, Packt Open Source and Packt Enterprise, in order to continue its focus on specialization. This book is part of the Packt Open Source brand, home to books published on software built around Open Source licences, and offering information to anybody from advanced developers to budding web designers. The Open Source brand also runs Packt's Open Source Royalty Scheme, by which Packt gives a royalty to each Open Source project about whose software a book is sold.

Writing for Packt

We welcome all inquiries from people who are interested in authoring. Book proposals should be sent to author@packtpub.com. If your book idea is still at an early stage and you would like to discuss it first before writing a formal book proposal, contact us; one of our commissioning editors will get in touch with you.

We're not just looking for published authors; if you have strong technical skills but no writing experience, our experienced editors can help you develop a writing career, or simply get some additional reward for your expertise.

Drupal 7 Development by Example Beginner's Guide

ISBN: 978-1-84951-680-8   Paperback: 270 pages

Follow the creation of a Drupal website to learn, by example, the key concepts of Drupal 7 development and HTML5

1. A hands-on, example-driven guide to programming Drupal websites

2. Discover a number of new features for Drupal 7 through practical and interesting examples while building a fully functional recipe sharing website

3. Learn about web content management, multi-media integration, and e-commerce in Drupal 7

Drupal 7 Themes

ISBN: 978-1-84951-276-3   Paperback: 320 pages

Create new themes for your Drupal 7 site with a clean layout and powerful CSS styling

1. Learn to create new Drupal 7 themes

2. No experience of Drupal theming required

3. Discover techniques and tools for creating and modifying themes

4. The first book to guide you through the new elements and themes available in Drupal 7

Drupal 7 Fields/CCK
Beginner's Guide

ISBN: 978-1-849514-78-1   Paperback: 288 pages

Explore Drupal 7 fields/CCK and master their use

1. Step-by-step guide to building your own Drupal 7 website using the Drupal 7 fields system

2. Specifically written for Drupal 7 development and site building

3. In-depth coverage of theming fields in Drupal 7

4. Discover the new fields system from the database perspective

Drupal 7 Social Networking

ISBN: 978-1-84951-600-6   Paperback: 328 pages

Build a social or community website with friends lists, groups, custom user profiles, and much more

1. Step-by-step instructions for putting together a social networking site with Drupal 7

2. Customize your Drupal installation with modules and themes to match the needs of almost any social networking site

3. Allow users to collaborate and interact with each other on your site

4. Requires no prior knowledge of Drupal or PHP; but even experienced Drupal users will find this book useful to modify an existing installation into a social website

Please check **www.PacktPub.com** for information on our titles